INTERNATIONAL CENTRE FOR MECHANICAL SCIENCES

COURSES AND LECTURES No. 256

# TOPICS IN ARTIFICIAL INTELLIGENCE

EDITED BY

A. MARZOLLO

UNIVERSITY OF TRIESTE

SPRINGER-VERLAG WIEN GMBH

Originally published by Springer Verlag Wien New York in 1976

ISBN 978-3-211-81466-6 ISBN 978-3-7091-4358-2 (eBook)
DOI 10.1007/978-3-7091-4358-2

# *PREFACE*

*The mechanization of some tasks which are considered as typical of the human intelligence has been a challenge for a long time, at least since the times of Leibniz and Pascal. At present, within the vast developments of computer science, the discipline called Artificial Intellingence (A.I.) has inherited this challenge and is now confronting itself with matters like automatic problem solving, "understanding" and translating natural languages, recognizing visual images and spoken sounds, etc. . . It does so by borrowing its theoretical tools from other sciences and, also, by trying to build its own theoretical bases. The present volume reflects this situation and aims at offering an appreciation of the wide scope of A.I. by collecting contributions of various researchers active in this field.*

*The two first contributions, by Meltzer and by Marzollo and Ukovich are both concerned with the general problem of giving appropriate definitions of mathematical objects and its importance in connection with the task of automatic theorem proving. B. Meltzer tends to broaden our view of the reasoning activity involved in mathematics and gives a closer look at what a proof is, trying to discover general principles governing its design. The contribution of Marzollo and Ukovich deals with computable functions and proposes a new look at their properties. These are considered as independent of any description of the functions themselves and simply follow from the existence of a finite sentence unambiguously indicating their behaviour in correspondence to each natural number.*

*The three next contributions (by Mandrioli, Sangiovanni Vincentelli and Somalvico, by Kulikowski and by Levelt) consider more specific aspects of A.I.: problem solving, visual images recognition and natural languages understanding.*

*The first one extensively illustrates an algebraic approach to problem solving, based on the state-space, naive, syntactic and semantic descriptions.*

*J. Kulikowski shows an interesting approach to the problem of pattern recognition which is based on a linguistic description and which treats a picture as a set of local and global features. He suggests a general scheme of pattern recognition based on semi-ordering relations between pictures. The last contribution by W. Levelt deals with the theory of formal grammars and the linguistic aspects of mathematical psychology. It clarifies the empirical domain of linguistic theory and the empiric interpretation of the elements and relations which appear in it.*

*A. Marzollo*
*March 1978*

## CONTENTS

**BERNARD MELTZER(*)**

# PROOF, ABSTRACTION AND SEMANTICS IN MATHEMATICS AND ARTIFICIAL INTELLIGENCE

(*) School of Artificial Intelligence, Department of Computational Logic. University of Edinburgh.

**Abstract**

The paradigm of a chain of inference from axioms is inadequate as an account of proof. A re-analysis of what proof is leads to a proposal for a semantic framework, which in a natural way accommodates abstraction, generalization and specialization involved in proof. It can be applied to other languages than that of mathematics, and in fact appears likely to be useful in considering the problems of free-ranging reasoning in programming languages of artificial intelligence.

**Introduction**

Researchers in artificial intelligence, in designing their programs and examining their results, are constantly made aware of how rich and how poorly understood are the cognitive activities involved in doing mathematics and other kinds of reasoning. Demonstrating a truth in mathematics involves far more than drawing a chain of inferences from a given collection of axioms. For example, introspection of one's mental activities in solving a school geometry problem might reveal that all of, and maybe more than, the following are involved: a perception, a thought experiment, a guess, rationalization of the guess by means of a vague concept, failure to intuit a proof, induction and generalization, drawing from memory a related complex concept, back-tracking because a line of attack looks like being clumsy and tedious, feeling of discomfort that a proof arrived at is peripherally not water-tight, examining special cases and carrying out a proof only in outline. In fact, it is often the case that one finally has a satisfying demonstration without even having carried through the small nitty-gritty chains of inference which constitute the major part of many modern automatic theorem- proving programs.

Of course it is the aim of A.I. research in the first place to develop computational models of such and other activities and try to discover general principles governing their design. The considerations below constitute an attempt to broaden our view of the reasoning activity involved in mathematics and similar kinds of reasoning beyond the framework of the proof and model theory of formal logic. No pretence is made that the kind of conceptual framework this leads to is adequate for all the rich structure of cognitive activity we are interested in, but it is a tentative in this direction. The point of departure is a closer look at what proof is, epistemologically speaking.

**What are Proofs About?**

Suppose one proves a theorem in plane geometry about all squares. If the proof made use of the fact that a square is a four-sided rectilinear figure and its sides are equal, but not that its angles are right-angles, then - in any strict sense - the theorem proved is not about squares but about rhombuses. And this is a general feature of mathematical proofs: they do not use all the properties of the object the theorem is supposed to be about, but only a selection of them. In fact they could not use them all, since mathematical objects have in general an infinite number of properties and a finite proof can use only a finite number of them. So, inherent in a proof of a theorem there is involved some abstraction, namely a selection of features of the object the theorem is supposed to be about. The rhombus is obtained by abstraction from the square when the feature of right- angledness is left out of the selection; and our theorem is about this 'more general' object, its application to the square involving a 'special instance' of this object.

The implication of this insight is more far-reaching than might at first appear. To illustrate: suppose in arithmetic we prove something about the number 2, for instance that its square root is irrational. Now 2 certainly has an infinite number of properties (including, for example, that it is less than 3, that it is less than 4, that it is less than 5, etc.) and only a finite number of them are used in the proof. The theorem proved is therefore essentially not about 2 as we intuitively understand it but about some other 'more general' object $2^1$, say, for which unfortunately we may not have a generally accepted name like 'rhombus' in the previous example. In this case actually a proof might use of 2 only the facts that it is a natural number and that it is a prime; so that it would be more correct to say that the theorem proved is not about 2 but about any prime number. Even this would not be entirely correct since only some of the properties of prime numbers are used, as indeed for that matter in the earlier example only some of the properties of a rhombus are used; but, provided we are clear about the epistemological situation, we have to reconcile ourselves to the inadequacy and ambiguity of natural language in such cases.

Thus, proof implicitly involves not only deduction but abstraction and generalization, traditionally thought of as the province of induction; and the proof of any theorem implicitly creates a new mathematical object, namely that one defined by the (explicit and implicit) premises actually used in the deduction. Recognizing this feature of mathematical reasoning, or for that matter of the kind of reasoning implemented in many A.I. programs, has interesting consequences.

## Semantics

For a fuller grasp of the epistemological situation we need to have a general notion of what we mean by 'mathematical object'. The above discussion and a classical definition of Leibniz's suggest what this might be. Leibniz defined identity as follows: two things are identical if everything that can be truthfully asserted about either can be similarly asserted about the other. It seems natural then to take the meaning of a mathematical object, like a number or a triangle or a vector or whatnot, to be the collection of true assertions about it. Then the operation of abstraction, which occurs in proofs as illustrated above, consists in making a selection from this collection. The meaning of 'a square' is the collection of true statements about squares, the meaning of a 'rhombus' is a sub-collection of the latter. The square, being a special case of the rhombus, has to have more said about it than the rhombus, to help identify it from among all possible types of rhombus. One has to say, though it sounds at first a little odd, that the 'meaning' of 'rhombus' is contained in that of 'square', when the latter is a special case of the former. (But it seems sound epistemology to do so, since selection is of the essence of the acquisition of knowledge at all levels, starting at the most elementary levels of perception).

A few comments: firstly, this notion of meaning is on the face of it language-dependent; for example, the meaning of 'triangle' would be a different collection of assertions if one's language was English than if it was French. This is not a serious defect. The important consequences and issues depend only on the fact that one language is posited, not on which it is; and in any case one might have some standard language into which other languages can be translated.

Secondly, it has been left open whether the collection is of all true assertions about the object, or only of all known true ones, or even of all known true but putatively not irrelevant ones. This is deliberate, since the choice should be determined by the purpose, mathematical, philosophical or practical of the user. For instance, in some of the most successful modern A.I. programs the implicit semantics used is of the third kind.

## The Role of Axiomatization

From the present point of view, the long rich history of axiomatization in mathematics from Greek times to the present, might be looked upon as an effort to put in a more manageable form the general notion of a mathematical object. That is to say, since the object's meaning is in general infinite, deal instead with its definition - the latter being a hopefully finite subset of the assertions constituting the meaning, from which by 'logical inference' all the other true assertions could, in principle, be derived. If A be the collection of axioms constituting the definition of the object, and A* its 'logical closure', i.e. the collecting of assertions consisting of those of A and all others which can be truly inferred from A, then A* constitutes the meaning of the object. Proofs in an axiomatized theory can then be looked upon as efforts to explore and display some of the meaning of the objects the theorems are about.

The analysis of the nature of logical closure for formal languages is one of the important achievements of 20th century logic, so that we have a good understanding of the relationship between definition and meaning in the above sense[1]. But, in spite of the triumphs of axiomatization in algebra and other fields, it is clear from other logical studies that it is not possible or even desirable to replace the notion of meaning by that of definition, since - for example - for integer arithmetic one would need a non-denumberably infinite number of axioms in the definition!

The formal representation of mathematical objects requires, in our semantics, a systematic method of naming them, since in fact - as we have seen - only some of them, like rhombus and 2, have conventional names. This requirement is similar to that met by Church's lambda-calculus in the naming of functions, and can be dealt with in a similar way. We need an operator, say $\eta$ ('eta') which binds a variable in an assertion or conjunction of assertions. Thus: let S(x) be an assertion or conjunction of assertions about the unspecified object represented by the variable x. Then by

$$\eta x \; . \; S(x)$$

we mean that object which has the properties asserted by S. Note that this is the

---

[1] It is perhaps a misnomer to call this traditional (Tarskian) model theory 'semantics', since it does not really deal with the mea-ings of terms or sentences, but only with conditions those meanings satisfy if they are to agree without intuitive notion of logical consequences: in fact it deals essentially only with the meanings of logical constant and quantifiers. But it is interesting that some of the contributors to this theory seem to have used Tarskian models which are collections of assertions; cf. Henkin's proofs of completeness of 1st-order and type logic, and Hintikka's model sets.

same object represented by

$$\eta x \ . \ \left[S(x)\right]^*$$

where the star symbol again represents logical closure. The former expression uses definition, this one meaning.

Incidentally, it would be very interesting for a philosopher-historian, by means of case-studies, to find out why certain objects are selected, and others not, for conventional naming[1].

Note that the study of what object a theorem is about has some interesting aspects. If A is the collection of axioms the prover proposes to use, then the ostensible object is the one determined by the closure of A. But if only a subset A' is used in proof, the object of the proved theorem is the more abstract one determined by the closure of A', this also being contained in the closure of A. But this may not be the most abstract object of which the theorem is true, for the proof obtained may have used more axioms than were necessary, and a smaller subset A'' may have been sufficient, yielding a still more abstract object. So one may set oneself the task not merely of proving an alleged theorem about a contingently created mathematical object, but proving it about 'minimal', most abstract objects[2].

### The Lattice of Objects Described By a Language

We are now in a position to give a comprehensive characterization of the universe of objects described by a given language. The collection of true sentences describing a particular object will be termed an 'obj'.

Since obj's are collections of assertions, the relation of inclusion generates a partial ordering among them. Furthermore, this becomes a lattice if we define the least upper bound of two obj's as the obj which is their set-intersection,

---

[1] The $\eta$-operator has some similarity to Hilbert's $\epsilon$-operator, which also yields objects from assertions, but it differs both in nature and purpose. The $\eta$-operator is introduced as a tool for semantics, and it creates new objects. The $\epsilon$-operator's function is to be a syntactic aid in consistency proofs, introduced only to be later eliminated; it is a special kind of choice operator, not a creation operator.

[2] This is, in effect, what is meant for example in resolution logic by the extraction of a 'minimally unsatisfiable set' from an 'unsatisfiable set of clauses'.

and the greatest lower bound as the obj which is the logical closure of their set-union. The top obj of the lattice, the one which contains no assertions, represents the completely general, the universal ('Platonic') object about which nothing is specified. The bottom obj represents the object about which all assertions are true, i.e. the 'null' object, since for every assertion in it there will also be the negation of that assertion.

Going up the lattice represents the process of selection of assertions, abstraction of generalization discussed earlier, e.g. going from a square to a rhombus. Going down the lattice represents the process of addition of assertions, specialization or instantiation. All the obj's in the sub-lattice below a given obj represent instances of the object described by that obj. Similarly, such an obj represents a particular instance of each of the objects represented by the obj's in the sub-lattice above it.

Furthermore, if we wish to find the least abstract generalization of several objects, we need merely carry out the appropriate set-intersections of their obj's, moving up the lattice to a unique node.

This representation, when applied to mathematics, suggests what may be a fruitful view of part of mathematical activity. Namely, the demonstration of a mathematical truth is not primarily a matter of deducing it by rules of inference from given premises, but a matter of searching the lattice for the object or objects of which it is true. As discussed in detail earlier, we do not in advance know of just which object the theorem is true, although we have a rough idea of some of its meaning. The latter will be an indicator of what region of the lattice should be searched. Since search may involve going up as well as down the lattice, this paradigm of mathematical reasoning involves alternations of abstraction and specialization, generalization and instantiation. Which is indeed what does occur to a great extent in actual mathematical practice.

A beautiful example of this kind of thing is a proof of Pythagoras' Theorem in one of Polya's books on plausible reasoning, illustrated in Figures 1, 2 and 3.(*) One wishes to show, for the areas of the three squares erected on the sides of the given right-angled triangle in Fig. 1, that $A = B + C$. First one generalizes the problem to the case of the erection of any three polygons which are similar on the sides of the triangle (illustrated in Fig. 2). If the area of the polygon on the hypotenuse is K times that of the square on the hypotenuse, then by the properties

(*) All figures quoted are to be found at the end of this chapter.

of similar polygons the areas of the three polygons will be KA, KB and KC. Now since KA = KB + KC is logically equivalent to A = B + C, the truth of the generalized theorem is equivalent to the truth of our original theorem. Now we specialize to the case of triangles, and in particular to the three similar to the three similar right-angled triangles generated by drawing a perpendicular to the hypotenuse from the opposite vertex - cf. Fig. 3, noting that the truth of this case is also equivalent to the truth of the general case. But the proof of this case is immediate, since the two 'non-hypotenuse' triangles divide the 'hypotenuse' triangle into two parts.

**Relevance to Artificial Intelligence**

It is significant that one of the most remarkable recent programs of automatic proof, that of Boyer and Moore for proving correctness of LISP programs, incorporates some generalization - the first ever to do so. Its other outstanding feature, the generation of its own induction hypotheses, is also outside the prevailing paradigm of automatic proofs doing only deduction from given premises.

But, although the illustrations of the present approach given above have been mathematical, it is applicable to other languages and in particular to the languages used in artificial intelligence. For example, one may reasonably interpret the recent trend of putting much more 'knowledge' into the programs, as due to the realization that 'definitions' of the objects dealt with are not enough but have to have much more of their 'meaning' added to them for the programs to be effective. And, for example, one of the most interesting recent programs, that of Winston's for concept formation in a world of structures made from bricks, wedges, etc., relies essentially on the set-intersection, abstraction operation of going up the lattice of sentences. And Plotkin and Meltzer's work on inductive generalization and more general types of induction can also be fitted into the lattice schema. The semantics proposed seems to offer a good framework for use in considering the problems of programming free-ranging reasoning including deduction, induction, generalization and hypothesising.

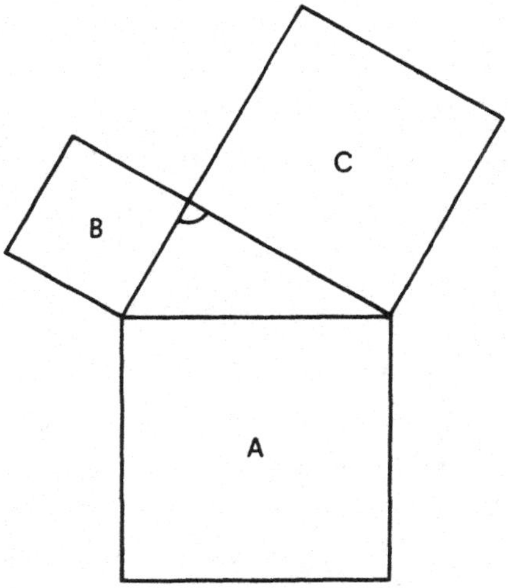


Fig. 1

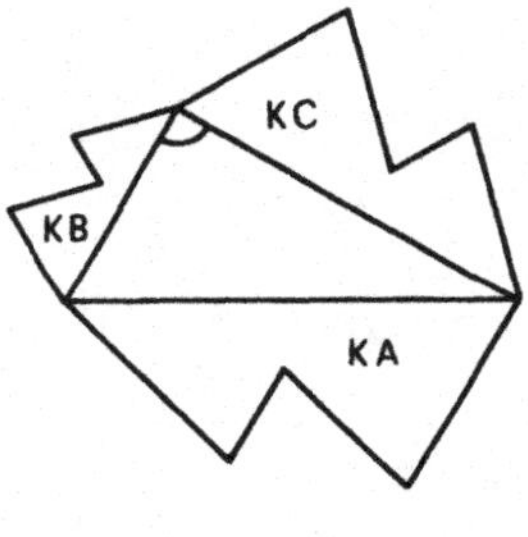


Fig. 2

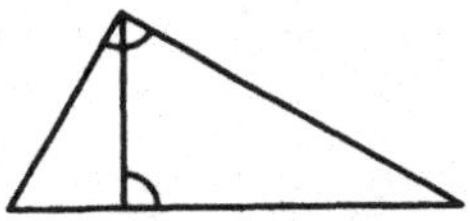

Fig. 3

ANGELO MARZOLLO (*)

WALTER UKOVICH (**)

# AN INTRODUCTION TO SOME BASIC CONCEPTS AND TECHNIQUES IN THE THEORY OF COMPUTABLE FUNCTIONS

(*) Istituto di Elettrotecnica ed Elettronica, University of Trieste, Italy, and International Centre for Mechanical Sciences, Udine, Italy

(**) Istituto di Elettrotecnica ed Elettronica, University of Trieste, Italy

## CHAPTER I

### 1. Introduction

We will talk about a class of function defined on subsets of the set of nonnegative integers, and assuming nonnegative integer values: the so-called "computable functions". We define a function to be computable if there exists an "effective description" for it, that is a finite sentence unambiguously indicating (possibly only some explicit way) what is its "behaviour" in correspondence to each natural number. In other words, an effective description must allow us to deduce, for any given argument, whether the described function is defined on it and, if it is so, the value it assumes there. Perhaps the careful reader will observe that this definition is very different from the one usually found in the literature: in fact, it may seem strange to call "computable" those functions for which we didn't explicitly prescribe the precise means for computing them, for example, some particular procedure or model of an abstract "computing device". Moreover, even the general concepts of "effective procedure", "algorithm", or "abstract computing device" are not needed for the definition we gave of a computable function.

A trivial answer to such arguments could be: try to accept the definition without considering the usual meaning of the word "computable"; possibly, it could be remarked that in this case a different expression, as "effectively describable" or something like that, would be more appropriate.

A more satisfactory argument is that we will eventually see that our computable functions are effectively computable in the usual sense, but now it is interesting to see that this somehow vague and perhaps unsatisfactory definition suffices not only to fully characterize a class of functions, but also to draw some important conclusions about their properties without introducing inessential concepts. In other words, we are looking now for properties of computable functions which do not depend on any specific description of them, but which simply follow from the fact that these functions are effectively described in the mentioned sense.

Obviously, such properties are of some interest mainly if they refer to a large number (hopefully infinite) of computable functions. This implies that we must deal with infinite collections of definitions, which we will call "defining systems". In other words, a defining system is a potentially infinite set of effective descriptions; since it is potentially infinite, we cannot hope to have it explicitly, but we need a synthetic definition of it. The property we require for the definition of a defining system is that it provides (possibly in an implicit way) an effective method allowing to decide whether a given finite sentence belongs or does not belong to it.

Observe that introducing the properties of the effective description of a function and of a describing system we did the same conceptual operation, consisting in reducing an infinite set (the set of "behaviours" of the computable functions, and the set of descriptions) to a finite description of it, and the only properties which are needed are to allow us to get any element of the described set from the description. This operation is necessary, since we want to talk about such infinite sets not referring to them simply with conventional "names", but with meaningful and exhaustive descriptions.

## 2. Enumeration of Computable Functions

A first important conclusion can now be drawn: given any defining system (i.e. given its description), we can enumerate the descriptions it contains, that is we can establish an effective one-one correspondence between integers and descriptions, such that there is a number for each description, and (if the defining system is infinite) there is a description for each number. This can be done extracting our definitions from any totally ordered set containing them, for example from the set of all strings of letters of the alphabet in which they are given, supposing we established a lexicographic order on it. The importance of having a description of the defining system with the required property is obviously essential in doing this. We can say that the number of a definition exactly expresses the number of definitions preceding it in the given ordering. In other words, having the description of the defining system, we may associate a definition with each given integer and an integer with any given definition. This implies that any defining system can contain at most countably many descriptions, and therefore the set of functions it describes can at most have countably many elements. Since there are nondenumberably many functions from subsets of the set of nonnegative integers assuming nonnegative integer values, we conclude that "almost all" of them cannot be described by a given defining system.

Let us now make a digression from the main course of our discussions for considering an interesting problem arising in a natural way from the enumerability of the descriptions of a defining system: can also the described functions be enumerated? In fact, such an enumeration would be very useful in our theory, allowing us to introduce a strong structure (of total ordering) in the set of functions corresponding to any describing system. At first sight, whereas it is easy to see how this could be done, it is very difficult to decide whether the proposed procedure can effectively be carried out. We would try to erase, from the enumeration of descriptions we showed to be possible, all descriptions of the functions already described in the enumeration. This would require that we detect whether any two descriptions refer to the same function. How could this be done? Obviously, we cannot verify that the "behaviour" indicated by each description is identical in both cases, since this requires carrying over infinitely many such checks, one for each integer. We may just hope that some effective procedure exists, based on considering only the descriptions per se, that are finite,and not also what they describe. It is important to notice that when we say that we are looking for an "effective" procedure of enumeration, we mean something similar to the concept of "satisfactory description", we introduced: we ask that such a procedure produces a definite result every time it is applied.

Surprisingly enough, it can be proved that there is no effective procedure solving the problem of the identity of functions given by different descriptions. This result is not easy to prove at this point, although it is a trivial corollary of a fundamental fact that will be exposed within a few pages. Anyway, we don't need to justify it now since it only precludes a possible solution (perhaps the more immediate) to the problem of enumeration of computable functions, which is not essential for the consistance of our subsequent arguments.

## 3. The Diagonalization Procedure

Let us now introduce a very fundamental consequence of the enumerability of the descriptions of a defining system, which constitutes one of the most important points of our introduction to the computable function theory. Consider the following statement: given a defining system and an enumeration of its definitions, define a function d whose behaviour is different from that of the elements of the diagonal of the matrix having rows corresponding to descriptions and columns corresponding to arguments. That is, the functions this statement would define have, for any given x, a different behaviour than the function corresponding to the x-th definition in the given enumeration, for the same argument. For the sake of clarity, particularize the definition of d for example in this way:

$$d(x) = \begin{cases} 0 & \text{if } f_x \text{ is undefined in } x \\ f_x(x) + 1 & \text{otherwise} \end{cases}$$

where $f_x$ is the function corresponding to the x-th definition in the given enumeration of the given defining system. This procedure defining a function is called "diagonalization", for obvious reasons, and it is widely applied in the theory we are introducing.

It is clear that the definition of d cannot belong to the definitory system from which it comes out, since its behaviour is different from the behaviour of any function described in the system, at least at the argument corresponding to the diagonal element. In fact, supposing that there is a y such that $f_y = d$ leads to the contradiction

$$f_y(y) \neq f_y(y)$$

Observing that this result simply follows from the properties of the definitions of functions and of defining systems, we could conclude that no defining system contains the definitions of all computable functions, since we may always produce, by diagonalization, the definition of a new function that does not correspond to any definition of the system. But remark that this conclusion is essentially based on the fact that we accept that the statement later introduced effectively defines a computable function. Let us now consider such assumption more deeply.

First of all, the diagonal procedure has a quite strange structure, since it refers to a defining system or, to say it clearly, to the set of its definitions as a whole. In other words, some perplexity should arise from the fact that we used the definition of the defining system in the definition of d, because a defining system involves infinitely many effectively computable functions. This does not mean that we cannot define functions referring to other computable functions, but perhaps having infinitely many of them could be too much for computability, if there is no way of reducing their number. On the other hand, this does not mean that no definition referring to a defining system is valid: for example, it is clear that the function $d'(x) = f_x(x)$ (that is, undefined in x if $f_x$ is also), for every x, is certainly well defined, even if its definition has a structure quite similar to that of d.

There may be something paradoxical in puzzling over the computability of a function each value of which we can compute, but remember that this is only a consequence of computability, for which the possibility of a finite and self-contained description is also needed.

There is another fundamental aspect related to the definition of d: we made no distinctions in dealing with the cases in which f is defined or undefined, implicitly considering undefiniteness at a point as if it were the value the function assumes there. This would imply, for example, that for a given computable and everywhere defined function we could obtain infinitely many functions simply by differently restricting its domain, and there is no doubt that each of them would be effectively described. This would lead to another quite surprising conclusion: starting from a system defining all constant functions, we could get by this technique the descriptions of nondenumerably many functions. Therefore there are nondenumerably many computable functions, and any defining system can only contain the infinitesimal part of them.

This result would erase any effective meaning from our theory, based on computability and defining systems: we try to avoid this drawback by supposing that there exists a "complete" defining system, that is containing the definitions of all computable functions. In what will follow, we shall always consider complete defining systems.

## 4. Church's Thesis and the Unsolvability Result

Before considering all consequences of the assumption made at the end of the previous section, let us emphasize that there is no logical necessity for it: we could try to construct another new theory without it. Nevertheless, there are many arguments supporting the convenience of accepting it. Beside what we exposed, there is at least another kind of consideration, starting from particular instances of defining systems, as those introduced by Turing, Markov, Kleene, Post, but we will expose only later one of them. However, all such indications share some obscure, informal and perhaps unconvincing appearance. This happens because the assumption usually referred to as "Church's Thesis", has, in some sense, an "extra-theoretical" character, that is, it asserts something about the real world, not intrinsic to the theory we are developing, but concerning the effective existence (even if in the sense of a platonic idea) of a mathematical object.

Let us now consider what Church's Thesis implies about our diagonal definition. Of course such a procedure must be rejected as effectively defining a recursive function in order to avoid the contradiction

$$(\exists y)\ [f_y(y) \neq f_y(y)]$$

How can this be justified? From our previous informal argumentations, it should be intuitively clear that the crucial point must concern the question wheth - $f_x$ is defined at x. In fact, if we accept that it is always possible to effectively solve this question, we have no more ways of denying that d is effectively defined i.e. computable. (Observe that in such kind of statements the fundamental term "effectively" gets some more precise definiteness, since its meaning is in some sense related to the existence of a computable function). To formally explain the last statement, consider the everywhere defined function:

$$u(x) = \begin{cases} 1 & \text{if } f_x(x) \text{ is defined} \\ 0 & \text{if } f_x(x) \text{ is undefined} \end{cases}$$

where now $f_x$ is the function corresponding to the x-th definition of our complete defining system. Obviously, there are plenty of simple ways effectively defining d using u, and therefore we must exclude that u can have an effective definition. Once more remark that this does not mean that we can't find the value that u assumes corresponding to any argument x, by considering any special structure of $f_x$ and manipulating it in some particular way. What we exclude is that such manipulation may be generalized to be applicable to any argument x. This conclusion is usually called "unsolvability result", since it expresses the unsolvability of the problem: for any x, is $f_x$ (x) defined? , by means of a computable function. (In the theory arising from the Turning's definition of a particular defining system, to be exposed later, this is called "unsolvability of the halting problem").

## 5. Other Unsolvable Problems and the s-m-n Theorem

There are many other problems which may be proved to be unsolvable (in the given meaning) by reducing them to our unsolvability result, but there also exist some "more unsolvable" problems, that is problems that would be still unsolvable even if some "oracle" would give us a definition for the function u. In the present paper, however, we will not be concerned with such problems. Rather than that, let us consider the above introduced problem of deciding, for any x and y, whether $f_x$ and $f_y$ describe the same function. (Remember that this problem would allow us to introduce an effective enumeration of all computable functions).

We need a preliminary result,usually known as the s-m-n theorem,in order to be able to face this problem. Consider the description of any computable function of two variables: $\psi(x,y)$. If we fix the value of its first argument, what we get is the description of a new function of a single variable. Suppose z to be such that

$$\lambda y\,[\psi(x,y)] = f_z(y)$$

that is $\psi$, considered as function only y, corresponds to the z-th definition of our complete defining system. Obviously, the index z depends on the value we fixed for x, in the sense that from different values for x we obtain different functions of one variable, and therefore we can say that

$$z = s(x)$$

and, what is very interesting, we can prove that s is computable. In fact, an effective definition of s can be given in two steps: first, obtain from the definition of $\psi$ a definition for $f_z$ simply by stating that the first variable has to be maintained at the prefixed value, as a parameter. After this, find a number for this new definition of $f_z$ in the numbering of the complete defining system.

We can now prove that the problem of identity of functions corresponding to different descriptions is unsolvable. The proof is carried out by contradiction, so suppose that there exists a computable and everywhere defined function f of two arguments such that

$$f(x,y) = \begin{cases} 1 & \text{if } f_x = f_y \\ 0 & \text{otherwise} \end{cases}$$

Then define a new function $\psi$ of two variables in this way:

$$\psi(x,y) = \begin{cases} 0 \text{ if } f_x(x) \text{ is defined} \\ \text{undefined} \quad \text{otherwise} \end{cases}$$

Remark that this definition is completely valid, even if its structure is quite similar to the definition of u; in fact, we do not require $\psi$ to be everywhere defined, and this avoids the contradiction we found in the definition of u. By the s-m-n theorem, there exists a function h such that

$$\lambda y\, [\psi(x,y)] = f_{h(x)}(y),$$

that is h(x) gives the number of a definition of a function that is everywhere equal to zero if $f_x$ (x) is defined and is nowhere defined if $f_x$ (x) is undefined. Observe that a definition for u cannot be effectively obtained in a simple way from a definition for h, since this would imply considering still now undefiniteness as a value assumed by our functions; therefore the existence of an effective definition for h is not contradictory. Choosing now any number $y_1$ such that $f_{y_1}$ is everywhere equal to zero, we obtain that:

$$u(x) = f(h(x), y_1)$$

is an effective definition, since we may detect whether $f_{h(x)}$ describes the everywhere null function. This contradicts the unsolvability result, and therefore the proposed description of f cannot be effective.

The unsolvability of this problem can also be deduced as a trivial corollary of Rice's Theorem, which will be presented later. Nevertheless, we believe that this proof is very interesting in its own right, and therefore that it has been worthwhile spending some time in exposing it.

We will present now another important result making somehow more precise the arguments about undefiniteness we introduced to informally making acceptable the Church's thesis. Remark however that this result cannot be used to justify the Church's Thesis, from which it directly follows. We show that undefiniteness is something essentially intrinsic to the type of functions we are dealing with, by proving that there exist computable functions for which there is not an everywhere defined function assuming the same values in their domain. In fact, consider the definition

$$v(x) = \begin{cases} f_x(x) + 1 & \text{if } f_x(x) \text{ is defined} \\ \text{undefined} & \text{otherwise} \end{cases}$$

Observe that accepting that this definition is effective does not lead to any contradiction even if v(x) is quite similar to the "diagonal" function u(x). This is because we can have $v(x) = f_y(x)$ for some y such that $f_y(y)$ is undefined. But if we suppose that y' is a number corresponding to the definition of an everywhere defined function coinciding with v(x) in its domain, we get the same paradoxical conclusion obtained for u(x): since $f_{y'}(y')$ is defined, also v(y') must be defined and

$$f_{y'}(y') = v(y') = f_{y'}(y') + 1$$

where the last equality holds by definition of v(x) and the first one by definition of y'.

A very important aspect of the last arguments is that we know we can get new functions by diagonalization only if we allow them to be undefined at least where the corresponding element of the diagonal is also undefined. Imposing differently defined behaviours depending on definiteness or undefiniteness over the diagonal leads to non computable functions. We could say, in a not completely rigorous but meaningful sense, that it is impossible in general to get definiteness from undefiniteness. This situation recalls the entropy principle of thermodynamics, but further work is required to ascertain the real meaning of this analogy.

Remembering that everywhere defined functions were often involved in unsolvable problems, it will not surprise that they are so ill-behaved that it is not even possible to enumerate the descriptions of all of them. In fact, if it would be possible, we could get by diagonalization a new everywhere defined function such that, supposing that a description of it is present in the enumeration, leads to a contradiction. In other words, define:

$$u'(x) = f'_x(x) + 1$$

where $f'_x$ is the x-th description in our enumeration of everywhere defined functions; supposing y to be such that

$$f'_y = u'$$

implies

$$f'_y(y) = u'(y) = f'_y(y) + 1$$

Observe that this conclusion does not depend on Church's thesis, but it implies the rather paradoxical situation in which a subset of an enumerable set (the complete defining system of Church's thesis) is not enumerable. This suffices to prove that there is no effective way to solve the problem whether any given $f_x$ is everywhere defined (since this would allow us to get an enumeration for the definitions of all everywhere defined functions from the enumeration of the complete defining system). Moreover, we may conclude that there is no effective way of deciding what is the domain of the function corresponding to any given description. Of course, the description of a function determines its domain, but what we mean is that saying that there must be an everywhere defined function $\psi$ of two variables such that

$$\psi(x,y) = \begin{cases} 1 & \text{if } f_x(y) \text{ is defined} \\ 0 & \text{otherwise} \end{cases}$$

does not effectively define a computable function. Remark that this result also follows from the unsolvability of the halting problem.

## 6. The Rice's Theorem: A First Proof

Rice's theorem is a quite general result about the unsolvability of a class of problems concerning relations between computable functions and their descriptions, and it can be proven by a quite simple procedure, which is very similar to those exposed in our previous considerations. Let $C$ be any class of computable functions (examples: the class of computable functions never assuming the value zero, or, simply, the only everywhere defined function always equal to ten), and define the set of integers

$$P_C = \{x \mid f_x \in C\}$$

that is, the set all indices of the functions belonging to $C$ in a given enumeration of the complete definging system. Consider now the function

$$g(x) = \begin{cases} 1 & \text{if } x \in P_C \\ 0 & \text{if } x \notin P_C \end{cases}$$

Rice's theorem asserts that in all nontrivial cases (that is, when C is nonempty and with nonempty complement), such a g is not computable! This is a very surprising result, but, as we shall see, it is directly implied by the unsolvability result. An equivalent statement says that the set $P_C$ is non recursive if C is nontrivial. The proof uses a slightly modified form of the function $\psi(x,y)$ we introduced to prove the unsolvability of the problem of identity of functions corresponding to different descriptions. (Remark that we said that this is a trivial corollary of Rice's theorem: if we choose

$$C = \{f_y\},$$

$f_x \in C$, simply means $f_x = f_y$). Suppose that f is in C and that the everywhere undefined function is not (if this were not the case, the proof could be carried over by obvious modifications), then define

$$f(x) + \psi(x,y) = \psi'(x,y) = \begin{cases} f(x) & \text{if } f_x(x) \text{ is defined} \\ \text{undefined} & \text{otherwise} \end{cases}$$

By the s-m-n theorem, the everywhere defined function h' such that

$$f_{h'(x)} = \lambda y\,[\psi'(x,y)]$$

is computable. But

$$u = gh'$$

In fact, h'(x) is in $P_C$ iff $f_x(x)$ is defined, and $g(y) = 1$ iff y is in $P_C$; otherwise, $g(y) = 0$. If g were computable, this would be an effective definition for u, which is absurd.

Another simple but interesting corollary of Rice's theorem is the unsolvability of the problem of deciding, for any given integer x, whether $f_x$ is extendible to an everywhere defined describable function (remember we showed that this is not always possible).

## CHAPTER II

### 1. Introduction

We shall now consider the computable functions from a different, and less abstract, point of view. In fact, we will be concerned with a particular complete defining system and the possible ways of enumerating its descriptions.

We think that in this way we shall not only make the properties of our computable functions more evident, but also that such a simple and satisfactory description will be an useful help to realize what we are talking about. Quite obviously, there is the risk of considering some peculiar properties of this particular description as having universal validity or, au contraire, of having some important general characteristics as shadowed in our representation. It is because of such possible drawbacks that, after giving the announced representation, we shall spend a great deal of time in order to extract from it the general properties we are really interested in. This is easily done, as we shall see, using the specific properties of this representation. In this way the main results of this chapter could be considered as general and abstract as the previous ones.

### 2. Computable functions described by Turing Machines

We shall describe our functions by specifying how their values can be computed, for each value of their arguments.

This is done in a "uniform" way, since for each function we use the same "defining model"; this means that each function has to be computed following the same general schema. We use the concept of Turing Machine (T M), as defining model.

A TM is a quadruple $(Q,X,P,q_o)$ where Q and X are disjoint sets having a finite number of elements

$$Q = \{q_o, q_1, q_2 \dots q_n\}$$

$$X = \{b, 1, x_1, \dots, x_m\}$$

(observe that we imposed $q_o \in Q$), and P is a sequence of quintuples each one of which has the following structure: $- q_i x_j q_k x_h D$, for any values of i, j, h, k

such that $q_i$ , $q_k \in Q$ and $x_j$ , $x_h \in X$; moreover, $D \in \{R, L, N\}$ . Finally, no two quintuples in P can have the same first two elements.
Example:

$$Q = \{q_0, q_1\} \qquad X = \{b, 1\}$$

$$P = (-q_0 1\, q_1 1 R - q_1 1\, q_0 b R - q_0 b\, q_0 b R)$$

A TM $M_f$ defines a function f in the following way: suppose we want to know the value of f in correspondence to the argument a: then build up the string

$$\ldots\ bbbbb\ q_0\ \underbrace{111\ \ldots\ 11}_{a\ \text{elements}}\ bbb\ \ldots\ ;$$

(that is, the finite string $q_0$ 111 ... 11 is supposed to be preceded and followed by an infinite string of b). After that, search in P for a quadruple whose two first symbols are the (unique) element of Q present in the string and its successor, and replace them with the third and fourth symbols of the quadruple. If no such quadruple exists, take the number of 1's present in the string as the value of f(a). Finally, interchange the element of Q present in the string with its predecessor if the fifth symbol of the string we are using is L, with its successor if it is R, and do nothing if it is N. We have so described a single "cycle" of our computation; after a cycle is carried out, the same procedure is iterated, until we find a string having no correspondence in P. If the computation cannot stop, then f is undefined at a. This is the way we associate a function to a TM, which is said to define the function it "computes".

It can be easily shown that the TM in preceding example defines the function: f(a) = a/2, that is only defined for even values.

## 3. The Standard Numbering

We shall now associate a number to each TM. First of all, observe that the only sequence P is sufficient to describe a TM, since we can define from it the set Q as containing the first and the third symbol we meet after every sign - in P, and similarly X.

Convert now all indices into full-size numbers following in P the symbol they refer to. Then we may consider this new form of P as a number written in base 16, with symbols 0,1,2,3,4,5,6,7,8,9,q,x,R,L,N,-.

We conclude that we have enumerated the set of functions computable by TM's, since as we saw, for each machine there is a function and a well defined number associated with it. We will refer to such functions as "partial recursive functions", and to such numbers as "standard numbers", and we will indicate by $\alpha_i$ the function defined by the TM $M_i$, that is by the machine whose standard number is i and defined by the sequence P obtained by expressing i in base 16, with symbols 0,1,2,3,4,5,6,7,8,9,q,x,R,L,N,.-.

Let us now consider in some detail the characteristics of the correspondence we have introduced between integers (indices) and functions via TM's, in order to fully understand its real usefulness in representing partial recursive functions.

First of all, it is clear that we are now able to know whether a given number does or does not correspond to a function (it suffices to see whether the number, expressed in base 16, possesses the characteristic structure and properties of any sequence P for TM's). This possibility is synthesized saying that the domain of the standard numbering is recursive. Moreover, we may effectively derive from the number the function it represents (that is, a TM computing it). The only thing we must do is to express the given index in base 16 and interpret it as a sequence of quintuples. This fact can help us to accept the following statement, given here without proof: there exists a "universal" TM U defining a function $\phi_u$ of two arguments (TM's dealing with more than one argument are a trivial extension of the TM we described), such that

$$(\forall i)\ [\lambda x\ [\phi_u\ (i,x)] = \varphi_i]$$

In an informal but suggestive way, we could say that U can "stimulate" what the machine described by its first argument would do about the second argument. (Remark that this fact suggests how U can be defined).

A very important aspect of this result has been emphasized by Rogers: the existence of U implies that, computing partial functions of one variable, there is a critical degree of "mechanical complexity" (that of U), beyond which all further complexity can be absorbed into increased size of program (i.e. of arguments).

On the other hand, it is obvious that the converse is also true: given any function (that is, given the description of any TM computing it), we are able (as we saw) to effectively produce a number associated with it.

We may therefore conclude that each standard number i can be identified with the corresponding TM. This point is of fundamental importance, since it allows us to deal with partial recursive functions as with integers; for example, we will consider partial recursive functions as arguments for TM's.

**4. Effective Numberings**

The question now arises about the generality of the standard numbering, since it is clear that any change in the representation or codification of TM's will produce different numberings. i.e. different ways of mapping integers onto the set of partial recursive functions, having the same three properties: recursiveness of the domain of such mappings, existence of a universal function $\phi$ such that $\lambda_x\ [\phi(i,x)]$ coincides with the function whose number (in the new numbering, of course) is i, and existence of a procedure giving a number corresponding to the function computed by a given TM $M_i$ i.e. to the function having a given standard number i. We may observe that the last statement follows, in an obvious sense, from the identification we have just made between standard numbers and TM's. Let us formalize this third property: there must exist an everywhere defined computable function f such that

$$(\forall i)[\lambda(x)[\phi(f(i),x)] = \varphi_i]$$

Any numbering enjoying the two first properties is said to be semi-effective, whereas if it satisfies also the third one, it is fully effective. Therefore it will be interesting to characterize the class of fully effective numberings.

Let us start considering in some detail the third property required for a fully effective numbering: it is always possible to effectively produce, from any standard number, a number corresponding to the same function in the new (fully effective numbering). We synthesize such a situation saying that the standard numbering is "derivable" from any fully effective numbering.

It is interesting to see that also the converse is true: any fully effective numbering is derivable from the standard numbering. This is easily proven, since we can effectively produce a TM computing the function corresponding to a given number in the fully effective numbering (by the second property), and then find its standard number. Observe that the same proof is valid in the case of semi-effective numberings.

## 5. Equivalence Classes of Numberings - Goedel Numberings

If we agree to call "equivalent" two numberings such that each of them is derivable from the other, we may conclude that the concept of derivability introduces a partial ordering between the classes of this equivalence (we obviously extend the definition of derivability to equivalence classes), since it is a transitive, reflexive and anti-symmetric binary relation.

We may conclude that the class of full effective numberings is contained in the equivalence class also containing the standard numbering. We may now ask: is this inclusion proper? The answer is negative, since if a nonstandard numbering is derivable from the standard numbering, it is semi-effective: in fact we can effectively produce a standard number (i.e. a TM) for the function corresponding to a given nonstandard number. On the other hand, if a numbering "derives" the standard numbering, this exactly means that there is an effective procedure generating a nonstandard number for a given function (via a standard number for it).

We have now the desired characterization for the class of fully effective numberings: a numbering is fully effective if it is equivalent to (i.e. it derives and it is derivable from) the standard numbering. Any numbering in such a situation is often referred to as "Goedel numbering".

Could we now even pretend to formulate concept of Goedel numbering in an "intrinsic" way, that is fully independent on the standard numbering? In fact, not only have we explicitly mentioned the standard numbering in its definition, but also the characterization as fully effective numbering is referred to the standard numbering (via the third property). Otherwise stated, could we characterize the class of fully effective numberings by means of semi- effective numberings? We will show we can.

Consider the partial order induced by the derivability relation over the equivalence classes of semi-effective numberings; then the class of Goedel numberings is the (unique) maximal equivalence class of such ordering, that is a Goedel numbering is a semi-effective numbering such that every semi-effective numbering can be derived from it.

We prove this statement by exploiting the derivability of the standard numbering from any other Goedel numbering (following from the definition of Goedel numbering). This fact allows to restrict ourselves to prove that any semi-effective numbering is derivable from the standard numbering, since in this way we will conclude that any given semi-effective numbering is derivable from any Goedel numbering.

The proof is completed by remembering the remark made after proving that any fully effective numbering is derivable from the standard numbering. From that we conclude, as desired, that there is an effective procedure giving a standard number for the function corresponding to any given number in a semi- effective numbering.

# CHAPTER III

## 1. Introduction

A very important part of the discussions of the first chapter was devoted to "diagonal" functions, that is, functions whose behaviour corresponding to an argument x were dependent on the behaviour corresponding to the same argument of the function whose description was the x-th in an enumeration of a complete defining system. In fact, the unsolvability result asserts that the function u is not computable and the proof of Rice's theorem introduces the function $\psi'$, which is a generalization of the corresponding function $\psi$. Comparing these functions and remembering what we said commenting the unsolvability result,we may consider the definition of the functions h and h'(obtained from $\psi$ and $\psi'$by the s-m-n theorem) as a trick to avoid the contradictions produced requiring that u be everywhere defined. In fact, h' is an everywhere defined and computable function having different behaviours corresponding to the definiteness or undefiniteness of the diagonal elements as we required for the function u , since it gives an index for a well defined function f if $f_x(x)$ is defined, and for the everywhere undefined function if $f_x(x)$ is undefined. Nevertheless, this does not lead to any contradiction because we cannot effectively know the complete behaviour of the function corresponding to any given description (as Rice's theorem states).

The proof of the recursion theorem that we shall expose in this chapter provides a further generalization of the functions $\psi$and h, leading the procedure of diagonalization to justify a useful and basic statement. Before exposing the recursion theorem, we introduce some other interesting results that will be useful for the proof of the recursion theorem.

## 2. "Padding" Functions

The first result is quite general and concerns the structure a complete defining system may have. As we know, a complete defining system must contain the definitions of all computable functions, but this leaves the question unsettled of how many descriptions of any function it can contain. We feel that this depends on the particular defining system we are considering, but the most interesting result is that there are complete defining systems containing infinitely many descriptions of each computable function. In fact, given any effective description of a function, we may construct a new description for the same function simply by adding some redundant statements that are not influencing the behaviour of the described function in any way. Since we may carry over this procedure infinitely many times, it can be concluded that, starting with any complete defining system, we may get as many descriptions for any computable function as needed. Moreover, since the exhibited procedure (often referred to as "padding" technique) can be made fully explicit in an effective way, once the defining system we begin with is specified, what we get is a new complete defining system with the required characteristics.

It must be emphasized that the padding technique effectively generates a new description from an old one; this means that an everywhere defined computable function $t'(x,y)$ exists and gives the indices of different descriptions f  as y varies. In fact, a description for t' could be the following: $t'(x,0)$  x  1, and to obtain $t'(x,y)$ apply y times the padding procedure to the x-th description in the enumeration of the defining system and then find the number of the obtained description. Moreover, we can obtain another computable function $t(x,y)$ having the same properties as t' and assuming only once each of its values (one-one property). An effective definition for t requires an effective enumeration of all ordered pairs of integers. Although this is a quite simple work, we will present it in some detail since it is a special case of a procedure that will be often useful in our theories, called "dovetailing procedure". It can also be used to show that there are only denumerably many rational numbers. The procedure consists in successively scanning the antidiagonals of the doubly infinite matrix whose element in the i-th row and j-th column is the pair (i,j) (we admit, for simplicity, that there exists the 0-th row and column). We obtain that the pair (i,j) is the k-th in this enumeration, with

$$k = 1/2\ (i^2 + 2ij + j^2 + 3i + j)$$

We will often indicate k as $\langle i, j \rangle$.

The function t can now be defined as follows: $t(0,0) = 1$, and to compute $t(x,y)$ check whether $t'(x,y) \neq t(x',y')$ for all values of x' and y' such that $\langle x',y' \rangle < \langle x,y \rangle$; if it is so, define $t(x,y) = t'(x,y)$; otherwise, repeat the test with $t'(x,y + 1)$, $t'(x,y + 2)$ and so on until a new value for $t(x,y)$ is found. This is an effective definition for t, since we have to carry over at most $\langle x,y \rangle$ tests, because $y_1 \neq y_2$ implies $t'(x,y_1) \neq t'(x,y_2)$. Moreover, t has the one-one property since $t(x,y) \neq t(x',y')$ for all x' and y' such that $\langle x',y' \rangle < \langle x,y \rangle$.

### 3. Composition of Functions

Another result required in the proof of the recursion theorem is given by an interesting application of the s-m-n theorem in a generalized form. Consider the function f of three arguments such that

$$f(x,y,z) = f_x(f_y(z))$$

(by this equation we mean that f is defined iff $f_y(z)$ is defined and $f_x$, is defined on it). That is, $\lambda z[f(x,y,z)]$ is the "composition" of $f_x$ and $f_y$. It is clear that $\lambda z\,[f(x,y,z)]$ is a computable function, since $f_x$ and $f_y$ are; moreover, also $\lambda xyz[f(x,y,z)]$ is a computable function, since we may define the operation of "composing" functions independently on the functions to be composed. It is now very easy to see that the s-m-n theorem can be generalized and made applicable also to the function f. We may therefore conclude that there exists an everywhere defined computable function c(x,y) such that

$$f_{c(x,y)}(z) = f_x(f_y(z))$$

### 4. The Recursion Theorem

We can now state and prove the recursion theorem. It says that there exists an everywhere defined one-one computable function of two variables n(x,y) such that, if $f_x$ is everywhere defined, then

$$f_{n(x,y)} = f_{f_x(n(x,y))}$$

for all y. This is not the first time we encounter a computable function manipulating the index of another computable function, but in this theorem the situation is perhaps more evident; there is nothing surprising in this, because we know that the effective enumeration of a defining system associates an integer to each description; nevertheless, remark that the above relation makes sense only if $f_x$ is everywhere defined. The bulk of the proof of the recursion theorem is the construction of an everywhere defined computable function $\tilde{g}(u)$ giving the index of a definition for $f_{f_u(u)}$ if $f_u(u)$ is defined, and for the everywhere undefined function otherwise. We know that this can be done applying this s-m-n theorem to the function

$$\tilde{\psi}(u,z) = \begin{cases} f_{f_u(u)}(z) & \text{if } f_u(u) \text{ is defined} \\ \text{undefined} & \text{otherwise} \end{cases}$$

following the same procedure used in the proof of Rice's theorem. We can say that if $f_u(u)$ is defined, the description whose index is $\tilde{g}(u)$ differs from the one whose index is $f_u(u)$ only in that it prescribes first to check the definiteness of $f_u(u)$. Observe now that for any given x, the function $f_x \tilde{g}$ is also computable; suppose v is such that $f_v = f_x \tilde{g}$ ; then if $f_x$ is everywhere defined, also $f_v(v)$ is, and therefore $f_{\tilde{g}(v)} = f_{f_v(v)} = f_{f_x(\tilde{g}(v))}$. This is a simpler form of the result we are looking for: it simply states that there is a point $n = \tilde{g}(v)$ such that

$$f_n = f_{f_x(n)}$$

Our version of the recursion theorem states that there are infinitely many such points (the values of the one-one function $\lambda y[n(x,y)]$)and that they can effectively be found from the value of x. This second requirement is easily proven by means of the function c found in the previous section, and giving the index of a definition of any "composed" function. In fact, if we fix $\tilde{g}$ , the index v will be an everywhere defined computable function of only x:

$$f_{v(x)} = f_x \tilde{g}$$

Try now to define $n(x,y) = \tilde{g}(t(v(x),y))$; is it a satisfactory solution? It is not, because such a function n is not one-one: in fact, we cannot exclude that, for different arguments, $\tilde{g}$ gives the index of the same description. The drawback is easily overcome by using a one-one function g' instead of g; for example $g'(u) = t(g(u),u)$. Then $n(x,y) = g'(t(v'(x),y))$ with v' such that $f_{v'(x)} = f_x g'$ concludes the proof, since it is one-one, and $f_{n(x,y)} = f_{g'(t(v'(x),y))} = f_{f_{t(v'(x),y)}(t(v(x),y))}$ by the property of g' and g, but: $f_{t(v(x),y)} = f_{v'(x)}$ by definition of t and therefore

$$f_{n(x,y)} = f_{f_x(\tilde{g}'(t(v'(x),y)))} = f_{f_x(n(x,y))}$$

as required.

Roughly speaking the recursion theorem states that for any given description of an everywhere defined function f there are infinitely many "fixed points" n, that can be effectively found starting from the given description, such that

$$f_{f(n)} = f_n$$

## 5. Rice's Theorem: Second Proof

An interesting application of the recursion theorem provides an alternative proof of Rice's theorem. It is noticeable that this new proof gets a contradiction without using the unsolvability result.

Suppose, by contradiction, that the function g of the Rice's theorem:

$$g(x) = \begin{cases} 1 & \text{if} \quad x \in P_C \\ 0 & \text{if} \quad x \notin P_C \end{cases}$$

is computable. Moreover, call i an index such that $f_j \in C$ and j an index such that $f_j \notin C$. Then define the function

$$h(x) = \begin{cases} j & \text{if} \quad g(x) = 1 \\ i & \text{if} \quad g(x) = 0 \end{cases}$$

Therefore h is an everywhere defined computable function mapping the elements of $P_C$ into $P_C$ and the elements $P_C$ into $P_C$ x, but since the recursion theorem is applicable we get a contradiction.

## 6. Isomorphism of Goedel Numberings

The recursion theorem can also be used to prove a further result about the matter exposed in Chapter II. We found there that the class of Goedel numberings can be fully characterized without any reference to the standard numbering. Nevertheless one feels that the standard numbering is in some sense more naturally "intrinsic" to the description of computable functions given by TM's as we did, than some other Goedel numbering. We will prove that this is not completely true, since there is an effective one-one correspondence between any two Goedel numberings, and therefore also between any Goedel numbering and the set of TMs. Observe that this is a peculiar property of the equivalence class of Goedel numbering, and it is not true for any equivalence class. Indeed, the equivalence only requires the existence of two computable functions mapping a numbering into the other whereas by one-one equivalence or, better said, recursive isomorphism, we mean a single one-one recursive function, mapping a numbering onto the other.

We now go into the details of the proof of this statement, since it uses some interesting techniques of the theory of computable functions that is of great usefulness in a wide area of problems.

We exploit the fact that the equivalence class we are dealing with contains the standard numbering showing that any Goedel numbering is recursively isomorphic to it. In fact, from this we may conclude that any two Goedel numberings are recursively isomorphic, since recursive isomorphism is a symmetric and transitive binary relation (as it can be easily shown).

We first show that if any numbering is derivable from the standard numbering, then there exists a one-one computable function mapping the former into the latter. In other words, if there is a computable function g mapping a numbering into the standard numbering, a one-one function g' can be found which does the same.

Such a function is defined in a simple way by means of the "padding" function t, defined in the section 2 of the present Chapter.

To compute g'(x), first check whether $g(x) \neq g'(y) \quad \forall y < x$; if it is so, we define $g'(x) = g(x)$. Otherwise define $g'(x) = t(g(x), z)$, with z sufficiently large in order to guarantee $g'(x) \neq g'(y) \quad \forall y < x$. Observe that the procedure defining g' is effective since both g and t are computable and everywhere defined.

We will now prove the converse of the former statement: if the standard numbering is derivable (by some computable function h) from any other numbering; then there is also a one-one recursive function h' mapping the former into the latter. The proof has to be somehow different from the previous one, in which we essentially exploited the fact that the range of g was contained into the set of standard numbers. Nevertheless, we need also in this case a computable "padding" function t of two variables having the same properties as t; moreover, $\bar{t}$ must be such that, for different values of its second argument, it produces standard numbers that are not only different, but that are mapped by h into different numbers. This suffices in order to give a definition for h' perfectly parallel to that of g'. The crucial point is now the definition of $\bar{t}$, that is given by applying two times the recursion theorem in its simpler version.

To compute $\bar{t}_{(i,x)}$ suppose to know the values of $\bar{t}_{(i,y)}$, $y<x$ and define the following everywhere defined function:

$$\varphi_{r(z)} = \begin{cases} \varphi_i & \text{if} \quad h(z) \notin \{h\bar{t}(i,y) \mid y z x\} \\ \text{undefined everywhere} & \text{otherwise} \end{cases}$$

observe that the condition can be effectively checked, and therefore r is computable; then apply the recursion theorem, obtaining an n such that $\varphi_n = \varphi_{r(n)}$. If the condition is satisfied, define $\bar{t}(i,x) = n$ (in fact this implies $\varphi_n = \varphi_i$). Otherwise, we can conclude that $\varphi_i$ is everywhere undefined, since h(n) is an index for it in the nonstandard numbering, and therefore n is a standard number for it. In this case define

$$\varphi_{r'(z)} = \begin{cases} 0 \text{ everywhere if } h(z) \in \{h\bar{t}(i,y) \mid y < x\} \\ \text{undefined everywhere otherwise} \end{cases}$$

and apply once more the recursion theorem; getting an m such that $\varphi_m = \varphi_{r'(m)}$. Now supposing that $h(m) \in \{h\,\bar{t}(i,y) \mid y<x\}$ is contradictory, since this implies $\varphi_m = \varphi_i$ and $\varphi_i$ is undefined, whereas $\varphi_m$ would be equal to zero everywhere. We therefore define $\bar{t}(i,x) = m$ and the proof of this second statement is concluded.

We have now all elements needed to prove that for any Goedel numbering there is a recursive one-one function mapping it onto the standard numbering (obviously, we also require that indices corresponding each other in this isomorphism describe the same function! ). From what we showed until now we know that there are two one-one computable functions g' and h' mapping respectively either numbering into the other. We define the required one-one onto function f by applying the so-called "finite correspondence procedure". This consists in building up an arbitrarily long sequence of pairs $(x_i, y_i)$ $i = 1...n$ such that $x_i$ is a standard number and $y_i$ is a (nonstandard) number for the same function, and $i \neq j \Rightarrow x_i \neq x_j$, $y_i \neq y_j$ ; moreover all standard and nonstandard numbers must appear in the sequence for some value of n. It is clear that such a sequence gives a definition of the function we are looking for. We show here just one half of the procedure, that uses only h' and leads to a sequence in which not necessarily all nonstandard numbers are present. It is very simple to generalize it in order to get all required properties. Suppose we have the finite correspondence $(x_i, y_i)$ $i = 1... n-1$, and we are looking for the correspondent of the standard number $x_n$ ($x_n \neq x_i$ $i = 1...n-1$). In order to do that, check whether $h'(x_n) \notin \{y_i \,/\, i = 1...n-1\}$. If it is so, take $y_n = h'(x_n)$. Otherwise, supposing $y_j = h'(x_n)$, compute $h'(x_j)$ and check whether $h'(x_j) \notin \{y_i \,/ i = 1...n-1\}$.This procedure must be iterated until the conditions is satisfied; the desired $y_n$ is eventually found after a finite number of steps (at most n) since h' is one-one.

# CHAPTER IV

## 1. Introduction

In the present chapter we shall exploit some implications of the trivial fact that a computable function can be computed in some way. In fact, since a computable function can be effectively described, we may always consider such a description as a procedure allowing us to get the behaviour the function assumes for any given argument. In other words, an effective description must provide a method by which we may know whether the described function is defined for a given value of its independent variable, and, if it is so, we may get its value.

Considering the description as a procedure simply means that we emphasize, instead of only what must be done by a description, also the way in which this must be done. We cannot imagine an effective definition not corresponding to a computing procedure, and this feeling is supported by a version of the Church's thesis a little different frol the one given in Chapter I, and stating that every effectively computable function can be defined by a Turing Machine.

## 2. "Step-Counting" Function M

Observe now that using a procedure to compute the behaviour of a function obviously means performing a sequence of some prescribed elementary operations and manipulations on symbols or numbers. This is a fundamental point, since in this way we can characterize the behaviour of a function for a given argument from the point of view of the effort required to compute it, simply counting how many elementary operations have been performed. Although this opens some promising ways for a theory of the complexity of computable functions, now we will not go furhter into this direction. We are only interested in observing that from the previous considerations we can conclude that an everywhere defined function of four variables M(x,y,z,u) exists and assumes value 1 if using the definition $f_x$ to perform the first u elementary operations (or "steps") prescribed for the computation of $f_x$ (y) , the result z is obtained and if it is not so, M(x,y,z,u) = 0. Moreover, such a "step-counting" function M is also computable if we specify what must be considered as a single "elementary operation" for the definitions of the defining system we are using; and since this can always be done, we conclude that such a computable M may be defined. Obviously, the values M assumes depend on how we define an elementary operation, but its computability immediately follows from the fact that this definition can always be given.

A modified form of the function M is a basic tool in the theory of computational complexity, but the fundamental idea, of considering the computation of the value a computable function assumes as a sequence of elementary operations, is very often useful to show the computability of many other functions.

**3. An Application of M and the "Dovetailing Procedure"**

We now prove a fundamental property of computable functions: for any given computable function f having a nonempty domain we can find a computable function g such that

range g = domain f.

moreover, such a g is everywhere defined.

To define g, carry over the following "dovetailing procedure" on f: compute the first step in the computation for f(0), then the first two steps in the computations for f(0) and f(1), then the first three steps for f(0), f(1), f(2), and so on until a computation (say for f(y)) stops, proving that f(y) converges, that is $y \in$ domain f. Then define g(0) = y. To compute g(x), suppose that g(0), g(1), g(2)...g(x-1) are known. After that, compute the first x steps of the computation for f(0); if this computation stops at or before the x-th step, check whether $0 \neq g(i)$ for i = 0,1,....x-1. If it is so, define g(x) = 0. Otherwise, compute the first x steps of the computation for f(1); if this computation stops in or before the x-th step, repeat the check for $1 \neq g(i)$, i = 0,1,....x-1. If it is so, define g(x) = 0. Otherwise, repeat the same procedure for f(2), f(3)....f(x-1). After this if g(x) has not been defined until now, define g(x) = g(0).

It is clear frol this definition that the range of g coincides with the domain of f. Remark that the values this g assumes depend on the particular definition of "elementary operation" we are using for f, but this does not invalidate the statement we proved.

**4. The Post's Problem - Statement**

Another interesting application of dovetailing procedures may be used to solve the so-called "Post's problem". Roughly speaking the Post's problem deals with the possibility of finding two sets of natural numbers such that there is no method of establishing between them any effective relation. however vague it could be. The crucial point in this formulation of Post's problem is to exactly specify the mathematical form of the above mentioned relation, making it so general to make the possible existence meaningful of the two sets we are looking for. In order to do this, let us define first of all, the "characteristic function" c of any given set A as the everywhere defined function

$$c_A(x) = \begin{cases} 1 & \text{if } x \in A \\ 0 & \text{if } x \notin A \end{cases}$$

Remark that this definition is the mere formalization of a concept often used in this paper: we introduce it here only to simplify our arguments.

The other fundamental concept required to state the Post's problem is the so-called "relative computability". Let A be any given set. Then the function $f^A$ is said to be A-computable if its behaviour is effectively determined once the behaviour of $c_A$ is known. That is, a step of a procedure defining $f^A$ can simply consist in checking whether any number is member of A, and this is supposed to be always possible even if $c_A$ is not computable. Remark that if $c_A$ is computable, then the "A-computability" coincides with plain computability, whereas if it is not so, we can imagine that a description for $f^A$ contains different behaviours, depending on the values assumed by $c_A$ corresponding to some arguments resulting from previous steps of the computation. We assume that for any given set A, all the descriptions of all A-computable functions can be effectively enumerated by the usual techniques, and we call $f_x^A$ the x-th description in such a complete enumeration. Consider now two sets A and B such that $c_B$ is an A-computable function: this means that we may know whether any given number belongs or does not belong to B if we can solve the same problem with respect to A, for any given integer (not only for x). We synthesize such a situation by saying that the set B is "Turing-reducible" to the set A. The Post's problem can be now stated as follows: enumerate two sets that are not Turing reducible each to the other. This problem can effectively be solved by an interesting procedure based on a sophisticated version of the dovetailing technique, and using a somehow implicit A diagonalization.

## 5. The Post's Problem - Solution.

First of all, observe that the Post's problem is solved if two sets A and B are found such that there exist two functions f and g having the properties that

$$(\forall x)[f(x) \in A \iff f(x) \in \text{domain } f_x^B] \text{ and}$$

$$(\forall x)[g(x) \in B \iff g(x) \in \text{domain } f_x^A]$$

In fact, from the first formula we can conclude that

$$(\forall x)[\bar{A} \neq \text{domain } f_x^B]$$

because if it were not so, that is if

$$(\exists x')[\bar{A} = \text{domain } f_{x'}^B]$$

we would have f(x') either belonging to the domain of $f_{x'}^B$ but not to $\bar{A}$ or to $\bar{A}$ but not to domain $f_x^B$. Moreover, supposing that there is a y such that $c_A^B = f_y^B$ would imply that there exists also an index y' for the B-computable function described as follows:

$$f_{y'}^B(x) = \begin{cases} \text{undefined} & \text{if } f_y^B(x) = 1 \\ 0 & \text{if } f_y^B(x) = 0 \end{cases}$$

but in this case we would have $\bar{A}$ = domain $f_{y'}^B$, contradicting the existence of f. A parallel argument for g leads to the conclusion that if f and g can be shown to exist, then the sets A and B solve Post's problem.

We now define A and B by an iterative procedure listing their elements and at the same time defining the function f and g. A singular character of this procedure is that f and g are defined "by successive approximations", in the sense that a finite sequence of different values can successively be assigned to them for each argument, and they are defined to have the last assumed of these values. Two other auxiliary everywhere defined functions h and k are defined during the procedure.

At the beginning of the procedure we have f(0) = g(0) = h(0) = k(0) = 0, and the two sets $A_0$ and $B_0$ are defined to be empty. Suppose now that f(x), g(x), for x = 0, 1...n and to h(n), k(n) some values have been assigned, and that two sets $A_n$ and $B_n$ have been defined. Then define f(n + 1) = h(n), and apply the first n steps of the dovetailing technique to each of the $B_n$-computable functions $f_i^{B_n}$ for i = 1,2...n. From these operations we get the sets $W_i^{B_n}$ of integers for which we have found that $f_i^{B_n}$ is defined, that is

$$W_i^{B_n} = \{x \mid \text{the procedure to compute } f_i^{B_n}(x) \text{ stops in not more than n steps}\}.$$

We may now look for the least element of the sets

$$\{f(x) \mid x = 0,1\ldots n\}$$

call it f(j) such that it is also in $W_j^{B_n}$, but not yet in $A_n$ and define $A_{n+1} = A_n \cup \{f(j)\}$, or $A_{n+1} = A_n$ if no such f(j) can be found. After that, define

$$V_n = \{x \mid x \notin B_n \Rightarrow f(j) \in W_j^{B_n}\}$$

that is the set of numbers that in the first n steps of the computation of $f_j^{B_n}(f(j))$ have been found to belong to $\bar{B}_n$, the complement of $B_n$. If $j \leqslant n$, re-define $g(j) = k(n)$, $g(j+1) = k(n)+1 \ldots g(n) = k(n) + n\text{-}j$, and make $k(n+1)$ to be equal to the least number greater than g(n) and not belonging to $V_n \cup B_n$.

The same operations are repeated for $g(n+1)$, which the value $k(n+1)$ is assigned to, and $B_{n+1}$ is defined to be $B_n \cup \{g(j)\}$ where g(j) has the same properties as f(j), with respect to the sets $W_i^{A_{n+1}}$ and to $B_n$. Moreover, if $j < n+1$, $f(j+1) \ldots f(n+1)$ are re-defined to have the values defined in a way similar to the one used for $k(n+1)$.

To show that this procedure is effective, observe first of all that only finitely many values have been assigned to f and g, for each argument. In fact, the value of f(x) is changed only when an index $\bar{j} < x$ is found, and the value of g(x) is changed only when an index $j \leqslant x$ is found. This never happens for f(0), whereas for g(0) it can happen only once, since the j's as well as the j's cannot assume the zero value more than once. In general, f(x) can change its value only once for each of the values assumed by g(0), g(1)... g(x-1), and for g(x) this is also possible only once for each of the values assumed for f(0), f(1),...... f(x). This suffices to conclude that f and g are well defined.

Now define $A = \bigcup_{n=0}^{\infty} A_n$, and $B = \bigcup_{n=0}^{\infty} B_n$: this means that at each stage of our procedure a new element can be defined to belong to A and B. To conclude our proof suppose that z is the last value assumed by f(x), and that $z = f(x) \in A$. This implies that $(\exists n)[A_{n+1} = A_n \cup \{f(x)\}]$ that is, f(x) has been introduced in A at the n-th stage of our procedure. To show that $f_x^B$ (f(x)) is defined, we observe that no element of $B \cap \bar{B}_n$ were involved in the computation of $f_x^{B_n}(f(x))$, since no element, call it y, of $V_n$ has ever been introduced in B. In fact, suppose it were not so: then $y = g(\bar{x})$ for some $\bar{x}$ but $\bar{x} \geq x$ does not hold, since in the n-th stage we defined $g(\bar{x}) > \max V_n$ for all $\bar{x} \geq x$, and if $\bar{x} < x$ then $g(\bar{x})$ must have added to B after the n-th stage, but in this case all values of f(x), $x > \bar{x}$ would have been changed, contradicting the fact that z is the last value assumed by f(x). Since $f_x^{B_n}$ (f(x)) is defined, so must be also $f_x^B$ (f(x)). Conversely, suppose that $f_x^B$ ((f(x)) is defined: then this implies that $(\exists n)[\, f(x) \in W_x^{B_n}]$ , and it follows from this and from our previous arguments about $f_x^B(f(x))$ and $f_x^{B_n}(f(x))$ that f(x) must have been added to A at some stage of the procedure. This concludes the proof of

$$(\forall x)[\, f(x) \in A \Longleftrightarrow f(x) \in \text{domain } f_x^B]$$

The proof of the similar property for g can be carried out by the same arguments. Therefore the sets A and B just defined effectively solve Post's problem.

# CHAPTER V

## References and Suggestions for Further Readings

As it must be clear, we did not intend to give here a complete and systematic presentation of the computable functions theory, but only to introduce some very basic concepts about it as tools to understand and fully appreciate some few results about the Goedel numberings, the recursion theorem and the Post's problem [+]. Nevertheless, we hope that this would induce some reader to look for a deeper knowledge about those and related topics. To this reader we emphasize that our exposition of the Church's Thesis with its premises and consequences is somehow unconventional, since we tried to summarize in Chapter I the common abstract features of different approaches to the problem of defining what must be meant by "effective computability".

This problem was solved in quite different ways by Kleene [9], Church [4], Turing [18], Post [13], Markov [11], Curry [5], and some others*, that formally introduced some instances of what we called "complete defining system". A careful study of these works would perhaps make clearer the motivations and the reasons of our point of view. A great deal of work was spent to show that the class of functions defined by these systems was always the same. Beside the just mentioned papers, the books by Kleene [10] and Davis [6] are interesting also for these kinds of arguments. In our approach, this problem is by-passed by our version of the Church's Thesis: this is not intended to suggest an alternative solution, but rather to make clearer and more evident the reasons and the arguments of the usual approach.

A very interesting discussion of those topics can be found in the first chapters of the book by Rogers [15] that is mainly devoted to the recent developments about unsolvability.

A different approach to the functions computable by Turing Machines is through the characterization of languages recognizable by a class of abstract automata: the pioneering works by Robin and Scott [14], Chomsky [2][3] are summarized and settled in the books by Minsky [12], Hopcroft and Ullman [8], Arbib [1], Salomaa [16] and others.

To conclude this brief list of indications, we mention the recent works by Scott [17] that opened new promising ways in this field.

## REFERENCES


[1] ARBIB, M., Theories of Abstract Automata, Prentice-Hall, Engelwood Cliffs, NY, 1969.

[2] CHOMSKY, N.,"On Certain Formal Properties of Grammars", Inf. and Control, 2.2 (1959), pp 137-167.

[3] CHOMSKY, N., "Formal Properties of Grammars", Handbook of Math Psych, 2, (1963), Wiley, New York, pp 323-418.

[4] CHURCH, A., "An Unsolvable Problem of Elementary Number Theory", American Journal of Mathematics.

[5] CURRY, H., and R. FEYS, "Combinatory Logic, Vol. 1" North Holland, Amsterdam, 1968.

[6] DAVIS, M., "Computability and Unsolvability", McGraw-Hill, New York, 1958.

[7] DAVIS, M., "The Undecidable", Raven Press, Hawlett, 1965. 8.

[8] HOPCROFT, J., and ULLMANN, J., "Formal Languages and Their Relation to Automata", Addison-Wesley, Reading, 1969.

[9] KLEENE, S., "General Recursive Functions of Natural Numbers", Mathematische Aunalen, Vol. 112, (1936), pp 727-742.

[10] KLEENE, S., "Introduction to Metamathematics" Van Nostrand, Princeton NY, 1952.

[11] MARKOV, A., "The Theory of Algorithms" (Russian), Trudy Mathematicheskogo Instituta, imeni V.A. Steklova, vol. 38 (1951), pp 176-189; Engl. transl., Jerusalem, 1962.

[12] MINSKY, M., "Computation: "Finite and Infinite Machines", Prentice-Hall, Englewood Cliffs, NY, 1967.

[13] POST, E., "Finite Combinatory Processes-Formulation", I, "The Journal of Symbolic Logic" Vol. I, (1936), pp 103-105.

[14] RABIN, M., and SCOTT, D., "Finite Automata and Their Decision Problems", IBM Journal of Research and Development, Vol. 3, (1959), pp 114-125.

[15] ROGERS, H., Jr.: "Theory of Recursive Functions and Effective Computability", McGraw-Hill, New York, 1967.

[16] SALOMAA, A., "Theory of Automata", Pergamon Press, Oxford, 1968,

[17] SCOTT, D., "The Lattice of Flow Diagrams", in E. Engeler (ed.), "Symposium on Semantics of Algorithmic Languages", Lecture Notes in Mathematics No. 168, Springer-Verlag, Wien, 1971.

[18] TURING, A. "On Computable Numbers, with an Application to the Entscheidungsproblem", Proceedings of the London Mathematical Society, ser. 2, Vol. 42, (1936), pp 230-265; Vol. 43 (1936) pp 544-546.

* The Goedel numberings are deeply discussed in the paper: H. ROGERS, Jr.: "Goedel Numberings of Partial Recursive Functions", The Journal of Symbolic Logic, Vol. 23 (1958), No. 3, pp 331-341, whereas the other two topics are extensively covered in the book by Rogers 15 .

* Several papers by these and other authors are reprinted in a book edited by Davis 7 .

# TOWARD A THEORY OF PROBLEM SOLVING

by

D. Mandrioli, A. Sangiovanni Vincentelli, and M. Somalvico

Milan Polytechnic Artificial Intelligence Project
MP-AI Project
Milan, Italy

## ABSTRACT

The new research activity, which has been developed within the area of artificial intelligence, in general, and within the domain of problem solving, in particular, has awakened the need for a new theoretical effort centered around the notion of problem which more and more appears to be of central importance within computer science.

The studies about the theory of problem solving to which belongs the algebraic approach that we shall present in this paper, are intended to achieve the following main goals :

- a rather precise understanding of the human behaviour in problem solving;
- a clear definition of what we mean by an automatic problem solver (APS) ;
- a proposal of an internal structure of an automatic problem solver which can perform the three activities of selection, search, and learning ;
- a constructive comparison between the theoretical possibility of an absolutely general automatic problem solver and the practical requirement of a tool useful for the man ;
- the formulation of a theory of problems which can be helpful as a theoretical base in the design of an automatic problem solver.
- further investigations about the automatic problem solver as a non-deterministic interpreter of an high-level representation language, and as an automatic programmer.

More precisely, the purpose of this paper is to present the results which have been obtained, within the Milan Polytechnic Artificial Intelligence Project (MP–AI Project), by the authors in developing such a theory of problem solving, in the last two years.

The notions, which will be presented, can be briefly sketched as follows :

- naive description of problem solving ;
- algebraic framework for the illustration of the main notions and properties involved both in problem representation and in solution search ;
- extended formalization for the description of a more informed problem representation ;
- automatic evaluation and use of heuristic information for improving

the efficiency of the solution search ;

– generalization and development of a learning ability during the problem-solving activity.

The presented results provide more understanding of some focal points on which a theory of problem solving can be founded.

Such a theory will constitute a formal basis for the design of automatic problem solvers, intended as the interpreters of the representation languages in which the represented problems have been communicated to the computer.

## Chapter 1

## INTRODUCTION

**Computer science**, considered as that unitary discipline which deals with all the basic problems tightly interconnected with the existence of the computer, has been developed in the last thirty years, under the stimulating pressure of many theoretical and applicative exigencies.

The rapidity and extension of the technological progress has, therefore, produced a quite tumultuous and badly organized development of computer science which, at the present moment, still lacks of a well structured understanding of the fundamental notions on which this new discipline stays.

It is, in fact, very surprising, that only recently, i.e., in the last ten years, a **theory of programs** (also indicated as **mathematical theory of computation**) has been proposed and conspicuously developed over the basic notion of program.

Still more recently, in the last decade, a new research work has been proposed and carried on in a field denoted as **artificial intelligence**, which has been considered as the research area related with some of the most open problems of computer science that have to be faced in order to further enhance the capability of computer activity [1].

More precisely, artificial intelligence research is devoted to the study of theoretical foundations and of the related techniques which enable the computer to perform mechanisms and activities which are considered as exclusive, or even not available, to human intelligence [3], [4].

**Problem solving** consititutes one of the research topics in artificial intelligence which has been investigated with most intensity and which has provided some of the most promising results [8].

Its aim is to develop techniques which give to the computer the ability of finding, in an automatic and efficient way, the solution of a problem which has been described to the computer in a suitable form [9].

The central aspect of problem solving is constituted by the goal of giving to the computer a **representation**, i.e., a formal description, of the **problem**, which is well settled in order to present all the necessary and useful informations which enable the computer to find the **solution**.

In any case, whichever rich and organized we shall construct our representation, we shall always leave a gap between the formal description and the intuitive notion that we have of a problem ; this gap can never be completely eliminated, but can only be reduced.

The new research activity, which has been developed within the area of artificial intelligence, in general, and within the domain of problem solving, in particular, has awakened the need for a new theoretical effort centered around the notion of problem, which more and more appears to be of central importance within computer science.

This newly developing **theory of problems** provides a better understanding of the path followed by computer science in its development, which seems to us coming out, now, from its prehistoric phase [10 ], [11] , [12] .

The studies about the **theory of problem solving**, to which belongs the algebraic approach that we shall present in this paper [2] ,[ 5 ], [ 6 ], [7] , are intended to achieve the following main goals :

- a rather precise understanding of the human behaviour in problem solving ;
- a clear definition of what we mean by an **automatic problem** solver (**APS**) ;
- a proposal of an internal structure of an automatic problem solver which can perform the three basic activities of **selection, search,** and **learning** ;
- a constructive comparison between the theoretical possibility of an absolutely general automatic problem solver and the practical requirement of a tool useful for the man ;
- the formulation of a theory of problems which can be helpful as a theoretical base in the design of an automatic problem solver ;
- further investigations about the automatic problem solver as a non-deterministic interpreter of an high-level representation language and as an automatic programmer.

More precisely, the purpose of this paper is to present the results which have been obtained, within the Milan Polytechnic Artificial Intelligence Project (MP–AI Project), by the authors in developing such a theory of problem solving, in the last two years.

The notions which will be presented, can be briefly sketched as follows :

- naive description of problem solving ;
- algebraic framework for the illustration of the main notions and properties involved both in problem representation and in solution search ;
- extended formalization for the description of a more informed problem

representation ;

- automatic evaluation and use of heuristic information for improving the efficiency of the solution search ;
- generalization and development of a learning ability during the problem-solving activity.

In the paper, we will firstly discuss the implication of problem-solving research in computer science.

Then, a simple and intuitive description of the **state-space approach to problem solving** (SSPS), denoted as **SSPS naive description**, will be presented.

Successively, we will propose a formal definition of SSPS, which providės a precise formalization of the notion of problem representation and of problem solution.

This description, that we shall call **SSPS syntatic description**, constitutes a formal framework in which we can state some interesting properties and characteristics of SSPS.

In the sequel, a more rich and informed formal description of SSPS, called **SSPS semantic description**, will be presented. The SSPS semantic description constitutes a framework useful to structure a rich content of informations about a given problem, and is shown to be equivalent to the SSPS syntactic description.

Furthermore, a method is presented, which is based on the SSPS semantic description, and which makes possible to extract in an automatic way, i.e., by computation, the heuristic information useful to guide the search in the state space (SS).

More precisely, the method consists in a procedure which associates to a main problem an auxiliary problem, whose solution, easy to be found, i.e., computed, yields an estimate for the main problem.

The estimate is essentially the formal quantification of heuristic information which, according to the well known Hart-Nilsson-Raphael algorithm, allows one to perform an efficient heuristically guided search.

Successively, we will illustrate the results concerning learning activity within the problem-solving process.

Learning is considered as a fundamental part of the functions performed by an automatic problem solver.

In principle, learning activity is shown to be the ability of the artificial system in improving its performance and efficiency during the ongoing process of solving a problem or a class of problems.

The previous works related to learning in problem solving have been dedicated to the study and design of particular systems, namely of problem solvers capable of learning performance and acting in the semantic domains of game playing of poker, in the case of Waterman, and of checkers, in the case of Samuel.

We will describe our effort in providing a more general approach to learning in problem solving, and we will illustrate the **learning-oriented problem-solving system.**

The final remarks, about our future research directions, will conclude the exposition of our results.

Therefore, in the Introduction, we will present a description of the role and of the implication of problem-solving research in computer science, together with the outline of the basic functions and fundamental structure of problem solvers and representation-languages interpreters.

In Chapter 2, the SSPS naive description will be illustrated ; moreover. some examples devoted to illustrate the notions of problem representation and solution search will be discussed ; the most important search algorithms will be presented as well.

In Chapter 3, the SSPS syntactic description will be exposed together with some interesting algebraic properties and characteristics of SSPS ; moreover, the search algorithms, which are based on the preceeding theoretical concepts, will be illustrated.

In Chapter 4, the SSPS semantic description will be presented together with some clarifying examples ; the technique devoted to the computation of the heuristic function will be discussed as well.

In Chapter 5, the learning-oriented problem-solving system will be presented ; moreover, we will introduce two typical and opposite learning methods performed by the system ; also, some general techniques for designing a learning system will be discussed ; an example devoted to evidentiate the preceeding focal points, and intended to outline future research directions, will be illustrated as well.

In the Conclusions, we will outline the motivations and goals for our successive and future research work, and we will present some conclusive remarks.

In this Chapter we are now going to illustrate the implication of problem-solving research in computer science.

The standpoint of our considerations is the following one : **computer science is an experimental discipline which is centered around an unitary and global goal : man-computer interaction in solving problems.**

As any experimental discipline, therefore, computer science can be viewed as involved in the passage between two distinct worlds, namely, the **world of reality**, and the **world of cognition of reality**.

Between these two worlds it exists a **gap** which can be overcome only by human ingenuity and creativity, but absolutely not, by means of any mechanical or artificial technique.

The activities required by any experimental discipline can be very well exposed within the framework of many philosophical models.

We will utilize, for our purpose , the **Galileian inductive-deductive experimental method.**

The Galileian method is represented by a directed graph with three vertices and three arcs.

In Fig. 1.1, we illustrate such a graph in the case of physics, as example of an experimental discipline.

In such example, the three vertices of the graph correspond to the notion of **phenomenon** (in the physical reality), of **model** (of such a phenomenon), and of **law** (which can be derived within such a model).

The three arcs represent three conceptual activities, which are related to the interaction between the world of reality and the world of cognition of reality.

**Formalization** is the first activity, which is exclusive of human creativity and invention, and which enables man to substitute the informal and intuitive notion of phenomenon with the rigorous and precise concept of model within a selected formal framework.

**Induction-deduction** is the second activity, which lies within the world of cognition of reality, and which allows both man and mechanical tools, to infer a law as a consequence or property of a formalized reality.

**Matching** is the third activity, which allows man, again by means of human creativity, to confront the validity and the utility of the formally obtained law with the phenomenon, considered as the source of the whole experimental cognition process.

The **whole cycle** is under the scrutiny of the man by means of continuous **critique** which may bring up the convenience of an improved repetition of the whole cycle itself.

The new experimental discipline of computer science can be embedded in a similar way, by simply introducing new conceptual notions in correspondence of each vertex of the graph.

More precisely, with respect to the case of physics, we have the following substitutions :

- to the notion of phenomenon, we substitute the notion of **intuitive problem** ;
- to the notion of model, we substitute the notion of **represented problem** ;
- to the notion of law, we substitute the notion of **solved problem.**

The intuitive problem is an entity which independently faces the man, and can be viewed as an undefined and unlimited source of information.

From it, through the activity of formalization, the man operates an extraction of a finite and precisely described amount of information, namely the represented problem (i.e.,the representation of the problem). This information is chosen as valuable and sufficient in order to provide, through mechanical or interactive computation, the construction of the solved problem (i.e., the solution of the problem).

It is very important to observe that, because of the overall meaning of the Galileian method, the whole passage between the represented problem and the solved problem lies within the world of cognition of reality, i.e., within a completely defined and formalized environment.

Hence, in principle, such a passage, i.e., the solution construction, can be performed in an artificial and completely automatic way.

On the other hand, the two other activities of formalization and matching, belong exclusively to the man.

These are the fundamental conceptual considerations which illustrate the role of an automatic problem solver within computer science.

In the same way, it has been shown what can be considered as the ultimate expandibility of the role of the computer within the man-computer interaction in solving problems.

However, this ultimate goal can be considered only as the final target of the development of automatization within computer science. On the other hand, it is important to observe that at the present state of the art, the passage between represented problem and solved problem still requires, in the practical and available technological impact of computer science, a widely extended and intense cooperation between man and computer.

The role of the man in such cooperation, while avoidable in principle, bears on itself the responsibility of the conceptually most important activities.

The trend of the computer science research can be therefore considered, with an overall synthesis of its historical development, as based on the criterion of continuously reducing the impact of man, and increasing the ability of computer.

In particular, the trend of artificial-intelligence research can be considered as centered on the aim of completely eliminating the role of man, in such a construction of a solved problem for a represented problem.

In Fig. 1.2, we illustrate the present state of such cooperation process.

The responsibility of the man is shown to be :

(i) **invention of the representation of the problem** ;

(ii) **invention of an algorithm**, for the construction of the solution of the problem, as it has been represented ;

(iii) **construction of a source program**, written in a symbolic and, generally, high-level programming language ;

(iv) **critical matching of the solution of the problem** with the intuitive problem embedded in its semantic domain.

Please note that, because of the previously exposed philosophical considerations, while activities (i) and (iv) belong always to the man, activities (ii) and (iii) can potentially be taken over by the computer.

The responsibility of the computer is shown to be :

– **translation of the source program**, into an object program written in machine language ;

– **execution of the object program** ;

– **construction of the solution of the problem.**

During its growth, computer science has been based and guided by appropriate **theories** in order to understand and organize the **methodology** followed by human activities, and to construct specific **artificial systems** responsible of the computer activities.

Specifically, the following theories have been particularly important :

–(i) **theory of computability**, for understanding the limit and power of invention of algorithms ;

–(ii) **theory of complexity**, for providing a basis for critical evaluation of efficiency in the invention of algorithms ;

–(iii) **theory of formal languages**, for providing frameworks and tools useful in order to design and to construct such artificial systems as the translators (**compilers, assemblers, interpreters**), from source programs to object programs;

–(iv) **switching theory**, for providing frameworks and tools useful in order to design and to construct such artificial systems as the **hardware systems** and **firmware systems** capable of the execution of object programs and the construction of the problem solution.

More recently, a new theory has been proposed, and embrionically developed, namely :

–(v) **theory of programs (mathematical theory of computation)**, for providing a basis for critical evaluation of invention of programs, and for providing frameworks and tools useful in order to design and to construct such artificial systems (though not yet available, at the present state of the art) as the **program checkers** and the **program verifiers**.

The recent results of problem solving, within artificial-intelligence research, make more and more necessary and important the development of a new theory which, in principle, can provide us with the bypassing of all the classical and, also, quite recent theories.

Such new theory can be defined as :

–(vi) **theory of problems**, for providing a basis for critical evaluation of the techniques capable of directly and automatically obtaining the solved problem from the represented problem, and for providing frameworks and tools useful in order to design and to construct such artificial systems (thought as available in a not too much distant future) as the **interactive problem solvers** and the **automatic problem solvers**.

In this way, we have achieved the purpose of illustrating the role of problem solving within computer science, by means of an illustration of its meaning and importance in the scenario of development of computer science.

Let us now present a more detailed understanding of the functions and of the structure of an automatic problem solver.

We will illustrate first the basic conceptual functions involved in an automatic problem-solving activity and we shall, by consequence, present a structure for an automatic problem solver.

We want to point out, just now, that all the considerations that we are going to illustrate, can be more deeply understood in a critical way, if one shall think to semantic domains, from where intuitive problems arise, which are not already set up by means of any rigorous description (e.g., like semantic domains originated from the world of mathematics, or of logic).

Namely, one should think to such kind of semantic domains (e.g., robotics, natural languages understanding, human situations, actions, behaviours, etc.) where :

– the representation of any problem is a real invention for the man, requiring an effort of creativity and ingenuity ;
– any represented problem still leaves completely unidentified, also in an implicit way, the solved problem (that might eventually be obtained), which may as well be completely out of reach even from human immagination.

The invention of the represented problem consists in the precise description of a finite quantity of information which the man formulates by means of the observation of two distinct entities, namely :

(i) the intuitive problem, embedded in its semantic domain, and considered as an unlimited source of formalizable or representable information ; this entity, considered as a "natural" entity, is provided by the world of reality ;

(ii) the automatic problem solver, intended as a general-purpose tool which can deal with represented problems originated from various semantic domains ; this entity, considered as an "artificial" entity, is provided by the artificial-intelligence scientist.

The invention of the represented problem requires that the man performs two basically different activities, in its formalization process.

The first activity is devoted to the specification of the methods and ways which shape the automatic problem solver, considered as an originally general-purpose tool, into a well precised special-purpose tool, which is oriented by the semantic domain from which the intuitive problem is originated.

In other words, this activity is devoted by the man to "tune" the general-purpose tool into a special-purpose tool, in a way of utilizing the human ingenuity and understanding of the best mode in which the artificial tool should work more efficiently in attacking the solution process for the particular intuitive problem.

By means of this activity, the general problem solver is transformed into a special problem solver.

The information described by consequence of this first activity, is called **control information**, and it is the first part of the information contained in the represented problem.

The second activity is dedicated to the selection, from the intuitive problem, of a finite quantity of information, well defined, which is considered by the man as useful, and, hopefully, efficient and sufficient, in order to allow the special problem solver to achieve its goal of providing an automatic solution of the problem.

The information, described by consequence of this second activity, is called **problem information**, and it is the second part of the information contained in the represented problem.

It is conceptually important to observe that both the two previously described activities are done by the man, with the conscience of being faced by ignorances of three different types, namely :

- whether the control and problem informations, contained in the represented problem, are **sufficient** in order to make the computer able to solve the problem ;
- what part, of these informations, is actually **relevant** to the computer and shall be utilized in order to solve the problem ;
- what is the actual way in which the relevant part of these informations shall be **processed** (possibly **efficiently**) in order to construct the (possibly **optimum**) solved problem, in the evenience that such a construction might be attainable.

It is important to observe that the first type of ignorance is a direct consequence of the existing gap between the world of reality and the world of cognition of reality.

In order to overcome this ignorance, the man needs to wait the end of the whole experimental cycle ; by means of the activity of matching, he will be able to check if an acceptable solution of the intuitive problem has been obtained, and, thus, he will be able to overcome this first type of ignorance.

The two other types of ignorances are very important, because they are useful to point out two functions, performed by the automatic problem solver, which are intended to give artificial answers to these ignorances.

The first function, which is devoted to produce an automatic answer to the second type of ignorance, consists in an appropriate selection of one part of the information, contained in the represented problem, and considered, by the automatic problem solver, as useful and relevant for its activity of solving problems.

This activity is performed by a first part of the automatic problem solver, called **Selector**, as it is shown in Fig. 1.3, where all the structure of an automatic problem solver is illustrated.

Therefore, we will call **global represented problem** the input of the Selector and **selected represented problem** the output of the Selector.

The second function, which is devoted to produce an automatic answer to the third type of ignorance, consists in a skillful search of the cooperation process, embracing the already selected information, which essentially makes up the solution algorithm and, thus, yields the solution of the problem.

This activity is performed by a second part of the automatic problem solver, called **Searcher**, as it is shown in Fig. 1.3.

Therefore, while the input of the Searcher will be the selected represented problem, the output of the Searcher will be the solved problem.

As it has been previously illustrated, the control information is the information which enables the man to specify the special configuration of the problem solver oriented towards a particular semantic domain.

In orther words, the Selector and the Searcher are two general–purpose artificial metasystems which, by means of the control information, are specialized into two special-purpose artificial systems.

This specialization, of the structure of the Selector and of the Searcher by the man, can be considered just as an initial specification which, during the ongoing solution process, can possibly be changed and improved.

This **modificating and enhancing activity** is the typical **activity of learning** which is able to provide a **dynamic evolution** of the structure of the Selector and of the Searcher.

This **selfchanging activity** is performed by a third part of the automatic problem solver, called **Learner**, as it is shown in Fig. 1.3.

Therefore, the inputs of the Learner are constituted by the global represented problem, by the selected represented problem, and by the solved problem.

In this way the inputs of the Learner are obtained not only from the human activity of formalization of the intuitive problem into a represented problem, but also from the artificial activity of the problem solver itself ; in this second case, these inputs can take account both of partial and of total results obtained from the artificial activity.

The outputs of the Learner are the automatically constructed and modifiable **specifications** of the Selector and of the Searcher.

Thus, the kernel of an automatic problem solver appears to be an **artificial metasystem** which is initialized by the man as an initial system, and, afterwards, can evolve *itself*, in a way appropriate to enhance its artificial performance in solving problems.

Therefore, learning can be viewed as the ability of **selfawereness** of the whole automatic problem solver.

In fact, in principle, the Learner can be considered itself, as an automatic problem solver, which has been tuned on the semantic domain of problem solving, and which has to automatically solve the problems of constructing (or, better, specifying) Selectors and Searchers.

Thus, such sophisticated level in designing a Learner, can envisage automatic problem solvers acting completely as self-developing artificial systems.

In conclusion, we can assert that an automatic problem solver can operate on a represented problem and can provide a solved problem.

Whichever has been the method followed by the man in performing its formalization task for the construction of the represented problem, it is necessary for him to choose an appropriate **formalism** apted both to provide a "good" represented problem and to catalyze a "valid" artificial activity for the automatic problem solver.

Therefore, we can rightfully call such formalism as a **representation language**, which man needs for cooperating with computer.

While the classic **programming languages** have been conceived to channel to the computer the human invention of **solution algorithms**, the representation languages can be conceived to channel to the computer the human invention of represented problems.

Therefore, we can look at automatic problem solvers as at the **interpreters** of the representation languages in which the represented problems have been communicated to he computer.

Thus, it is natural to look at first-order predicate logic and at the PLANNER-like goal-oriented languages, as at preliminary examples of representation languages.

The interpreters of such representation languages (e.g., the theorem provers, in the case of first-order predicate logic) need, in the present state of the art, to be conceived and structured on the more formal basis of a theory of problems.

This paper is, indeed, centered around a part of this developing new theory, and the presented results provide more understanding for the design of both automatic problem solvers and representation-languages interpreters.

# CHAPTER 2

## SSPS NAIVE DESCRIPTION

In this Chapter we will present a simple and intuitive description of the state-space approach to problem solving which we will indicate as the SSPS naive description.

The SSPS is important and widely adopted since it provides some very intuitive and simple notions, together with efficient techniques, which assist the man during the task of constructing the representation of the problem, and of performing the search of the solution.

In order to obtain a description of the problem in the SSPS, we have to individuate some particular elements that are present in the "informal description" (i.e., the intuitive knowledge) of the problem itself, namely:

1. the problem configurations ;
2. the initial configuration ;
3. the goal configuration ;
4. the transformations that change a configuration into another one.

In order to clarify these primitive notions, we will present a simple problem example: the **Eight-Puzzle**.

This puzzle consists of a 3x3 frame of an 8–numbered tiles set movable in the frame.

In the frame, one cell is empty and will be called "blank" in the following.

The problem configurations are all the possible positions of the tiles set in the frame.

The initial configuration is a well defined position of the tiles set and the goal configuration is, usually, the situation in which the tiles are ordered from 1 to 8 in the three rows in a precise way.

The possible transformations consist of the change of the blank with one of the numbered tiles adjacent to it (it is also possible to consider the blank as an empty space that can be occupied by its adjacent tiles).

We can divide the transformations, according to the shift of the blank, into four classes: R (right), L(left), U(up), D(down).

As an example, we can pass from the configuration shown in Fig. 2.1, to the configuration shown in Fig. 2.2, with the transformation L to the configuration of Fig. 2.1. We have to note that it is not possible to apply the transformations L and U to the configuration of Fig. 2.2.

Therefore, some preliminary conditions have to be satisfied in order to apply a transformation. These conditions are called legal conditions.

We can now give a first formalization to the fundamental elements previously described, i.e., we are going to introduce the SSPS naive description.

1. An element s called state is associated to every configuration. The set S constituted by all these elements, i.e., by all the states, is called state set of state space.

2. The state corresponding to the initial configuration according to the correspondence 1, is selected and called initial or source state.

3. The state corresponding to the goal configuration according to the correspondence 1, is selected and called final or goal state.

4. A function $\gamma_i$ called operator is associated with every class of transformations. Thus, an operator changes a state into another one. The set of all the operators $\gamma_i$ will be indicated with $\Gamma$ and will be called the operators set.

Now, we can point out that it is possible to represent a problem, described with SSPS, with an oriented graph. Its vertices correspond to the states of the problems and its arcs correspond to the operators such that an arc $a_j$ is directed from a vertex $v_h$ to a vertex $v_k$ if and only if its corresponding operator $\gamma_i$ transforms $s_h$ into $s_k$.

In Fig. 2.3, we show a partial graph obtained from the Eight-Puzzle. It has to be noted that in the complete graph some states of the problem are not connected with the initial state. The why is that some states are not reachable from a chosen initial state via the successive application of the operators.

As an example, in Fig. 2.4 it is shown a state that cannot be reached from the initial state described in Fig. 2.2.

Normally, the graph associated to the state space is not stored in a way that is called explicit description, i.e., with the complete list of all the vertices and all the arcs.

It is worth to observe that the graph of the problem can be represented more usefully in a way which is denoted as implicit description.

In this case, we will give only the initial vertex i, the final vertex f and the operators set $\Gamma$.

Thus, the graph can be built up at first applying to i all the elements of $\Gamma$ that satisfy the legal condition. Secondly, we can apply in the same way the operators to the set of vertices previously obtained.

The iteration of this procedure constitutes the transformation from the implicit to the explicit description.

Another very interesting example of problem described in SSPS is the **Hanoi-Tower-Puzzle.**

This puzzle consists of three discs of different sizes that can be stacked on three pegs. It is not possible to put a disc having smaller size on another one having a larger size.

Initially, the discs are all on a peg, the largest is on the bottom, the smallest is on the top. The goal is to transfer all of the discs to another peg. We are allowed to move discs one at a time; moreover, only the top disc can be moved.

We are going now to set up the SSPS formulation of the problem by introducing states, operators, initial and goal state.

In this case, a state is corresponding to an ordered triple of numbers (x,y,z) which individuates the pegs on which the discs are stacked (x = position of the largest one, y = position of the medium one, z = position of the smallest one). The pegs can be numbered from 1 to 3 from left to right.

The initial state is corresponding to, e.g., the triple (1,1,1), i.e., all of the discs are on the peg 1 and the final state is corresponding to the triple (3,3,3), i.e. all of the discs are on the peg 3.

The operators are corresponding to the three classes of reversible transformations 1-2, 1-3, 2-3 indicating the two pegs between which it exists the transfer of the top disc; also in this case, each operator is bounded by the legal conditions, namely, that a larger disc cannot be over a smaller one.

In Fig. 2.5, we show the explicit graph of the Hanoi puzzle with the corresponding states.

Now, we can consider the "search" aspect of SSPS, i.e., the search of a solution for a problem described in SSPS.

We intend as solution of a problem, a sequence of operators that have to be applied consecutively to the initial state (i.e., we have to apply the first operator to the initial state, the second one to the state so obtained and so on) in order to obtain the final state.

If we consider the graph of the problem (both in the explicit and implicit way) a solution is, clearly, a path (i.e., a sequence of consecutive arcs) that starts from the initial vertex and ends in the final vertex. An example is constituted by the graph of the Hanoi-Tower-Puzzle in Fig. 2.5, in which one path from i to f (i.e., one solution) is marked.

We are often interested in obtaining a particular solution of the problem, called the optimum solution.

The notion of optimum solution arises when we associate a cost to the application of an operator, i.e., we label every arc in the graph with a cost.

Then, the optimum solution is the solution of minimum cost represented by the minimum cost path from i to f in the graph.

Thus, it is trivial to observe that the search of a solution (possibly an optimum one) in the SSPS is equivalent to the search of a "minimum cost" path between two vertices of a graph.

Since the dimension of the state space, for real problems, is usually of big magnitude, the problem arises of limiting the storage requirement and the computation time of the path finding algorithm.

Thus, normally, the graph associated to the state space, is not stored in the explicit way but in the implicit one.

Therefore the search strategy is quite different from the usual algorithms for the computation of a minimum cost path between two vertices in a graph.

Thus, in SSPS, the search strategy consists of two processes which are developed in parallel:

1) incremental construction of the path (i.e., of the solution);
2) incremental explicitation of the graph.

Because of this incremental procedure, the search strategies are called expansion techniques. A node of the graph is expanded when all the nodes adjacent to it are generated.

The most used expansion techniques are:

1) **Breadth-first method;**
2) **Depth-first method;**
3) **Uniform-Cost (Dijkstra-Dantzig) method;**
4) **Heuristically-guided (Hart-Nilsson-Raphael) method.**

The method 1 follows a fixed expansion strategy: the nodes are expanded in the order in which they are generated.

We shall now describe the steps of a simple algorithm for searching a graph breadth first.

STEP 1 Put the initial node in a list called OPEN.

STEP 2 If OPEN is empty, then the search fails: no solutions of the problem exist; otherwise continue.

STEP 3 Remove the first node on OPEN and put it on a list called CLOSED. Call this node "n".

STEP 4 Expand node n applying to it all the operators $\gamma_i$ . If there are no successors go to STEP 2.

STEP 5 If some generated nodes are already in OPEN, throw them away. All the other nodes are put at the end of OPEN in the order in which they are generated and provide "pointers" from these successors back to "n".

STEP 6 If any of the successors is a goal node, the search is successful, exit and the solution is obtained by tracing back through the pointers; otherwise go to STEP 2. □

It is very simple to check that this algorithm finds always a minimum cost path only if the costs associated to the operators are equal, otherwise it is not possible to obtain an optimum solution.

However, this method finds a solution whenever a solution exists.

The depth first method follows a fixed strategy, too: the most recently generated nodes are expanded as first ones.

In order to realize this strategy, we have to introduce the depth of a node with a recursive definition, as follows:

(i) the initial node has zero depth;

(ii) the depth of any other node is one plus the depth of its shallowest parent.

Thus, the currently deepest node in the search is the one selected for the next expansion.

Now, we can give a very simple description of the steps of an algorithm for searching a graph depth first.

**STEP 1** Put the initial node in a list called OPEN.

**STEP 2** If OPEN is empty, then the solution does not exist and the search fails; otherwise continue.

**STEP 3** Remove the first node on OPEN and put it on a list called CLOSED. Call it "n".

**STEP 4** Expand and generate all of its successors. Put these at the beginning of OPEN and provide pointers back to n.

**STEP 5** If any of the successors are goal nodes, then the solution is found and it can be obtained by tracing back the pointers; otherwise go to STEP 2.

□

This algorithm does not find a minimum cost path, but can find a solution, if a solution exists.

An inconvenience associated with this method is the possibility of going down along a fruitless path for a long time.

In order to avoid this situation, we can introduce a number, the depth bound, that specifies when we have to abandon a path and to follow another one.

The sequence of steps is modified in the following way: between STEP 3 and STEP 4, we introduce a new step, i.e., STEP 3 BIS.

**STEP 3 BIS** If the depth of n equals the depth bound, go to STEP 2; otherwise continue.

□

With this modification the algorithm cannot find a solution if its search should require to go below the depth bound.

The Uniform-Cost method is introduced in order to obtain an optimum solution when the costs associated with the operators are not equal. This method belongs to the class of evaluation function methods. In these methods, the nodes are expanded according to an evaluation function which guides the selection of the nodes that have to be expanded (i.e., it guides the order of node expansion). This function is defined for every node which has been already expanded and is related to data, parameters and informations already contained in the graph of the problem.

The particular evaluation function g(n) of Uniform-Cost method is derived from the costs of the arcs belonging to the path from i to the considered node n.

More precisely, g(n) is the cost of a path from i to n that has minimum cost among all the paths so far obtained.

The Uniform-Cost method expands nodes in order of increasing g(n) and can be described in this way:

STEP 1 Put the initial node i on a list called OPEN.

STEP 2 If OPEN is empty, then a solution for the problem does not exist and the search fails, otherwise continue.

STEP 3 Remove the node having the smallest value of g and put it on a list called CLOSED. Let is be "n" (if more than one node has the same minimum value of g, pick n arbitrarily but always in favor of any goal node).

STEP 4 If n is a goal node, the optimum solution is found and is obtained by tracing back through the pointers; otherwise continue.

STEP 5 Expand node n and generate all of its successors. If there is not a successor, go to STEP 2. Otherwise, for each successor $n_j$ , compute:

$$g(n_j) = g(n) + c(n, n_j)$$

STEP 6 where $c(n, n_j)$ is equal to the cost of the arc from n to $n_j$. If any of $n_j$'s is already in OPEN, check if the new value of $g(n_j)$ is less than the previous one.
If this value is less than the previous one, cancel $n_j$ from OPEN and its old value of $g(n_j)$.
Otherwise do not consider $n_j$ as successor of n.

STEP 6 If any of successors is already in CLOSED, do not consider $n_j$ as successor of n.

STEP 7 Put the successors not eliminated in STEP 5 and STEP 6 on OPEN associating them the $g(n_j)$ values just obtained and provide the pointers back to n.

STEP 8 Go to STEP 2. □

In STEP 6, we disregard the generated nodes that are already in CLOSED. It is possible to prove that this procedure does not remove the capability of finding an optimal solution, but we do not prove this statement for brevity.

It has to be noted that if the costs of the arcs are equal, this method is a breadth-first method.

All of the methods previously described are "blind" in the sense that they do not "look ahead" at the goal but only "look behind" at the path already done.

This characteristic causes the expansion of too many nodes before a solution is found. Thus, we will add to the previous representation of a problem some new information which is a kind of information obtained from the particular "semantic domain" of the investigated problem. This information is usually called heuristic information and the related search strategy, heuristic search.

We will use the heuristic information to measure "the promise" of a node to be on a shortest path. Such an information will be embedded in the evaluation function previously introduced.

It has to be noted that the heuristic information has been considered in order to reduce the search effort (i.e., the number of nodes expanded) but it may happen as well that the derived algorithm cannot find a shortest path. Therefore, we have to face two problems: how to reduce the cost of the search and how to obtain an optimal solution.

An algorithm similar to the Uniform-Cost method, which uses an evaluation function computed on the basis of heuristic information is now described. As usual, this algorithm orders the nodes for expansion in increasing order of the values of the evaluation function, which we will indicate as f(n).

STEP 1 Put the initial node i on a list called OPEN.

STEP 2 If OPEN is empty, then the solution does not exist and the search fails; otherwise continue.

STEP 3 Remove from OPEN the node having the smallest value of f and put it on a list called CLOSED. Call it "n". (If more than one node has the same minimum value of f pick n arbitrarily, but always in favor of any goal node).

STEP 4 If n is a goal node, the solution is found. It is possible to obtain the shortest path by tracing back through the pointers; otherwise continue.

STEP 5 Expand node n and generate all of its successors. If there are no successors, go to STEP 2; otherwise, for each successor $n_j$, compute $f(n_j)$.
If any of $n_j$'s is already in OPEN, check if the new value of $f(n_j)$ is less than the previous one.
If this value is less than the previous one, cancel $n_j$ from OPEN and its old value of $f(n_j)$. Otherwise do not consider $n_j$ as successor of n.

**STEP 6** If any of successors is already in CLOSED, check if the new value of $f(n_j)$ is less than the previous one. If this value is less than the previous one, cancel $n_j$ from CLOSED and its old value of $f(n_j)$. Otherwise do not consider $n_j$ as successor of n.

**STEP 7** Put the successors not eliminated in STEP 5 and STEP 6, in OPEN associating them the $f(n_j)$ values just obtained and provide the pointers back to n.

**STEP 8** Go to STEP 2. □

It is obvious that this algorithm cannot find an optimum cost solution according to the unprecised definition of f. However, if f(n) is an "estimate" of the minimum path from n to the goal node, the search is less "expensive" than in the Uniform-Cost method.

It is also possible to select a precise definition of f such that the algorithm can find an optimum cost solution whenenver it exists.

This definition is due to Hart, Nilsson and Raphael.

Let $f(n) = g(n) + \hat{h}(n)$ where g is the evaluation function of Uniform-Cost method and $\hat{h}$ is a lower bound of the cost h(n) of the optimum solution for a problem which has n as initial state and the previous goal node as final state.

It has been proved that this algorithm is admissible, i.e., it finds an optimum solution whenever it exists.

It is also possible to simplify the algorithm previously described modifying the STEP 6 and eliminating the STEP 7, if we assume that n satisfies this condition:

$$(\forall s_1)\ (\forall s_2)\ ((s_1 \in S) \wedge (s_2 \in S) \wedge (\hat{h}(s_1) - \hat{h}(s_2) \leqslant K(s_1, s_2)))$$

where $K(s_1, s_2)$ is the minimum path between $s_1$ and $s_2$. This condition is called **consistency assumption** and it is always verified if $\hat{h}$ does not change during the search process.

STEP 6 becomes:

**STEP 6′** If any of successors is already in CLOSED, do not consider $n_j$ as successor of n. □

As an example, we can give an heuristic evaluation function that satisfies the previously stated conditions for the Eight-Puzzle.

The function f(n) is put equal to g(n) + w(n), where g is the length of the path in the search graph from the initial vertex i to vertex n, (all the costs equal to 1) and w(n) counts the number of misplaced tiles in the problem configuration corresponding to n. It has been proved that w(n) is a lower bound for the minimum cost path from n to the goal node.

Another important result is that a **more informed Hart-Nilsson-Raphael method**, i.e., an algorithm which uses an heuristic function $\hat{h}_1$ strictly larger than another one, e.g., $\hat{h}_2$, expands fewer nodes in finding a solution for the same problem.

This result is intuitive because a more efficient algorithm is based obviously on a more "precise" heuristic function and the precision of $\hat{h}$ is due to the amount of heuristic information embedded in it. Thus, it is possible to say that an heuristically guided algorithm is surely more efficient than an Uniform-Cost method.

An important question is, in the case of this algorithm, how to provide a technique to obtain a lower bound estimate $\hat{h}$. Usually, this estimate requires human ingenuity based on an appropriate inspection and processing of the semantic domain of the problem.

Therefore, the goal of a complete automatization of the problem-solving procedure is incompatible with the use of an heuristic information, which is not contained inside the computer, and which thus implies invention from man.

For the above considerations, it seems important to develop new techniques which enable in some way the computer to obtain, within an automatic procedure, the heuristic information itself.

The Chapter 4 illustrates a technique which is intended to achieve this objective.

# CHAPTER 3

# SSPS SYNTACTIC DESCRIPTION

In the previous Chapter 2 we have described, in an intuitive form, called SSPS naive description, the state-space approach to problem solving.

In this way, we have introduced the fundamental notions of state, operator, initial state, and final state.

Moreover, the two fundamental aspects of problem solving, namely the representation and the search, have been outlined.

The purpose of this Chapter 3 is to present a more precise and formal description of SSPS of mathematical, mainly algebraic nature. This description, that we call **SSPS syntactic description**, constitutes a formal framework on which we can state some interesting properties and characteristics of SSPS.

Moreover, it represents a basis on which we can insert a more detailed and comprehensive description, called SSPS semantic description (see the following Chapter 4).

Also, a general illustration of SSPS learning (see the following Chapter 5) is mainly based both on the SSPS syntactic and semantic descriptions.

This Chapter 3 is divided in four Subchapters, namely :

- Subchapter 3.1, where the basic notions of SSPS, of problem, and of problem solution are introduced;
- Subchapter 3.2, where the basic results on the necessary and sufficient conditions for the existence of a solution of a problem are illustrated;
- Subchapter 3.3, where the notion of resolvent set H and its algebraic properties are presented;
- Subchapter 3.4, where the algorithms which are based on the preceding theoretical concepts, are described, as a first result of this research effort toward a theory of problem solving.

## 3.1. Fundamental Notions of SSPS Syntactic Description

In this Subchapter, we shall give, in rigorous terms, the characterization of the basic concepts which constitute the kernel of SSPS.

**Definition 3.1.1.** A problem schema M is a couple $M = (S, \Gamma)$, where S is a non empty (possibly infinite) set of states, and $\Gamma$ is a set of functions, called **operators,** s.t.:

(3.1.1) $$\Gamma = \{\gamma_i \mid \gamma_i : A_i \longrightarrow S,\ A_i \subset S\}$$

□

**Theorem 3.1.1.** The set $\Gamma$ of operators yields a function $\Gamma_1$, s.t. :

(3.1.2) $$\Gamma_1 = S \longrightarrow P(S)$$

(3.1.3) $$\Gamma_1 = s_j \longmapsto A_j,\ A_j \subset S$$

**Proof.** For each $s_j \in S$, it is possible to determine a set $A_j$, s.t.:

$$A_j = \{s \mid (\forall s)(\exists \gamma_i)((\gamma_i \in \Gamma) \wedge (\gamma_i : A_i \longrightarrow S) \wedge (s_j \in A_i) \wedge (s = \gamma_i(s_j)))\}$$

(3.1.4)

Moreover, by Definition 3.1.1, the set $A_j$ is unique, since each $\gamma_i$ is a function, and by (3.1.1) and (3.1.4), $s \in S$, and therefore, $A_j \subset S$.

Thus:

(3.1.5) $$\Gamma_1 : s_j \longmapsto A_j,\ A_j \subset S$$

□

**Theorem 3.1.2.** The function $\Gamma_1$ yields a function $\Gamma_2$, s.t.:

(3.1.6) $$\Gamma_2 : P(S) \longrightarrow P(S)$$

(3.1.7) $$\Gamma_2 : A_i \longmapsto A_j,\ A_i, A_j \subset S$$

**Proof.** For each $A_i \subset S$, we shall determine an unique $A_j \subset S$. In fact, in correspondence of each $s_k \in A_i$, by Theorem 3.1.1, it exists an unique set $\Gamma_1(s_k) \subset S$. Therefore, we obtain an $A_j$, s.t.:

(3.1.8) $$A_j = \bigcup_{(s_k \in A_i)} \Gamma_1(s_k)$$

Thus:

$$\Gamma_2 \ : A_i \longmapsto A_j \ , \ A_i \ , A_j \subset S \qquad (3.1.9)$$

□

**Definition 3.1.2.** We define the n-step **global operator** $\Gamma^n$, s.t.:

$$\Gamma^n = S \longrightarrow P(S) \qquad (3.1.10)$$

in the following way:

$$\Gamma^1 = \Gamma_1 \qquad (3.1.11)$$

$$\Gamma^2 = \Gamma_1 \circ \Gamma_2 \qquad (3.1.12)$$

i.e.,$\Gamma^2$ is the concatenation of $\Gamma_1$ with $\Gamma_2$, and, in general

$$\Gamma^n = \Gamma_1 \circ \Gamma_2 \circ \ldots \circ \Gamma_2 \qquad (3.1.13)$$

i.e.,$\Gamma^n$ is the concatenation of $\Gamma_1$ with $\Gamma_2$ taken n-1 times. □

The problem schema M represents the "skeleton" of a problem in the SSPS.

We can now add, in our mathematical framework, the initial state.

**Definition 3.1.3. A source problem** I is a couple I = (M,i), where M is a problem schema, and i is an element of S, called **initial (or source) state** .

A source problem is associated with a particular set of states, which shall be very useful in the sequel.

**Definition 3.1.4** Given a source problem I = (M,i), we define as **n-reachable set from i**, the set $R_i^n$, s.t.:

$$\left(R_i^n \subset S\right) \wedge \left(i \stackrel{\Gamma^n}{\longmapsto} R_i^n\right) \qquad (3.1.14)$$

i.e., $R_i^n$ is the value of $\Gamma^n$ applied to i.

Each element $r_i^n$ , s.t.:

$$r_i^n \in R_i^n \qquad (3.1.15)$$

is called **n-reachable state from i.**

□

**Definition 3.1.5.** We define as **reachable set from i**,the set $R_i$ , s.t.:

(3.1.16) $$R_i = \bigcup_{n=1}^{\infty} R_i^n$$

Each element $r_i$, s.t.:

(3.1.17) $$r_i \in R_i$$

is called **reachable state from i.**

□

Therefore, the reachable set $R_i$ is made up by all those states, to which we can arrive from i, with the iteration of the application, in all the possible ways, of all the operators $\gamma_i \in \Gamma$ .

We associate now, to the problem schema the notion of final state (or of set of final states).

**Definition 3.1.6.** A **goal problem** F is a couple F = (M,f), where M is a problem schema, and f is an element of S, called **final (or goal) state** .

We can extend the notion of goal problem as a couple F = (M,K), where we consider, in place of f, a set $K \subset S$, called **set of final states.**

□

Similarly to the source problem, also the goal problem can be associated with a particular set of states.

**Definition 3.1.7.** Given a goal problem F = (M,f), we define as **n-generating set** of f, the set $G_f^n$, s.t.:

(3.1.18) $$\left(G_f^n \subset S\right)\wedge\left(\forall g_f^n\right)\left(\left(g_f^n \in G_f^n\right)\wedge\left(g_f^n \xrightarrow{\Gamma^n} O^n\right)\wedge\left(f \in O^n\right)\right)$$

Alternatively, if we take the definition F = (M,K), we substitute the (3.1.18) with the following relation, where $G_K^n$ is defined as n-generating set of K:

(3.1.19) $$\left(G_K^n \subset S\right)\wedge\left(\forall g_K^n\right)\left(\left(g_K^n \in G_K^n\right)\wedge\left(g_K^n \xrightarrow{\Gamma^n} O^n\right)\wedge\left(K \cap O^n \neq \phi\right)\right)$$

Each element $g_f^n$ (or $g_K^n$), s.t. :

(3.1.20) $$g_f^n \in G_f^n \qquad (g_K^n \in G_K^n)$$

is called **n-generating state** of f (or of K).

□

**Definition 3.1.8.** We define as **generating set of f (or of K)**,the set $G_f$ (or $G_K$), s.t.:

$$G_f = \bigcup_{n=1}^{\infty} G_f^n \qquad \left(G_K = \bigcup_{n=1}^{\infty} G_K^n\right) \qquad (3.1.21)$$

Each element $g_f$ (or $g_K$), s.t.:

$$g_f \in G_f \qquad (g_K \in G_K) \qquad (3.1.22)$$

is called **generating state of f (or of K)**.

□

Therefore,the generating set $G_f$ (or $G_K$) is made up by all those states, from which we can arrive to f (or to an element $k \in K$), with the iteration of the application, in all the possible ways, of all the operators $\gamma_i \in \Gamma$.

We can now add together the previously defined notions, and state the formal definition of problem.

**Definition 3.1.9.** A **problem** P is a triple P = (M,i,f),where M is a problem schema, i is an element of S called **initial (or source) state**, and f is an element of S called **final (or goal) state**.

We can extend the notion of problem as a triple P = (M,i,K), where we consider, in place of f, a set $K \subset S$, called **set of final states**.

□

We can now state two obvious properties.

**Theorem 3.1.3.** A problem P is composed of a source problem I associated with a final state f (or a set of final states K), i.e., a problem P is a couple P = (I,f) (or P = (I,K)).

**Proof.** It is obvious, because of Definitions 3.1.3 and 3.1.9.

□

**Theorem 3.1.4.** A problem P is composed of a goal problem F associated with an initial state i, i.e., a problem P is a couple P = (F,i).

**Proof.** It is obvious, because of Definitions 3.1.6 and 3.1.9.

□

After having introduced the formal definition of problem, we are going to state the formal definition of solution to a problem.

We shall consider, in the sequel, the definition of problem which is associated with only one final state f; it is anyhow obvious to obtain an extension to the case in which a problem is associated with a set of final states K.

**Definition 3.1.10.** An **n-step solution** of a problem P, is a sequence of functions, $\xi^n$, s.t.:

$$\xi^n = \langle a_1, a_2, \dots, a_j, \dots, a_n \rangle$$

where each function $a_j$, satisfies the following two conditions:

(3.1.23) (i) $(\forall_j \in \bar{n})(\exists \gamma_i)((\gamma_i \in \Gamma) \wedge (a_j = \gamma_i))$

where:

(3.1.24) $\bar{n} = \{1, 2, \dots, j, \dots, n\}$

(3.1.25) (ii) $i \xrightarrow{a_1} s_1 \xrightarrow{a_2} s_2 \ \dots \ s_{j-1} \xrightarrow{a_j} s_j \ \dots \ s_{n-1} \xrightarrow{a_n} f$

□

**Theorem 3.1.5** An n-step solution $\xi^n$, yields one and only one sequence of states, $S[\xi^n]$, s.t.:

(3.1.26) $S[\xi^n] = \{s_1, s_2, \dots, s_{n-1}\}$

$S[\xi^n]$ is called **n-step solution sequence,** and it is composed of n-1 states called **intermediate solution states.**

**Proof.** If $\xi^n$ is an n-step solution, because of Definition 3.1.10 and relation (3.1.25), it individuates a sequence of n-1 states; the sequence is unique since in (3.1.25) each $a_j$ is, because of (3.1.23), an operator $\gamma_i$, and, therefore, because of Definition 3.1.1, each $a_j$ is a function.

□

We shall now present some interesting relationship between the theory of problem solving that has been outlined up to now, and the classical theory of automata, with particular emphasis to the Rabin-Scott automaton.

**Defintion 3.1.11.** A **semiautomaton** E is a triple $E = (Q, \Sigma, T)$, where Q is a set of elements called **states,** $\Sigma$ is a set of elements called **symbols,** while $\Sigma$ is called **alphabet,** and T is a set of functions on Q. The cardinality of T is equal to the cardinality of $\Sigma$.

More precisely, we have:

$$Q = \{q_1, q_2, \ldots, q_m\} \quad (3.1.27)$$

$$\Sigma = \{\sigma_1, \sigma_2, \ldots, \sigma_n\} \quad (3.1.28)$$

$$T = \{T_{\sigma_1}, T_{\sigma_2}, \ldots, T_{\sigma n}\} \quad (3.1.29)$$

where:

$$T_{\sigma i} \; : \; Q \longrightarrow Q \quad (3.1.30)$$

□

**Theorem 3.1.6.** A problem schema M is equivalent to a semiautomaton $E_M$.

**Proof.** We want to prove, that it exists an equivalence between a problem schema $M = (S, \Gamma)$ and a semiautomaton $E_M = (Q_M, \Sigma_M, T_M)$. This equivalence is established, with the following three conditions, which determine $E_M$ from M and viceversa:

(i) S is the equivalent to $Q_M$, iff the states of the problem schema are in an one-to-one correspondence to the states of the semiautomaton.

(ii) Given $\Gamma = \{\gamma_1, \gamma_2, \ldots, \gamma_o\}$, we can associate to $\Gamma$ the set $\bar{o}$ of the first o natural numbers, i.e.:

$$\bar{o} = \{1, 2, \ldots, o\} \quad (3.1.31)$$

Iff o = n, then we have that $\bar{o}$ is equivalent to $\Sigma_M$, i.e., there is an one-to-one correspondence between the o first natural numbers, and the n symbols of the alphabet.

(iii) Iff condition (ii) holds, then we say that $\Gamma$ is equivalent to $T_M$, when for each $\gamma_i \in \Gamma$, s.t.:

$$\gamma_i : A_i \longrightarrow S \quad (3.1.32)$$

the correspondent (because of (ii)) $T_{M\sigma_i}$, s.t.:

$$T_{M\sigma_i} : Q \longrightarrow Q \quad (3.1.33)$$

satisfies the condition that its restriction $\bar{T}_{M\sigma_i}$ on $A_i$, s.t., $A_i \subset S$, i.e., because of (i), $A_i \subset Q$, is, s.t.:

$$\bar{T}_{M\sigma_i} : A_i \longrightarrow Q \quad (3.1.34)$$

and $\bar{T}_{M\sigma_i}$ is equal to $\gamma_i$ of (3.1.32).

□

**Definition 3.1.12. A Rabin-Scott automaton A, is a triple $A = (E, q_i, L)$, where E is a semiautomaton $E = (Q, \Sigma, T)$, $q_i$ is an element $q_i \in Q$, called initial state, and L is a set $L \subset Q$, called set of final states.**

□

**Theorem 3.1.7.** A problem P is equivalent to a Rabin-Scott automaton $A_P$.

**Proof.** We want to prove, that it exists an equivalence between a problem $P = (M,i,f)$ (or $P = (M,i,K)$) and a Rabin-Scott automaton $A_P = (E_P, q_{iP}, L_P)$.

This equivalence is established, with the following three conditions, which determine $A_P$ from P and viceversa:

(i) M is equivalent to $E_P$, iff $E_P$ satisfies the three conditions of Theorem 3.1.6, i.e., iff $E_P = E_M$.

(ii) i is equivalent to $q_{iP}$, iff, in satisfying the condition (i) of Theorem 3.1.6, the one-to-one correspondent to i is $q_i$.

(iii) In the case in which, $P = (M,i,f)$, f is equivalent to $L_p$, iff $\{f\}$ is equivalent to $L_P$, i.e., $L_P$ is a singleton, and its unique element, in satisfying the condition (i) of Theorem 3.1.6, is in the one-to-one correspondence to f.
In the case in which $P = (M,i,K)$, K is equivalent to $L_p$, iff the states of K are in an one-to-one correspondence to the states of $L_p$ .

□

**Theorem 3.1.8.** The n-step solution of a problem P is equivalent to the n-step control law of a Rabin-Scott automaton $A_P$.

**Proof.** The proof is obtained, by Theorem 3.1.7 and by the definition of n-step control law, which is typical of the theory of automata.

□

**Theorem 3.1.9.** The n-step solution of a problem P is equivalent to the n-step trajectory of a Rabin-Scott automaton $A_P$.

**Proof.** The proof is obtained, by Theorem 3.1.7 and by the definition of n-step trajectory, which is typical of the theory of automata.

□

This parallel between the theory of problem solving and the theory of automata, can be interesting for further researches in this direction.

## 3.2. Existence of a Solution of a Problem

This Subchapter is dedicated to the presentation of some basic results on the necessary and sufficient conditions for the existence of a solution of a problem.

These properties shall be illustrated with reference to the formal notions introduced in Subchapter 3.1.

In particular, the utility of the concepts of reachable set from i, $R_i$, and of generating set of f, $G_f$, shall be clarified.

**Theorem 3.2.1.** A problem P = (M,i,f) has solution iff the final state f belongs to the reachable set from i, $R_i$, i.e.:

$$f \in R_i \tag{3.2.1}$$

**Proof.a) Only if part.**

If an n-step solution for P exists, by Definition 3.1.10, it exists the sequence:

$$\xi^n = \langle a_1, a_2, \dots, a_j, \dots, a_n \rangle \tag{3.2.2}$$

By Theorem 3.1.3, the problem P is defined as a couple P = (I,f).

In corrispondence of I, because of Definitions 3.1.4 and 3.1.5, we can define, for the problem P, the reachable set from i, $R_i$.

We shall prove, that the state $s_j$, obtained by the application:

$$i \xrightarrow{a_1} s_1 \xrightarrow{a_2} s_2 \cdots s_{j-2} \xrightarrow{a_{j-1}} s_{j-1} \xrightarrow{a_j} s_j \tag{3.2.3}$$

belongs to $R_i^j$, i.e.:

$$s_j \in R_i^j \tag{3.2.4}$$

We shall prove, the previous sentence, by simple induction on j, i.e., on the length of the solution.

(i) **Case:** j = 1.
Because of Definition 3.1.10, $a_1$ is applied to i, and the value obtained, $a_1(i)$, by Definition 3.1.4, belongs to $R_i^1$.

(ii) **Case: j implies j +1.**

We suppose that the (3.2.4) holds for j, and we shall show, that it holds also for j + 1.

By the induction hypothesis, if the (3.2.4) holds for j, then:

(3.2.5) $$s_j \in R_i^j$$

and, by Theorem 3.1.1, we have:

(3.2.6) $$s_j \overset{\Gamma_1}{\longmapsto} A^{j+1}$$

By Theorem 3.1.1, 3.1.2 and Definitions 3.1.2 and 3.1.4, we obtain:

(3.2.7) $$A^{j+1} \subset R_i^{j+1}$$

In particular, we have:

(3.2.8) $$s_j \overset{a_{j+1}}{\longmapsto} s_{j+1}$$

with:

(3.2.9) $$s_{j+1} \in A^{j+1}$$

because of Theorem 3.1.2.

Therefore, from (3.2.7), we obtain:

(3.2.10) $$s_{j+1} \in R_i^{j+1}$$

and we have proved (3.2.4).

If we take the case: j = n-1, we shall have:

(3.2.11) $$s_{n-1} \overset{a_n}{\longmapsto} s_n$$

with $s_n$, s.t.:

(3.2.12) $$s_n \in R_i^n$$

But, by Definition 3.1.10, we have:

(3.2.13) $$s_n = f$$

Thus, from (3.2.12) and (3.2.13), we obtain:

(3.2.14) $$f \in R_i^n$$

and, by Definition 3.1.5, we have:

(3.2.15) $$f \in R_i$$

b) **If part.**

If $f \in R_i$, by Definition 3.1.5, it exists an $\bar{n}$, s.t.:

$$\bar{n} \in \{1,2,\dots,n,\dots\} \qquad (3.2.16)$$

and, s.t.:

$$f \in R_i^{\bar{n}} \qquad (3.2.17)$$

By Definition (3.1.4), relation (3.2.17) yields:

$$i \xrightarrow{\Gamma^{\bar{n}}} R_i^{\bar{n}} \qquad (3.2.18)$$

Let now be:

$$(k = \bar{n}) \wedge (r_i^{\bar{n}} = f) \qquad (3.2.19)$$

Let us consider the set $R^{k-1}{}_i$, and one of its elements $r^{k-1}{}_i$, s.t.:

$$\left(r^{k-1}{}_i \xrightarrow{\Gamma_1} A^k\right) \wedge \left(r^k{}_i \in A^k\right) \qquad (3.2.20)$$

Moreover, we have, by Definition 3.1.4:

$$A^k \subset R^k{}_i \qquad (3.2.21)$$

Because of Theorem 3.1.1 and Definition 3.1.1, it shall exist at least one particular function $\gamma_{\bar{j}}$, s.t.:

$$\left(\gamma_{\bar{j}} \in \Gamma\right) \wedge \left(r^{k-1}{}_i \xrightarrow{\gamma_{\bar{j}}} r_i^k\right) \qquad (3.2.22)$$

We can now construct a sequence $\mathfrak{G}$, in which, $\gamma_{\bar{j}}$ takes the k – th place.

Let us repeat, recursively, this procedure, by letting k = k-1 until k = 1. At that moment, we have obtained a sequence of functions $\mathfrak{G}$, s.t.:

$$\mathfrak{G} = \langle a_2, a_3, \dots, a_j, \dots, a_{\bar{n}} \rangle \qquad (3.2.23)$$

and, an element $r^1{}_i$, s.t.:

$$r_i^1 \in R_i^1 \qquad (3.2.24)$$

Let us consider, now, the set $R^o{}_i$, s.t.:

$$R_i^o = \{i\} \qquad (3.2.25)$$

Obviously, because of Definition 3.1.4, the unique element i satisfies the condition:

(3.2.26) $$\left(i \xrightarrow{\Gamma_1} A^1\right) \wedge \left(r_i^1 \in A^1\right) \wedge \left(A^1 \equiv R_i^1\right)$$

Moreover, because of Theorem 3.1.1 and Definition 3.1.1, it exists one particular function $\gamma_{\bar{j}}$,s.t.:

(3.2.27) $$\left(\gamma_{\bar{j}} \in \Gamma\right) \wedge \left(i \xrightarrow{\gamma_{\bar{j}}} r_i^1\right)$$

In this way, from (3.2.23) and (3.2.27), we have obtained a sequence $\mathcal{G}$ in which the $\gamma_{\bar{j}}$ , of (3.2.27),takes the first place, s.t.:

(3.2.28) $$\mathcal{G} = < a_1 , a_2 , \dots , a_j , \dots , a_{\bar{n}} >$$

By construction, the sequence $\mathcal{G}$, of (3.2.28), satisfies the condition:

(3.2.29) $$i \overset{a_1}{\longmapsto} s_1 \overset{a_2}{\longmapsto} s_2 \; \dots \; s_{\bar{n}-1} \overset{a_{\bar{n}}}{\longmapsto} f$$

and, therefore, $\mathcal{G}$ satisfies at the conditions of Definition 3.1.10, i.e., $\mathcal{G}$ is the $\bar{n}$-step solution of the problem P, i.e.:

(3.2.30) $$\mathcal{G} = \mathcal{G}^{\bar{n}}$$

□

Theorem 3.2.1 shows the conditions for the existence of the solution of a problem, by stating a constraint on f.

Because of the structure of a problem P, we can now illustrate a dual condition, which yields a constraint on i.

**Theorem 3.2.2.** A problem P has solutions iff the initial state i belongs to the generating set of f, $G_f$ , i.e.:

(3.2.31) $$i \in G_f$$

**Proof.** a) **Only if part.**

If an n-step solution for P exists, by Definition 3.1.10, it exists the sequence:

(3.2.32) $$\mathcal{G}^n = < a_1 , a_2 , \dots , a_j , \dots , a_n >$$

By Theorem 3.1.4, the problem P is defined as a couple P = (F,i).

In correspondence of F, because of Definitions 3.1.7 and 3.1.8, we can define, for the problem P, the generating set of f, $G_f$.

We shall prove, that the states $s_j$, obtained by the application:

$$i \overset{a_1}{\longmapsto} s_1 \overset{a_2}{\longmapsto} s_2 \quad \ldots \quad s_{j-2} \overset{a_{j-1}}{\longmapsto} s_{j-1} \overset{a_j}{\longmapsto} s_j \qquad (3.2.33)$$

belongs to $G^{n-j+1}_f$:

$$s_j \in G^{n-j+1}_f \qquad (3.2.34)$$

We shall prove, the previous sentence, by simple induction on the length of the solution, i.e., on k, s.t.:

$$k = n - j \qquad (3.2.35)$$

(i) **Case: k = 1 (i.e., j = n-1).**

Because of Theorem 3.1.1 and Definition 3.1.1:

$$a_n \in \Gamma \qquad (3.2.36)$$

and, because of Definition 3.1.10:

$$(\exists s_{n-1}) \left( (s_{n-1} \in S) \wedge \left(s_{n-1} \overset{a_n}{\longmapsto} f\right)\right) \qquad (3.2.37)$$

Because of Definition 3.1.7, we have:

$$s_{n-1} \in G^1_f \qquad (3.2.38)$$

(ii) **Case: k implies k + 1.**

We suppose that (3.2.34) holds for k, i.e., for n-j, and we shall show, that it holds also for k + 1, i.e., for n - j + 1.

If (3.2.34) holds for k, the state $s_j = s_{n-k}$ (n-k=j) obtained with the (3.2.33), belongs, by induction hypothesis, to $G^k_f$.

But, because of the (3.2.33):

$$s_{n-(k+1)} \overset{a_{n-k}}{\longmapsto} s_{n-k} \qquad (3.2.39)$$

Since $a_{n-k} \in \mathcal{G}^{n}$, and, by Theorems 3.1.1, 3.1.2 and Definition 3.1.2, we have:

$$\left(s_{n-(k+1)} \xmapsto{\Gamma^{k+1}} O^{k+1}\right) \wedge \left(f \in O^{k+1}\right) \tag{3.2.40}$$

Therefore, because of Definition 3.1.7, $s_{n-(k+1)}$ belongs then to $G^{k+1}_{f}$, and so:

$$s_{n-(k+1)} \in G^{k+1}_{f} \tag{3.2.41}$$

and we have proved the (3.2.34).

If we take the case: k = n, we have:

$$s_o \xmapsto{a_1} s_1 \tag{3.2.42}$$

with $s_o$, s.t. :

$$s_o \in G^{n}_{f} \tag{3.2.43}$$

But, because of Definition 3.1.10, we have:

$$s_o = i \tag{3.2.44}$$

Thus, from (3.2.43) and (3.2.44), we obtain:

$$i \in G^{n}_{f} \tag{3.2.45}$$

and, by Definition 3.1.8, we have:

$$i \in G_{f} \tag{3.2.46}$$

b) **If part.**

If $i \in G^{n}_{f}$, by Definition 3.1.8, it exists an $\bar{n}$, s.t.:

$$\bar{n} \in \{1,2,3,\dots,n,\dots\} \tag{3.2.47}$$

and, s.t.:

$$i \in G^{\bar{n}}_{f} \tag{3.2.48}$$

By Definition 3.1.7, relation (3.2.48) yields:

$$\left(i \xmapsto{\Gamma^{\bar{n}}} O^{\bar{n}}\right) \wedge \left(f \in O^{\bar{n}}\right) \tag{3.2.49}$$

Let now be:

$$(k = 0) \wedge (g^{\bar{n}-k}{}_f = i) \qquad (3.2.50)$$

Let us consider the set $G^{\bar{n}-(k+1)}{}_f$, and one of its elements $g^{\bar{n}-(k+1)}{}_f$;in correspondence of $g^{\bar{n}-(k+1)}{}_f$, we can define the set $A^k$, s.t.:

$$A^k \subset G^{\bar{n}-k}{}_f \qquad (3.2.51)$$

and, s.t.:

$$A^k = \left\{ a^k \mid \left(a^k \xmapsto{\Gamma_1} o^k\right) \wedge \left(g^{\bar{n}-(k+1)}{}_f \in o^k\right)\right\} \qquad (3.2.52)$$

$A^k$, moreover, yields:

$$g^{\bar{n}-k}{}_f \in A^k \qquad (3.2.53)$$

and, therefore, because of (3.2.52):

$$\left(g^{\bar{n}-k}{}_f \xmapsto{\Gamma_1} o^k\right) \wedge \left(g^{\bar{n}-(k+1)}{}_f \in o^k\right) \qquad (3.2.54)$$

Because of Theorem 3.1.1 and Definition 3.1.1, it shall exist at least one particular function $\gamma_{\bar{j}}$,s.t.:

$$\left(\gamma_{\bar{j}} \in \Gamma\right) \wedge \left(g^{\bar{n}-k}{}_f \xmapsto{\gamma_{\bar{j}}} g^{\bar{n}-(k+1)}{}_f\right) \qquad (3.2.55)$$

We can now construct a sequence $\mathfrak{G}$, in which, $\gamma_{\bar{j}}$ takes the k + 1 -th place.

Let us repeat, recursively, this procedure, by letting k = k + 1 until k = $\bar{n}$ - 1. At that moment, we have obtained a sequence of functions $\mathfrak{G}$, s.t.:

$$\mathfrak{G} = \langle a_1, a_2, \dots, a_j, \dots, a_{\bar{n}-1} \rangle \qquad (3.2.56)$$

and, an element $g^1_f$, s.t.:

$$g^1{}_f \in G^1{}_f \qquad (3.2.57)$$

Let us consider, now, the set $G^o_f$, s.t.:

$$G^o{}_f = \{f\} \qquad (3.2.58)$$

Obviously, because of Definition 3.1.7, the unique element f satisfies the condition:

(3.2.59) $$A^{\bar{n}-1} = G^1_f$$

where:

(3.2.60) $$A^{\bar{n}-1} = \left\{ a^{\bar{n}-1} \mid \left( a^{\bar{n}-1} \overset{\Gamma_1}{\longmapsto} o^{\bar{n}-1} \right) \wedge \left( f \in o^{\bar{n}-1} \right) \right\}$$

Let us consider $g^1_f$; because of Theorem 3.1.1 and Definition 3.1.1, it exists one particular function $\gamma_{\bar{j}}$, s.t.:

(3.2.61) $$\left( \gamma_{\bar{j}} \in \Gamma \right) \wedge \left( g^1_f \overset{\gamma_{\bar{j}}}{\longmapsto} f \right)$$

In this way, from (3.2.56) and (3.2.61), we have obtained a sequence in which the $\gamma_{\bar{j}}$, of (3.2.61), takes the n - th place, s.t.:

(3.2.62) $$\mathfrak{g} = < a_1, a_2, \ldots, a_{\bar{j}}, \ldots, a_{\bar{n}} >$$

By construction, the sequence $\mathfrak{g}$, of (3.2.62), satisfies the following condition:

(3.2.63) $$i \overset{a_1}{\longmapsto} \underset{s_1}{} \overset{a_2}{\longmapsto} \underset{s_2}{} \ldots \underset{s_{\bar{n}-1}}{} \overset{a_{\bar{n}}}{\longmapsto} f$$

and, therefore, $\mathfrak{g}$ satisfies the conditions of Definition 3.1.10, i.e., $\mathfrak{g}$ is the $\bar{n}$-step solution of the problem P, i.e.:

(3.2.64) $$\mathfrak{g} = \mathfrak{g}^{\bar{n}}$$

□

The fundamental Theorems 4.1 and 4.2 can also be stated in a different way, by utilizing the notions of the theory of automata.

**Theorem 3.2.3.** A problem P = (M,i,f) has solutions iff its equivalent Rabin-Scott automaton $A_P = (E_P, q_{iP}, L_P)$ holds the property that $L_P$ is reachable from $q_{iP}$.

**Proof.** The proof is obtained by Theorem 3.1.7 and by the definition of reachability of states, which is typical of the theory of automata.

□

**Theorem 3.2.4.** A problem P = (M,i,f) has solutions iff its equivalent Rabin-Scott automaton $A_P = (E_P, q_{iP}, L_P)$ holds the property that $q_{iP}$ is controllable to $L_P$.

**Proof.** The proof is obtained by Theorem 3.1.7 and by the definition of controllability of states, which is typical of the theory of automata.

□

Moreover, the properties on the existence of solutions of a problem P, yield some similar conditions on the notion of solution sequence.

**Theorem 3.2.5.** Each n-step solution sequence $S[\xi^n]$ is contained in the reachable set from i, $R_i$, i.e.:

$$S[\xi^n] \subset R_i \tag{3.2.65}$$

**Proof.** From Definition 3.1.10, Theorems 3.1.5, 3.2.1, because of (3.2.3), (3.2.4), we have:

$$S[\xi^n] \subset \bigcup_{j=1}^{n-1} R_i^j \subset R_i \tag{3.2.66}$$

□

**Theorem 3.2.6.** Each n-step solution sequence $S[\xi^n]$ is contained in the generating set of f, $G_f$, i.e.:

$$S[\xi^n] \subset G_f \tag{3.2.67}$$

**Proof.** From Definition 3.1.10, Theorems 3.1.5, 3.2.2, because of (3.2.33), (3.2.34), we have:

$$S[\xi^n] \subset \bigcup_{j=1}^{n-1} G_f^j \subset G_f \tag{3.2.68}$$

□

The formal framework,that has been presented in Subchapters 3.1 and 3.2, shall be further developed, in the following Subchapters 3.3 and 3.4, in order to provide some additional results on the task of effectively obtaining solutions of a problem P.

### 3.3. The Resolvent Set H

The notions, previously introduced, of reachable set $R_i$ and of generating set $G_f$, have allowed us, according to Subchapter 3.2, to define precisely the conditions for the existence and the uniqueness of the solution.

In this Subchapter we will show that it is possible, on the basis of $R_i$ and $G_f$, to consider all the solutions and, successively, to construct algorithms capable of obtaining the optimum solution when all the costs associated to the operator are equal.

**Definition 3.3.1.** The resolvent set is the set H defined as follows:

$$H = R_i \cap G_f \tag{3.3.1}$$

□

**Theorem 3.3.1.** Each element h, belonging to the resolvent set H, is contained in almost one solution sequence $S[\mathcal{S}^n]$.

**Proof.** By Definition 3.3.1, each element $h \in H$ satisfies the following condition:

$$(h \in R_i) \wedge (h \in G_f) \tag{3.3.2}$$

The condition $(h \in R_i)$ implies, by Theorem 3.2.1, the existence of a sequence $\mathcal{B}^{\bar{n}}$ constituted by $\bar{n}$ operators:

$$\mathcal{B}^{\bar{n}} = \langle b_1, b_2, \ldots, b_{\bar{n}} \rangle \tag{3.3.3}$$

Moreover, the elements of $\mathcal{B}^{\bar{n}}$ are such that the following condition holds:

$$i \xrightarrow{b_1} v_1 \xrightarrow{b_2} v_2 \; \ldots \; v_{\bar{n}-1} \xrightarrow{b_{\bar{n}}} h \tag{3.3.4}$$

Moreover, the condition $h \in G_f$ implies, by Theorem 3.2.2, the existence of a sequence $\mathcal{C}^{\tilde{n}}$ constituted by $\tilde{n}$ operators:

$$\mathcal{C}^{\tilde{n}} = \langle c_1, c_2, \ldots, c_{\tilde{n}} \rangle \tag{3.3.5}$$

Moreover, the elements of $\mathcal{C}^{\tilde{n}}$ are such that the following condition holds:

$$h \xrightarrow{c_1} w_1 \xrightarrow{c_2} w_2 \; \ldots \; w_{\tilde{n}-1} \xrightarrow{c_{\tilde{n}}} f \tag{3.3.6}$$

Thus, we are able to build up a solution $\mathcal{S}^n$, in the following way:

$$\mathcal{S}^n = \langle a_1, a_2, \ldots, a_n \rangle \tag{3.3.7}$$

$$n = \bar{n} + \tilde{n} \tag{3.3.8}$$

$$a_i = b_i \qquad 1 \leqslant i \leqslant \bar{n} \qquad (3.3.9)$$

$$a_{j+\bar{n}} = c_j \qquad 1 \leqslant j \leqslant \tilde{n} \qquad (3.3.10)$$

Moreover, it is also possible to obtain the solution sequence $S[\xi^n]$ from $\xi^n$ in the following way :

$$S[\xi^n] = \langle s_1, s_2, \ldots, s_{n-1} \rangle \qquad (3.3.11)$$

$$s_i = v_i \qquad 1 \leqslant i \leqslant \bar{n} - 1 \qquad (3.3.12)$$

$$s_{\bar{n}} = h \qquad (3.3.13)$$

$$s_{\bar{n}+j} = w_j \qquad 1 \leqslant j \leqslant \tilde{n} - 1 \qquad (3.3.14)$$

Therefore, because of relation (3.3.13), h is an element of the solution sequence $S[\xi^n]$.

□

We can now illustrate the main property of H, that justifies its denomination.

**Theorem 3.3.2.** The resolvent set H is equal to the union of all the possible solution sequences of a problem P = (M,i,f), i.e.:

$$H = \bigcup_{n=1}^{\infty} S[\xi^n] \qquad (3.3.15)$$

*Proof.* Let:

$$U_j = \bigcup_{i=1}^{\ell_j} S[\xi^j_i] \qquad (3.3.16)$$

i.e., $\xi^j_i$ is the i-th j-th step solution, and $U_j$ contains all the states belonging to a j-step solution sequence.

Let also:

$$U = \bigcup_{j=1}^{\infty} U_j \qquad (3.3.17)$$

The relation (3.3.15), that we have to prove, can therefore be expressed in the following way:

(3.3.18) $$H = U$$

Now, because of Theorem 3.3.1, it has been proved that:

(3.3.19) $$H \subseteq U$$

In order to prove the relation (3.3.18), we have only to prove that:

(3.3.20) $$U \subseteq H$$

i.e., each element u of U belongs also to H.

Let us suppose that an element u of U belongs to a solution sequence $S[\xi_i^j]$, i.e., let us suppose that u is the h-th element of the i-th j-step solution.

Therefore, because of Theorem 3.2.5 and Definition 3 2.4:

(3.3.21) $$u \in R_i^h$$

i.e., u belongs to the h-reachable set from i.

Moreover, because of Theorem 3.2.5 and Definition 3.2.7:

(3.3.22) $$u \in G_f^{j-h}$$

i.e., u belongs to the (j-h)-generating set of f.

Then, from relations:

(3.3.23) $$R_i^h \subset R_i$$

and:

(3.3.24) $$G_f^{j-h} \subset G_f$$

it follows, because of relations (3.3.21) and (3.3.23):

(3.3.25) $$u \in R_i$$

and, because of relations (3.3.22) and (3.3.24):

(3.3.26) $$u \in G_f$$

From relations (3.3.25) and (3.3.26), because of Definition 3.3.1, we obtain:

(3.3.27) $$u \in R_i \cap G_f = H$$

Since we can apply the same procedural steps for each h, for each i, and for each j, we have therefore proved the relation (3.3.20) and, by consequence, the theorem.

□

The two theorems, previously illustrated, have clarified the significance of the resolvent set H, which contains exactly only and all the states belonging to any solution sequence.

Therefore, this set represents the natural domain on which it is possible to formulate many interesting considerations related to:

1) solutions enumeration;
2) solutions search;
3) optimum solution search;
4) analysis of search algorithms and evaluation of their complexity.

Thus, it seems to be a question of natural and spontaneous interest to investigate the algebraic structure of H, and to extract more informations about its characteristics.

First of all, we shall introduce, in a convenient way, a partial ordering relation on H.

**Definition 3.3.2.** Given an element $h \in H$, and considered all the solution sequences $S[\xi^{n,h}]$, such that $h \in S[\xi^{n,h}]$, the **minimum solution sequence through h**, $\bar{S}[\xi^{\bar{n},h}]$ is defined as a sequence, containing h, such that $\bar{n}$ is the minimum possible number of steps.

□

**Definition 3.3.3.** We define as minimum solution relation $\Omega$, a binary relation on H, i.e. :

$$\Omega \subset H \times H \qquad (3.3.28)$$

such that $h\,\Omega\,k$ if and only if it exists a minimum solution sequence through h coincident with a minimum solution sequence through k, i.e., it exists:

$$\bar{S}[\xi^{\bar{n},h,k}] = \langle s_1, s_2, \ldots, s_i, \ldots, s_j, \ldots, s_{\bar{n}-1} \rangle \qquad (3.3.29)$$

such that:

$$s_i = h, \; s_j = k, \quad 1 \leqslant i \leqslant j \leqslant \bar{n} - 1 \qquad (3.3.30)$$

□

We can now illustrate an interesting property on the minimum solution relation $\Omega$.

**Theorem 3.3.3.** The minimum solution relation $\Omega$ is a partial ordering relation on H.
**Proof.** We shall prove that $\Omega$ satisfies the reflexive, antisymmetric, and transitive properties.

*1. Reflexive property.*

We have to prove that, for each $h \in H$:

(3.3.31) $$h \; \Omega \; h$$

This is true, because, by Definition 3.3.2, and by Definition 3.3.3, and because of relation (3.3.30), it obviously holds.

*2. Antisymmetric property.*

We have to prove that, for each $h \in H$ and for each $k \in H$, if:

(3.3.32) $$h \; \Omega \; k$$

and if:

(3.3.33) $$k \; \Omega \; h$$

then, the following relation holds:

(3.3.34) $$h = k$$

By Definition 3.3.3, and because of relation (3.3.30), it exists a minimum solution sequence:

(3.3.35) $$\bar{S}'[\wp^{\bar{n},h,k}] = < s_1', s_2', \ldots, s_i', \ldots, s_j', \ldots, s_{\bar{n}-1}' >$$

such that:

(3.3.36) $$h = s_i', \; k = s_j', \quad 1 \leqslant i \leqslant j \leqslant \bar{n} - 1$$

Moreover, by Definition 3.3.3, and because of relation (3.3.30), relation (3.3.33) implies that it exists a minimum solution sequence:

(3.3.37) $$\bar{S}''[\wp^{\bar{n},h,k}] = < s_1'', s_2'', \ldots, s_\ell'', \ldots, s_m'', \ldots, s_{\bar{n}-1}'' >$$

such that:

(3.3.38) $$k = s_\ell'', \; h = s_m'', \quad 1 \leqslant \ell \leqslant m \leqslant \bar{n} - 1$$

It has to be noted that, by Definition 3.3.2 and because of the property of minimum, it is correct that the number of steps of the two sequences (3.3.35) and (3.3.37) should be considered as equal.

We can observe, as well, that:

$$\ell = j \tag{3.3.39}$$

In fact, if relation (3.3.39) should not be true, let us assume that:

$$\ell < j \tag{3.3.40}$$

In this case, the solution sequence $\bar{S}'[\mathcal{G}^{\bar{n},h,k}]$ could not be a minimum solution sequence through k, because it should exist the following solution sequence:

$$\bar{\bar{S}}[\mathcal{G}^{\bar{n},k}] = < s_1'', s_2'', \ldots, s_\ell'' = s_j', s_{j+1}', \ldots, s_{\bar{n}-1}' > \tag{3.3.41}$$

such that:

$$k = s_\ell'' = s_j' \tag{3.3.42}$$

and its number of steps should be:

$$\bar{n} - (j - \ell) < \bar{n} \tag{3.3.43}$$

In the same way, it is possible to prove, as well, that it could not hold that:

$$\ell > j \tag{3.3.44}$$

Therefore, relation (3.3.39) has been proved.

With the same kind of considerations, we can prove also that:

$$\bar{n} - m = \bar{n} - i \tag{3.3.45}$$

and, therefore:

$$m = i \tag{3.3.46}$$

It has to be noted that, because of relation (3.3.36), it holds that:

$$i \leqslant j \tag{3.3.47}$$

Moreover, because of relation (3.3.38), it holds that:

$$\ell \leqslant m \tag{3.3.48}$$

Because of relations (3.3.39), (3.3.46), and (3.3.47), it holds that:

$$m \leqslant \ell \tag{3.3.49}$$

Because of relations (3.3.48) and (3.3.49), we can finally deduce that:

(3.3.50) $$m = \ell$$

Therefore, because of (3.3.38) and (3.3.50), we have proved relation (3.3.34).

*3. Transitivity property.*

We have to prove that $\Omega$ satisfies the transitivity property, i.e., for each $h \in H$, $k \in H$, and $\ell \in H$, if:

(3.3.51) $$h \;\Omega\; k$$

and if:

(3.3.52) $$k \;\Omega\; \ell$$

then:

(3.3.53) $$h \;\Omega\; \ell$$

It has to be noted that relation (3.3.51) implies, because of relation (3.3.30), that it exists a minimum solution sequence:

(3.3.54) $$\bar{S}'\,[\mathcal{G}^{\bar{n},h,k}] = < s'_1, s'_2, \ldots, s'_i, \ldots, s'_j, \ldots, s'_{\bar{n}-1} >$$

such that:

(3.3.55) $$h = s'_i, \quad k = s'_j, \quad 1 \leqslant i \leqslant j \leqslant \bar{n} - 1$$

Moreover, relation (3.3.52) implies, because of relation (3.3.30), that it exists a minimum solution sequence:

(3.3.56) $$\bar{S}'\,[\mathcal{G}^{\bar{n},h,k}] = < s''_1, s''_2, \ldots, s''_m, \ldots, s''_n, \ldots, s''_{\bar{n}-1} >$$

such that:

(3.3.57) $$k = s''_m, \quad \ell = s''_n, \quad 1 \leqslant m \leqslant n \leqslant \bar{n} - 1$$

First of all, by Definition 3.3.2 and because of the minimum property, it is correct that the number of steps $\bar{n}$ should be considered as equal for both the minimum solution sequences (3.3.54) and (3.3.56).

Let us now consider the following solution sequence

(3.3.58) $$\bar{\bar{S}}[\mathcal{G}^{\bar{n},h,k}] = < s'_1, s'_2, \ldots, s'_i, \ldots, s'_j, \quad s''_{m+1}, \ldots, s''_n, \ldots, s''_{\bar{n}-1} >$$

This solution sequence contains the states $h = s_i'$ and $\ell = s_n''$. Moreover, it is a minimum solution sequence, because we can prove with considerations similar to those utilized in the proof of relation (3.3.46), that:

$$j = m \tag{3.3.59}$$

Therefore, its number of steps is still the minimum value $\bar{n}$.

Hence, from relation (3.3.30), we have obtained relation (3.3.53).

The theorem has been proved.

□

It has to be noted that the initial and final states, i and f, are not included in the definition of solution sequence.

It seems useful, at this moment, to add these states to the solution sequence.

**Definition 3.3.4.** A **closed solution sequence** is a sequence $\tilde{S}[\mathfrak{g}^n]$, defined as follows:

$$\tilde{S}[\mathfrak{g}^n] = < s_o, s_1, s_2, \ldots, s_{n-1}, s_n > \tag{3.3.60}$$

and such that, $i = s_o$, $f = s_n$, and the sequence:

$$S[\mathfrak{g}^n] = < s_1, s_2, \ldots, s_{n-1} > \tag{3.3.61}$$

is a solution sequence.

□

**Definition 3.3.5.** A **closed resolvent set** is defined as the set $\tilde{H}$ such that:

$$\tilde{H} = H \cup \{i, f\} \tag{3.3.62}$$

□

**Definition 3.3.6.** A closed solution sequence is called **minimum closed solution sequence through h**, if and only if the corresponding (not closed) solution sequence is a minimum solution sequence through h.

□

**Definition 3.3.7.** We define as **minimum closed solution relation** $\tilde{\Omega}$, a binary relation on $\tilde{H}$, defined in the same way of the Definition 3.3.3 for H.

□

**Theorem 3.3.4.** The minimum closed solution relation $\tilde{\Omega}$ is a partial ordering relation on $\tilde{H}$.

**Proof.** The proof is just similar to the proof of Theorem 3.3.3.

□

It is, now, possible to illustrate, a very important algebraic property on $\tilde{H}$.

**Theorem 3.3.5.** The couple $\tilde{R} = (\tilde{H}, \tilde{\Omega})$ is a lattice.

**Proof.** Because of Theorem 3.3.4, $\tilde{\Omega}$ is a partial ordering relation on $\tilde{H}$.

Therefore, we have to prove that for every couple $h \in \tilde{H}$ and $k \in \tilde{H}$, it is possible to define a binary operation of meet:

(3.3.63) $$\sqcap : \tilde{H} \times \tilde{H} \longrightarrow \tilde{H}$$

and a binary operation of join:

(3.3.64) $$\sqcup : \tilde{H} \times \tilde{H} \longrightarrow \tilde{H}$$

i.e., we have to prove the two following relations:

(3.3.65) $$(h,k) \overset{\sqcap}{\longmapsto} p = h \sqcap k$$

(3.3.66) $$(h,k) \overset{\sqcup}{\longmapsto} q = h \sqcup k$$

In fact, we will define:

(3.3.67) $$p = h \sqcap k = \max_i \left\{ p_i \mid p_i \tilde{\Omega} h \wedge p_i \tilde{\Omega} k \right\}$$

(3.3.68) $$q = h \sqcup k = \min_j \left\{ q_j \mid h \tilde{\Omega} q_j \wedge k \tilde{\Omega} q_j \right\}$$

The operations introduced in this way are always defined because, for every h and k, it holds that:

(3.3.69) $$i \tilde{\Omega} h \quad , \quad i \tilde{\Omega} k$$

(3.3.70) $$h \tilde{\Omega} f \quad , \quad k \tilde{\Omega} f$$

Therefore, i is the universal lower bound of $\tilde{R}$ and f is the universal upper bound of $\tilde{R}$.

It has to be noted that in the particular case, when:

(3.3.71) $$h \tilde{\Omega} k$$

it holds that:

$$p = h \sqcap k = h \tag{3.3.72}$$

$$q = h \sqcup k = k \tag{3.3.73}$$

□

It is trivial to observe that the minimum cost solution sequences are all contained in H and that the domain of the search is, then, H.

A very important problem is that one of finding, among all the possible solutions, the optimum solution, i.e., the particular solution which represents the minimum of some cost function.

**Definition 3.3.8.** Let $\gamma_i \in \Gamma$ be an operator. We define, in correspondence of $\gamma_i$, a cost $c_{\gamma_i}$. Such cost is a label, which is associated to the application of $\gamma_i$ from s to t, i.e.:

$$s \overset{\gamma_i}{\longmapsto} t \tag{3.3.74}$$

□

**Definition 3.3.9.** Let $\xi^n$ be an n-step solution, i.e.:

$$\xi^n = \langle a_1, a_2, \ldots, a_n \rangle \tag{3.3.75}$$

We define a cost $C(\xi^n)$ for a solution $\xi^n$, such that:

$$C(\xi^n) = \sum_{1j}^{n} C_{a_j} \tag{3.3.76}$$

where $C_{a_j}$ represents the cost of an operator $a_j$.

□

**Definition 3.3.10.** We define as **optimum cost** $\bar{C}(\xi^{\bar{n}})$, the minimum of the costs $C(\xi^n)$, and we define as **optimum solution**, the corresponding solution $\bar{\xi}^{\bar{n}}$, and **optimum solution sequence**, the corresponding solution sequence $S[\bar{\xi}^{\bar{n}}]$.

□

**Theorem 3.3.6.** The optimum solution $\bar{\xi}^{\bar{n}}$ is determined with an algorithm which operates only on states which are elements of H.

The optimum solution sequence $S[\bar{\xi}^{\bar{n}}]$ is contained in H.

**Proof.** The proof is obtained, directly, from Theorem 3.3.2.

□

### 3.4. H-Based Algorithms

In this Subchapter we will present some algorithms, based on the previously exposed theoretical results, that can be used in order to achieve the following goals:

- the construction of H;
- the construction of a subset of H, $\bar{H}$, which contains all the minimum solution sequences;
- the construction of the minimum solution sequence.

The first algorithm, that we shall present, is the algorithm which constructs H.

This algorithm is based on the Definition 3.3.1 of H.

In order to prove the correctness of such algorithm, we shall first illustrate a further theoretical result.

**Theorem 3.4.1.** The resolvent set H:

$$H = R_i \cap G_f \tag{3.4.1}$$

can be expressed in the following way:

$$H = \bigcup_{\ell=1}^{\infty} H_\ell \tag{3.4.2}$$

where:

$$H_\ell = R^{*\ell}_{\ i} \cap G^{*\ell}_{\ f} \tag{3.4.3}$$

and:

$$R^{*\ell}_{\ i} = \bigcup_{j=1}^{\ell} R_i^j \tag{3.4.4}$$

and:

$$G^{*\ell}_{\ f} = \bigcup_{j=1}^{\ell} G^j_{\ f} \tag{3.4.5}$$

**Proof.** The proof of the theorem is obtained just by applying the usual properties of set union and set intersection.

□

**Algorithm 3.4.1.** Construction of H.

**STEP 1.** Let:

$$H = \phi; \; H_o = \phi; \; R^{*o}_{\ i} = \phi; \; G^{*o}_{\ f} = \phi; \; j = 1 \tag{3.4.6}$$

**STEP 2.** Compute $R_i^j$ and $G_f^j$.

**STEP 3.** Let:

$$R^{*j}_i = R^{*j-1}_i \cup R^j_i \tag{3.4.7}$$

$$G^{*j}_f = G^{*j-1}_f \cup G^j_f \tag{3.4.8}$$

**STEP 4.** Let:

$$H_j = H_{j-1} \cup \left(R^{*j}_i \cap G^{*j}_f\right) \tag{3.4.9}$$

**STEP 5.** Let:

$$H = H \cup H_j \tag{3.4.10}$$

**STEP 6.** Let:

$$j = j + 1 \tag{3.4.11}$$

**STEP 7.** Go to STEP 2.

□

It has to be observed that Algorithm 3.4.1 is of bidirectional nature, because of the structure of $R_i$ and $G_f$.

Moreover, it is obvious that, because of Theorem 3.4.1, this algorithm does not terminate, because both $R_i$ and $G_f$ have been defined as the union of an infinite number of sets.

In some cases, it may happen (and this is always the case when S is a finite set), that for j greater than a given value $\bar{j}$, $H_j$ is always contained in H.

However, it is not possible to decide that H has been completely constructed (with the exception of the case in which H is equal to S, and S is finite).

We shall now illustrate an efficient algorithm, which generates a particular finite set $\bar{H}$ such that:

$$\bar{H} \subseteq H \tag{3.4.12}$$

It shall be proved, successively, that the set $\bar{H}$ satisfies the important condition of containing the minimum solution sequence.

Moreover, it shall be proved, as well, that the algorithm for the construction of $\bar{H}$ terminates if and only if there exist some solutions to the problem.

The algorithm, for the construction of $\bar{H}$, is divided in two parts. In the first part, we shall determine the first non empty set $H^*_{\bar{n}}$ (i.e., $H^*_{\bar{n}}$ corresponds to the minimum integer $\bar{n}$ for which $H^*_{\bar{n}}$ is non empty), such that:

$$H^*_{\bar{n}} = R^{*\bar{n}}_{i} \cap G^{*\bar{n}}_{f} \tag{3.4.13}$$

In the second part, we shall construct $\bar{H}$ on the basis of the elements of $H^*_{\bar{n}}$.

In order to construct $H^*_{\bar{n}}$, we shall utilize two auxiliary sets, namely $\bar{R}^{\bar{n}}_{i}$, such that:

$$\bar{R}^{\bar{n}}_{i} = R^{\bar{n}-1}_{i} \cup R^{\bar{n}}_{i} \subset R^{*\bar{n}}_{i} \tag{3.4.14}$$

and $\bar{G}^{\bar{n}}_{f}$, such that:

$$\bar{G}^{\bar{n}}_{f} = G^{\bar{n}-1}_{f} \cup G^{\bar{n}}_{f} \subset G^{*\bar{n}}_{f} \tag{3.4.15}$$

The intersection of these two auxiliary sets satisfies, as we shall prove successively, the following interesting property:

$$H_{\bar{n}} = \bar{R}^{\bar{n}}_{i} \cap \bar{G}^{\bar{n}}_{f} = R^{*\bar{n}}_{i} \cap G^{*\bar{n}}_{f} = H^*_{\bar{n}} \tag{3.4.16}$$

**Algorithm 3.4.2.** Construction of $\bar{H}$.

**STEP 1.** Let:

$$\bar{H} = \phi; \ \bar{R}^{o}_{i} = \phi; \ \bar{G}^{o}_{f} = \phi; \quad j = 1 \tag{3.4.17}$$

**STEP 2.** Compute $R^{j}_{i}$ and $G^{j}_{f}$.

**STEP 3.** Let:

$$\bar{R}^{j}_{i} = R^{j-1}_{i} \cup R^{j}_{i} \ ; \ \bar{G}^{j}_{f} = G^{j-1}_{f} \cup G^{j}_{f} \tag{3.4.18}$$

**STEP 4.** Let:

$$H_{j} = \left(\bar{R}^{j}_{i} \cap \bar{G}^{j}_{f}\right) \tag{3.4.19}$$

**STEP 5.** If $H_j = \phi$, then let $j = j + 1$, and go to STEP 2. Otherwise CONTINUE.

**STEP 6.** Let:

$$H^{R}_{1} = H_{j} \ ; \ H^{G}_{1} = H_{j} \ ; \quad k = 1 \tag{3.4.20}$$

**STEP 7.** Let:

$$\bar{H} = \bar{H} \cup H_K^R \cup H_K^G \qquad (3.4.21)$$

**STEP 8.** If j-k = 0, then STOP with $\bar{H}$ completely constructed. Otherwise CONTINUE.
**STEP 9.** Compute $R^1_{H_k^R}$ and $G^1_{H_k^G}$, in the following way. Consider all the elements belonging to $H_k^R$ and, for each of them, generate all the successors. These new states are the elements of $R^1_{H_k^R}$.

Consider all the elements belonging to $H_k^G$ and, for each of them, find all the parents. These new states are the elements of $G^1_{H_k^G}$.
**STEP 10.** Let:

$$k = k + 1;\ H_k^R = R^1_{H^R_{k-1}} \cap G^{j-k}_f;\ H_k^G = G^1_{H^G_{k-1}} \cap R^{j-k}_i \qquad (3.4.22)$$

**STEP 11.** Go to STEP 7.

□

We shall now prove that the set $H_{\bar{n}}$, which has been constructed in the first five steps of Algorithm 3.4.2, is equal to the set $H^*_{\bar{n}}$, as expressed by relation (3.4.13), and, therefore, that the previously stated property, expressed by the relation (3.4.16), is satisfied.

**Theorem 3.4.2.** The set $H_{\bar{n}}$ with $\bar{n}$ equal to the minimum integer j, such that:

$$H_j \neq \phi \qquad (3.4.23)$$

where $H_{\bar{n}}$ has been computed as:

$$H_{\bar{n}} = \bar{R}^{\bar{n}}_i \cap \bar{G}^{\bar{n}}_f \qquad (3.4.24)$$

is equal to the set $H^*_{\bar{n}}$, computed as:

$$H^*_{\bar{n}} = R^{*\bar{n}}_i \cap G^{*\bar{n}}_f \qquad (3.4.25)$$

with $\bar{n}$ equal to the minimum integer j such that:

$$H^*_j \neq 0 \qquad (3.4.26)$$

*Proof.* Let us consider an element $h_{\bar{n}} \in H^*_{\bar{n}}$ ; we shall prove that such an element is also a member of $\bar{H}_{\bar{n}}$.

It is obvious that, because of the definition of $H^*_{\bar{n}}$, given by relations (3.4.25), (3.4.6), (3.4.7), and (3.4.8), and because of the definition of $\bar{H}_{\bar{n}}$, given by relations (3.4.24), and (3.4.18), every element $h_{\bar{n}}$, which is a member of $H^*_{\bar{n}}$, is also a member of $\bar{H}_{\bar{n}}$.

We shall prove, therefore, that it is not possible that $h_{\bar{n}} \in \bar{H}_{\tilde{n}}$, with $\tilde{n} < \bar{n}$.

This proof shall be divided in two parts. We shall prove, in the first part, that it is not possible that $h_{\bar{n}} \in \bar{R}^{\bar{n}}_i$ and $h_{\bar{n}} \in \bar{G}^{\bar{n}}_f$, with $\tilde{n} < \bar{n}$.

Therefore, we shall prove that, because of the definitions of $\bar{R}^j_i$ and of $\bar{G}^j_f$, given by relation (3.4.18), the following relation yields a contraddiction:

$$(\exists h_{\bar{n}})((h_{\bar{n}} \in H^*_{\bar{n}}) \wedge (h_{\bar{n}} \in R^{\alpha}_i) \wedge (h_{\bar{n}} \in G^{\beta}_f) \wedge (\alpha < \bar{n} - 1) \wedge (\beta < \bar{n} - 1))$$

(3.4.27)

In fact, if the relation (3.4.27) could hold, then it would be certainly possible to construct a set $H^*_{\tilde{n}}$, computed according to the relation (3.4.25), which would include, among its members, the element $h_{\bar{n}}$ which, because of relations (3.4.24), (3.4.18), (3.4.27), would be a member of $\bar{H}_{\tilde{n}}$, with $\tilde{n}$ such that:

(3.4.28) $$\tilde{n} = \max\,[\alpha, \beta]$$

Therefore, it would also hold that:

(3.4.29) $$H^*_{\tilde{n}} \neq \phi$$

with:

(3.4.30) $$\tilde{n} < \bar{n}$$

because of relations (3.4.25) and (3.4.27).

But, relations (3.4.29) and (3.4.30) are against the hypothesis that $\bar{n}$ is equal to the minimum integer j such that relation (3.4.26) holds.

Therefore, it must be that:

(3.4.31) $$\max\,[\alpha, \beta] = \bar{n}$$

Because of relation (3.4.31), if it should be that $h_{\bar{n}} \in \bar{H}_{\tilde{n}}$, with $\tilde{n} < \bar{n}$, there should be only two more possibilities left.

We shall prove now, in the second part, that also these two possibilities yield two contraddictions.

The first possibility is that relation (3.4.31) is satisfied in the following way:

$$\alpha = \bar{n} \; ; \; \beta < \bar{n} - 1 \qquad (3.4.32)$$

Let us call $h'_{\bar{n}}$ an element $h_{\bar{n}}$ of $H^*_{\bar{n}}$ which satisfies relation (3.4.27), but with $\alpha$ and $\beta$ satisfying, not relation (3.4.27), but relation (3.4.32).

Since $h'_{\bar{n}}$ satisfies relations (3.4.27) and (3.4.32), it shall be that:

$$(\exists T)\left(\left(T \subset R^{\bar{n}-1}{}_{i}\right) \wedge \left(t \in T\right) \wedge \left(t \overset{\Gamma_1}{\longmapsto} T^1\right) \wedge \left(h'_{\bar{n}} \in T^1\right)\right) \qquad (3.4.33)$$

because of Definition 3.1.4.

The set T, because of relations (3.4.27) and (3.4.32), and because of Definition 3.1.7, is such that:

$$T \subset G^{\beta+1}{}_{f} \qquad (3.4.34)$$

But, then, it shall be that:

$$R^{\bar{n}-1}{}_{i} \cap G^{\beta+1}{}_{f} \neq \phi \qquad (3.4.35)$$

and, therefore, because of relations (3.4.32) and (3.4.25), $\bar{n}$ would not be equal to the minimum integer j, such that relation (3.4.26) holds.

Therefore, the first possibility yields a contraddiction.

The second possibility is that relation (3.4.31) is satisfied in the following way:

$$\alpha < \bar{n} - 1 \; ; \; \beta = \bar{n} \qquad (3.4.36)$$

Let us call $h''_{\bar{n}}$ an element $h_{\bar{n}}$ of $H^*_{\bar{n}}$ which satisfies relation (3.4.27), but with $\alpha$ and $\beta$ satisfying, not relation (3.4.27), but relation (3.4.36).

Since $h''_{\bar{n}}$ satisfies relations (3.4.27) and (3.4.36), it shall be that:

$$(\exists W)\left(\left(W \subset G^{\bar{n}-1}{}_{f}\right) \wedge \left(h''_{\bar{n}} \overset{\Gamma_1}{\longmapsto} W\right)\right) \qquad (3.4.37)$$

by Definition 3.1.7.

The set W, because of relations (3.4.27) and (3.4.36), and by Definition 3.1.4, is such that:

$$W \subset R^{\alpha+1}{}_{i} \qquad (3.4.38)$$

But, then, it shall be that:

(3.4.39) $$R^{\alpha+1}{}_i \cap G^{\bar{n}-1}{}_f \neq \phi$$

and, therefore, because of relations (3.4.36) and (3.4.25), $\bar{n}$ would not be equal to the minimum integer j, such that relation (3.4.26) holds.

Therefore,the second possibility yields a contraddiction.

Thus, we have proved that it does not exist an element $h_{\bar{n}} \in H^*_{\bar{n}}$, which is also an element of $H_{\tilde{n}}$, with $\tilde{n} < \bar{n}$.

Then, such element $h_{\bar{n}}$ must be an element of $H_{\bar{n}}$.

Therefore, the theorem has been proved.

□

We shall, now, illustrate two more theorems, which shall prove both the correctness and the termination of Algorithm 3.4.2.

Theorem 3.4.3. Given a problem P, the set $\bar{H}$, obtained with Algorithm 3.4.2, contains only the minimum solution sequence $S[\mathfrak{g}^{\ell}]$, i.e., the solution sequence, with the minimum number of states.

**Proof.** Because of the Steps 3, 4, and 5, of Algorithm 3.4.2, the elements $h_{\bar{n}} \in H_{\bar{n}}$ have been obtained in such a way that they belong to $\bar{R}^{\bar{n}}_i$ and to $\bar{G}^{\bar{n}}_f$.

Therefore, two different cases can arise:

I) $$\left(\forall\, h_{\bar{n}} \in H_{\bar{n}}\right)\left(\left(h_{\bar{n}} \in R^{\bar{n}}{}_i\right) \wedge \left(h_{\bar{n}} \in G^{\bar{n}}{}_f\right)\right)$$
(3.4.40)

II) $$\left(\forall\, h_{\bar{n}} \in H_{\bar{n}}\right)\left(\left(\left(h_{\bar{n}} \in R^{\bar{n}}{}_i\right) \wedge \left(h_{\bar{n}} \in G^{\bar{n}-1}{}_f\right)\right) \vee \left(\left(h_{\bar{n}} \in R^{\bar{n}-1}{}_i\right) \wedge \left(h_{\bar{n}} \in G^{\bar{n}}{}_f\right)\right)\right)$$
(3.4.41)

*Case I.*

The elements $h_{\bar{n}}$ of $H_{\bar{n}}$ belong, because of relation (3.4.40), to $R^{\bar{n}}_i$.

Therefore, by Theorem 3.2.1, it exists an $\bar{n}$-step solution for each one of the problems:

(3.4.42) $$P_{h_{\bar{n}}} = (M, i, h_{\bar{n}})$$

which have, as final states, the elements $h_{\bar{n}}$.

The $\bar{n}$-step solution to each one of the problems $P_{h_{\bar{n}}}$, by Definition

3.1.10, is a sequence $\xi^{\bar{n}}$.

Thus, we can obtain, by Theorem 3.1.5, an $\bar{n}$-step solution sequence:

$$S[\xi^{\bar{n}}] = < s_1, s_2, \ldots, s_{\bar{n}-k}, \ldots, s_{\bar{n}-1} > \quad (3.4.43)$$

The states $s_1, s_2, \ldots, s_{\bar{n}-k}, \ldots, s_{\bar{n}-1}$, of the $\bar{n}$-step solution sequence, belong, by Theorem 3.2.5, respectively to $R^1_i, R^2_i, \ldots, R^{\bar{n}-k}_i, \ldots, R^{\bar{n}-1}_i$.

Let:

$$k = 1 \ , \ s_{\bar{n}}^{i} \sim h_{\bar{n}} \quad (3.4.44)$$

By Definition 3.1.7 and by Algorithm 3.4.2, we have, by construction, that:

$$s_{\bar{n}-k+1} \in H^G_k \quad (3.4.45)$$

Relation (3.4.45) is true, when $k = 1$, because of STEP 6 of Algorithm 3.4.2; it is also true, for $k > 1$, because of what we have proved in the previous steps.

Therefore, because of relation (3.4.45), we have:

$$s_{\bar{n}-k} \in G^1_{H^G_k} \quad (3.4.46)$$

From relations (3.4.21) and (3.4.22), we then obtain:

$$s_{\bar{n}-k} \in \bar{H} \quad (3.4.47)$$

In a recursive way, by letting $k = k+1$, until that $k = \bar{n}$, we obtain that the whole $\bar{n}$-step solution sequence $S[\xi^{\bar{n}}]$ belongs to $\bar{H}$.

Moreover, the elements $h_{\bar{n}}$ of $H_{\bar{n}}$ belong, because of relation (3.4.40), to $G^{\bar{n}}_f$ as well.

Therefore, by Theorem 3.2.2, it exists an $\bar{n}$-step solution for each one of the problems:

$$\bar{P}_{h_{\bar{n}}} = (M, h_{\bar{n}}, f) \quad (3.4.48)$$

which have, as initial states, the elements $h_{\bar{n}}$.

The $\bar{n}$-step solution, to each one of the problems $\bar{P}_{h_{\bar{n}}}$, by Definition 3.1.10, is a sequence $\bar{\xi}^{\bar{n}}$. Thus, we can obtain, by Theorem 3.1.5, an $\bar{n}$-step solution sequence:

$$S[\bar{\xi}^{\bar{n}}] = < \bar{s}_1, \bar{s}_2, \ldots, \bar{s}_k, \ldots, \bar{s}_{\bar{n}-1} > \quad (3.4.49)$$

The states $\bar{s}_1, \bar{s}_2, \ldots, \bar{s}_k, \ldots, \bar{s}_{\bar{n}-1}$ of the $\bar{n}$-step solution sequence belong, by Theorem 3.2.6, respectively, to $G^{\bar{n}-1}{}_f, G^{\bar{n}-2}{}_f, \ldots, G^{\bar{n}-k}{}_f, \ldots, G^1_f$.

Let:

(3.4.50) $$k = 1 \quad , \quad \bar{s}_o = h_{\bar{n}}$$

By Definition 3.1.4 and by Algorithm 3.4.2, we have, by construction. that:

(3.4.51) $$\bar{s}_{k-1} \in H^R_k$$

Relation (3.4.51) is true, when $k = 1$, because of STEP 6 of Algorithm 3.4.2; it is also true, for $k > 1$, because of what we have proved in the previous steps.

Therefore, because of relation (3.4.51), we have:

(3.4.52) $$\bar{s}_k \in R^1_H R_k$$

From relations (3.4.21) and (3.4.22), we then obtain:

(3.4.53) $$\bar{s}_k \in \bar{H}$$

In a recursive way, by letting $k = k+1$, until that $k = \bar{n}$, we obtain that the whole n-step solution sequence $S[\mathscr{G}^{\bar{n}}]$ belongs to $\bar{H}$.

Therefore, in correspondence of each element $h_{\bar{n}}$ of $H_{\bar{n}}$, we can obtain an l-step solution sequence $S[\mathscr{G}^{\ell}]$ for the problem P, by appropriately connecting the two previously described $\bar{n}$-step solution sequences, in the following way:

(3.4.54) $$S[\mathscr{G}^{\ell}] = < s_1, s_2, \ldots, s_{\bar{n}-1}, h_{\bar{n}}, \bar{s}_1, \bar{s}_2, \ldots, \bar{s}_{\bar{n}-1} >$$

with:

(3.4.55) $$\ell = 2\bar{n}$$

The whole l-step solution sequence $S[\mathscr{G}^{\ell}]$ belongs, because of what has been previously proved, to $\bar{H}$.

It also contains the minimum number of states. In fact, let us suppose that it could exist an l-step solution sequence:

(3.4.56) $$S[\mathscr{G}^{\ell'}] = < s'_1, s'_2, \ldots, s'_{\ell'-1} >$$

with:

(3.4.57) $$\ell' < \ell$$

In this evenience, by Definitions 3.1.4, 3.1.7, and 3.1.10, and by Theorems 3.2.5 and 3.2.6, we would have that $s'_1, s'_2, \ldots, s'_{\ell'-1}$ should belong, respectively, to $R^1_i$ and $G^{\ell'-1}_f$; $R^2_i$ and $G^{\ell'-2}_f$, ..., $R^{\ell'-1}_i$ and $G^1_f$.

Therefore, two different subcases may arise, namely:

i) l'is even;

ii) l'is odd.

*Subcase i.*

If l'is even, it obviously holds that:

$$(\exists n^*)\left(\left(s'_{n^*} \in G^{n^*}{}_f\right) \wedge \left(s'_{n^*} \in R^{n^*}{}_i\right)\right) \tag{3.4.58}$$

with:

$$n^* = \ell'/2 \tag{3.4.59}$$

Because of relations (3.4.18) and (3.4.19), n* would be the minimum value of j for which relation (3.4.23) (i.e., $H_j \neq \phi$) holds, i.e., it would be that:

$$n^* = \ell'/2 < \ell/2 = \bar{n} \tag{3.4.60}$$

which would be against the hypothesis that $\bar{n}$ is the minimum value of j for which relation (3.4.23) (i.e., $H_j \neq \phi$ ) holds.

*Subcase ii.*

If l' is odd, it obviously holds that:

$$(\exists n^*)\left(\left(s'_{n^*} \in R^{n^*}{}_i\right) \wedge \left(s'_{n^*} \in G^{n^*-1}{}_f\right) \wedge \left(s'_{n^*-1} \in R^{n^*-1}{}_i\right) \wedge \left(s'_{n^*-1} \in G^{n^*}{}_f\right)\right) \tag{3.4.61}$$

with:

$$n^* = (\ell' + 1)/2 \tag{3.4.62}$$

Now, if:

$$\ell' < \ell - 1 \tag{3.4.63}$$

then:

$$n^* < \bar{n} \tag{3.4.64}$$

which would be against the hypothesis that $\bar{n}$ is the minimum value of j for which relation (3.4.23) (i.e., $H_j \neq \phi$) holds.

Otherwise, if:

(3.4.65) $$\ell' = \ell - 1$$

then:

(3.4.66) $$n^* = \bar{n}$$

But, because of relation (3.4.61), there would be at least two elements ($s'_{n^*-1}$ and $s'_{n^*}$) which do not satisfy relation (3.4.40), but which satisfy relation (3.4.41).

This also is against the hypothesis of considering Case I.

*Case II.*

By Definitions 3.1.4 and 3.1.7, if it exists one element $h'_{\bar{n}}$, s.t.:

(3.4.67) $$\left(h'_{\bar{n}} \in R^{\bar{n}}{}_{i}\right) \wedge \left(h'_{\bar{n}} \in G^{\bar{n}-1}{}_{f}\right)$$

it exists, at least, one element $h''_{\bar{n}}$, s.t.:

(3.4.68) $$\left(h''_{\bar{n}} \in R^{\bar{n}-1}{}_{i}\right) \wedge \left(h''_{\bar{n}} \in G^{\bar{n}}{}_{f}\right)$$

Also, if it exists one element $h''_{\bar{n}}$, satisfying relation (3.4.68), it exists at least one element $h'_{\bar{n}}$, satisfying relation (3.4.67).

In fact, if $h'_{\bar{n}} \in R^{\bar{n}}_{i}$, by Definition 3.1.4, it holds that:

(3.4.69) $$(\exists \bar{s})\left(\left(\bar{s} \in R^{\bar{n}-1}{}_{i}\right) \wedge \left(\bar{s} \xmapsto{\Gamma_1} T\right) \wedge \left(h'_{\bar{n}} \in T\right)\right)$$

But, since $h'_{\bar{n}} \in G_{f}^{\bar{n}-1}$, by Definitions 3.1.4 and 3.1.7, we obtain that:

(3.4.70) $$\bar{s} \in G^{\bar{n}}{}_{f}$$

And, therefore, we have that:

(3.4.71) $$\bar{s} \in H_{\bar{n}}$$

Thus, it exists at least one element $h''_{\bar{n}}$, which satisfies relation (3.4.68), and s.t.:

(3.4.72) $$h''_{\bar{n}} = \bar{s}$$

The opposite case can be proved with similar considerations. Since the elements $h'_{\bar{n}}$

and $h''_{\bar{n}}$ of $H_{\bar{n}}$ belong, respectively, because of relation (3.4.41), to two sets $H'_{\bar{n}}$ and $H''_{\bar{n}}$, whose elements satisfy, respectively, relations (3.4.67) and (3.4.68), by Theorem 3.2.1, it exists an $\bar{n}$-step solution for each one of the problems:

$$P_{h'_{\bar{n}}} = (M, i, h'_{\bar{n}}) \qquad (3.4.73)$$

which have, as final state, the elements $h'_{\bar{n}}$ ; also, it exists an ($\bar{n}$-1)-step solution for each one of the probelms:

$$P_{h''_{\bar{n}}} = (M, i, h''_{\bar{n}}) \qquad (3.4.74)$$

which have, as final states, the elements $h''_{\bar{n}}$.

The $\bar{n}$-step solution to each one of the problems $P_{h'_{\bar{n}}}$, by Definition 3.1.10, is a sequence $\xi'^{\bar{n}}$.

The ($\bar{n}$-1)-step solution to each one of the problems $P_{h''_{\bar{n}}}$, by Definition 3.1.10, is a sequence $\xi''^{\bar{n}-1}$.

Thus, we can obtain, by Theorem 3.1.5, respectively, the following $\bar{n}$-step solution sequence:

$$S[\xi'^{\bar{n}}] = < s'_1, s'_2, \ldots, s'_{\bar{n}-k}, \ldots, s'_{\bar{n}-1} > \qquad (3.4.75)$$

and ($\bar{n}$-1)-step solution sequence:

$$S[\xi''^{\bar{n}-1}] = < s''_1, s''_2, \ldots, s''_{\bar{n}-k}, \ldots, s''_{\bar{n}-2} > \qquad (3.4.76)$$

The states $s'_1$ and $s''_1$, $s'_2$ and $s''_2$, ..., $s'_{\bar{n}-k}$ and $s''_{\bar{n}-k}$, ..., $s'_{\bar{n}-2}$ and $s''_{\bar{n}-2}$, and $s'_{\bar{n}-1}$ belong, by Theorem 3.2.5, respectively, to $R^1_i, R^2_i, \ldots, R^{\bar{n}-k}_i, \ldots, R^{\bar{n}-2}_i, R^{\bar{n}-1}_i$.

Let:

$$k = 1 \quad , \quad s'_{\bar{n}} = h'_{\bar{n}} \qquad (3.4.77)$$

By Definition 3.1.7 and by Algorithm 3.4.2, we have, by construction, that:

$$s'_{\bar{n}-k+1} \in H^G_k \qquad (3.4.78)$$

Relation (3.4.78) is true, when k = 1, because of STEP 6 of Algorithm 3.4.2; it is also true, for k >1, because of what we have proved in the previous steps and in the beginning of Case II.

Therefore, because of relation (3.4.78), we have:

$$s'_{\bar{n}-k} \in G^1_{H^G_k} \qquad (3.4.79)$$

From relations (3.4.21) and (3.4.22), we then obtain:

(3.4.80) $$s'_{\bar{n}-k} \in \bar{H}$$

In a recursive way, by letting $k = k+1$, until $k = \bar{n}$, we obtain that the whole $\bar{n}$-step solution sequence $S[\xi^{\bar{n}}]$ belongs to $\bar{H}$.

The same thing cannot, a priori, be stated for the ($\bar{n}$-1)-step solution sequence $S[\xi''^{\bar{n}-1}]$.

Moreover, since the elements $h'_{\bar{n}}$ and $h''_{\bar{n}}$ of $H_{\bar{n}}$ belong, respectively, because of relation (3.4.41), to two sets $H'_{\bar{n}}$ and $H''_{\bar{n}}$, whose elements satisfy respectively, relations (3.4.67) and (3.4.68), by Theorem 3.2.2, it exists an ($\bar{n}$-1)-step solution for each one of the problems:

(3.4.81) $$\bar{P}_{h'_{\bar{n}}} = (M, h'_{\bar{n}}, f)$$

which have, as initial states, the elements $h'_{\bar{n}}$; also, it exists an $\bar{n}$-step solution for each one of the problems:

(3.4.82) $$\bar{P}_{h''_{\bar{n}}} = (M, h''_{\bar{n}}, f)$$

which have, as initial states, the elements $h''_{\bar{n}}$. The ($\bar{n}$-1)-step solution to each one of the problems $\bar{P}_{h'_{\bar{n}}}$, by Definition 3.1.10, is a sequence $\bar{\xi}'^{\bar{n}-1}$.

The $\bar{n}$-step solution to each one of the problems $\bar{P}_{h''_{\bar{n}}}$, by Definition 3.1.10, is a sequence $\bar{\xi}''^{\bar{n}}$.

Thus, we can obtain, by Theorem 3.1.5, respectively, the following ($\bar{n}$-1)-step solution sequence:

(3.4.83) $$S[\bar{\xi}'^{\bar{n}-1}] = \langle \bar{s}'_1, \bar{s}'_2, \ldots, \bar{s}'_{\bar{n}-k}, \ldots, \bar{s}'_{\bar{n}-2} \rangle$$

and $\bar{n}$-step solution sequence:

(3.4.84) $$S[\bar{\xi}''^{\bar{n}}] = \langle \bar{s}''_1, \bar{s}''_2, \ldots, \bar{s}''_{\bar{n}-k}, \ldots, \bar{s}''_{\bar{n}-1} \rangle$$

The states $\bar{s}'_1$ and $\bar{s}''_1$, $\bar{s}'_2$ and $\bar{s}''_2$, . . . , $\bar{s}'_{\bar{n}-k}$ and $\bar{s}''_{\bar{n}-k}$, ..., $\bar{s}'_{\bar{n}-2}$ and $\bar{s}''_{\bar{n}-2}$ and $\bar{s}''_{n\ 1}$ belong, by Theorem 3.2.6, respectively to $G^{\bar{n}-1}{}_f$, $G^{\bar{n}-2}{}_f$, ..., $G^{\bar{n}-k}{}_f$, ..., $G^2_f$, $G^1_f$.

Let:

(3.4.85) $$k = 1 \quad , \quad \bar{s}''_o = h''_{\bar{n}}$$

By Definition 3.1.4 and by Algorithm 3.4.2, we have, by construction, that:

$$\bar{s}''_{k-1} \in H^R_k \qquad (3.4.86)$$

Relation (3.4.86) is true, when $k = 1$, because of STEP 6 of Algorithm 3.4.2; it is also true, for $k > 1$, because of what we have proved in the previous steps and in the beginning of Case II.

Therefore, because of relation (3.4.86), we have:

$$\bar{s}''_k \in R^1_{H^R_k} \qquad (3.4.87)$$

From relations (3.4.21) and (3.4.22), we then obtain:

$$\bar{s}''_k \in \bar{H} \qquad (3.4.88)$$

In a recursive way, by letting $k = k+1$ until $k = \bar{n}$, we obtain that the whole $\bar{n}$-step solution sequence $S[\xi''^{\bar{n}}]$ belongs to $\bar{H}$.

The same thing cannot, a priori, be stated for the ($\bar{n}$-1)-step solution sequence $S[\xi'^{\bar{n}-1}]$.

Let us now consider a particular element $h'^*_{\bar{n}}$ of $H'_{\bar{n}}$, and a particular element $h''^*_{\bar{n}}$ of $H''_{\bar{n}}$, which corresponds to $h'^*_{\bar{n}}$, as expressed by relation (3.4.69).

Therefore, by Theorems 3.1.5, 3.2.1, and 3.2.2, and by Definition 3.1.10, in correspondence of $h'^*_{\bar{n}}$ and $h''^*_{\bar{n}}$, we can obtain the following problems, $\bar{n}$-step solutions, and $\bar{n}$-step solution sequences:

$$\begin{aligned}
P_{h'^*_{\bar{n}}} &= (M, i, h'^*_{\bar{n}}), \quad \xi'^{*\bar{n}} \\
S[\xi'^{*\bar{n}}] &= \langle s'^*_1, s'^*_2, \ldots, s'^*_{\bar{n}-k}, \ldots, s'^*_{\bar{n}-1} \rangle \\
\bar{P}_{h''^*_{\bar{n}}} &= (M, h''^*_{\bar{n}}, f), \quad \bar{\xi}''^{*\bar{n}} \\
S[\bar{\xi}''^{*\bar{n}}] &= \langle \bar{s}''^*_1, \bar{s}''^*_2, \ldots, \bar{s}''^*_{\bar{n}-k}, \ldots, \bar{s}''^*_{\bar{n}-1} \rangle
\end{aligned} \qquad (3.4.89)$$

By Definitions 3.1.5 and 3.1.7, and because of relation (3.4.69), it is possible to construct the $\bar{n}$-step solution sequences $S[\xi'^{*\bar{n}}]$ and $S[\bar{\xi}''^{*\bar{n}}]$ of relation (3.4.89), in such a way that the following conditions hold :

$$s'^*_{\bar{n}-1} = h''^*_{\bar{n}}, \quad \bar{s}''^*_1 = h'^*_{\bar{n}} \qquad (3.4.90)$$

Therefore, in corrispondence of each pair of elements $h'^{*}_{\bar{n}}$ of $H'_{\bar{n}}$ and $h''^{*}_{\bar{n}}$ of $H''_{\bar{n}}$, we can obtain an 1-step solution sequence $S[\xi^{\ell}]$ for the problem P, by appropriately connecting the two previously described $\bar{n}$-step solution sequences, in the following way :

$$S[\xi^{\ell}] = < s'^{*}_1, s'^{*}_2, \ldots, s'^{*}_{\bar{n}-2}, h''^{*}_{\bar{n}}, h'^{*}_{\bar{n}}, \bar{s}''^{*}_2, \ldots, \bar{s}''^{*}_{\bar{n}-1} >$$

(3.4.91)

with:

(3.4.92) $$\ell = 2\bar{n} - 1$$

The whole l-step solution sequence $S[\xi^{\ell}]$ belongs, because of what has been previously proved, to $\bar{H}$.

It also contains the minimum number of states.

In fact, let us suppose that it could exist an l'-step solution sequence:

(3.4.93) $$S[\xi^{\ell'}] = < s'_1, s'_2, \ldots, s'_{\ell'-1} >$$

with:

(3.4.94) $$\ell' < \ell$$

In this evenience, by Definitions 3.1.4, 3.1.7, and 3.1.10, and by Theorems 3.2.5 and 3.2.6, we would have that $s'_1, s'_2, \ldots, s'_{\ell'-1}$ should belong, respectively, to $R^1_i$ and $G^{\ell'-1}_f$, $R^2_i$ and $G^{\ell'-2}_f$, ... , $R^{\ell'-1}_i$ and $G^1_f$.

Therefore, two different subcases may arise, namely:

i) l' is even ;
ii) l' is odd.

*Subcase i.*

If l' is even, relations (3.4.58), (3.4.59), and (3.4.60), obviously hold.

Now, if:

(3.4.95) $$\ell' < \ell + 1$$

then, because of relations (3.4.59) and (3.4.92), it would be that:

(3.4.96) $$n^{*} = \ell'/2 < (\ell' + 1)/2 = \bar{n}$$

which would be against the hypothesis that $\bar{n}$ is the minimum value of j for which relation (3.4.23) (i.e., $H_j \neq \phi$ ) holds.

Otherwise, if:

$$\ell' = \ell + 1 \qquad (3.4.97)$$

then:

$$n^* = \bar{n} \qquad (3.4.98)$$

But, because of relation (3.4.58), there woul be at least one element $s_{n^*}$, which does not satisfy relation (3.4.41), but which satisfy relation (3.4.40).

This also is against the hypothesis of considering Case II.

*Subcase ii.*

If l' is odd, relations (3.4.61), (3.4.62), and (3.4.63), obviously hold.

Then, because of relations (3.4.62), (3.4.63), and (3.4.92), it would be that:

$$n^* \doteq (\ell' + 1)/2 < (\ell + 1)/2 = \bar{n} \qquad (3.4.99)$$

which would be against the hypothesis that $\bar{n}$ is the minimum value of j for which relation (3.4.23) (i.e., $H_j \neq \phi$) holds.

$\bar{H}$ contains only elements $\bar{h}$ belonging to solution sequences with the minimum number of states.

In fact, by STEP 10 of Algorithm 3.4.2, if we are in Case I, it holds :

$$\left(\forall\, \bar{h} \in \bar{H}\right) \left(\left(\left(\bar{h} \in G^{\bar{n}+k}{}_f\right) \wedge \left(\bar{h} \in R^{\bar{n}-k}{}_i\right)\right) \vee \left(\left(\bar{h} \in G^{\bar{n}-k}{}_f\right) \wedge \left(\bar{h} \in R^{\bar{n}+k}{}_i\right)\right)\right) \qquad (3.4.100)$$

while, if we are in Case II, it holds :

$$\left(\forall\, \bar{h} \in \bar{H}\right) \left(\left(\left(\bar{h} \in G^{\bar{n}+k-1}{}_f\right) \wedge \left(\bar{h} \in R^{\bar{n}-k}{}_i\right)\right) \vee \left(\left(\bar{h} \in G^{\bar{n}-k}{}_f\right) \wedge \left(\bar{h} \in R^{\bar{n}+k-1}{}_i\right)\right)\right) \qquad (3.4.101)$$

By Theorems (3.1.5), (3.2.1), and (3.2.2), and by Definition (3.1.10), in correspondence of each element $\bar{h}$ of $\bar{H}$, we can consider the two problems $P_{\bar{h}} = (M, i, \bar{h})$ and $\bar{P}_{\bar{h}} = (M, \bar{h}, f)$, which have, respectively, as initial and final state, the element $\bar{h}$.

If we are in Case I, because of relations (3.4.54) and (3.4.55), we can obtain an $\bar{l}$-step solution sequence $S[\xi^{\bar{\ell}}]$ for the problem P, with $\bar{\ell} = 2\bar{n}$.

We have already proved that this sequence contains the minimum number of states.

If we are in Case II, because of relations (3.4.91) and (3.4.92), we can obtain an $\bar{\bar{l}}$-step solution sequence $S[\xi^{\bar{\bar{\ell}}}]$ for the problem P, with $\bar{\bar{\ell}} = 2\bar{n} - 1$. We have already proved that this sequence contains the minimum number of states. The proof of the theorem is now completely achieved.

□

Now, we have to prove the termination property of Algorithm 3.4.2.

**Theorem 3.4.4** Algorithm 3.4.2 terminates if and only if it exists an l-step solution:

$$\xi^{\ell} = \langle a_1, a_2, \dots, a_j, \dots, a_{\ell} \rangle \tag{3.4.102}$$

and if l is finite.

**Proof.**

**a) If part.**

Because of STEP 5 and STEP 8, Algorithm 3.4.2 terminates if and only if it is finite the value n* for which the following relation holds:

$$H_{n*} \neq \phi \tag{3.4.103}$$

Let us consider the l-step solution sequence $S[\xi^{\ell}]$ which is associated with the l-step solution $\xi^{\ell}$:

$$S[\xi^{\ell}] = \langle s_1, s_2, \dots, s_j, \dots, s_{\ell-1} \rangle \tag{3.4.104}$$

By Definitions 3.1.4, 3.1.7, and 3.1.10, we have that $s_1, s_2, \dots, s_j, \dots, s_{\ell-1}$ belong respectively to $R_i^1$ and $G^{\ell-1}{}_f$, $R_i^2$ and $G^{\ell-2}{}_f$, ..., $R_i^j$ and $G^{\ell-j}{}_f$, ..., $R^{\ell-1}{}_i$ and $G^1{}_f$

Then, if l is even, relations (3.4.58) and (3.4.59) hold.

Therefore, it will be that n* is the minimum value of j for which $H_j \neq \phi$.

Moreover, if l is finite, because of relation (3.4.59), also n* is finite, and, therefore, Algorithm 3.4.2 terminates.

If l is odd, relations (3.4.61) and (3.4.62) hold.

Therefore, it will be that n* is the minimum value of j for which $H_j \neq \phi$.

Moreover, if l is finite, because of relation (3.4.62), also $n^*$ is finite, and, therefore, Algorithm 3.4.2 terminates.

**b) Only if part.**

If Algorithm 3.4.2 terminates, there is, because of what we have proved in the if part of the proof, a value $n^*$, such that $H_{n^*} \neq \phi$, with $n^*$ satisfying either relation (3.4.59) or relation (3.4.62).

By Theorem 3.4.2, it is then possible to obtain an l-step solution $\xi^{\ell}$, with a minimum number of steps, where l satisfies either relation (3.4.55) or relation (3.4.92).

The theorem has been proved.

□

It is important to observe that Algorithm 3.4.2 is bidirectional, because of the independent characteristics and specifications of $R_i$ and $G_f$.

**Example 3.4.1.** Let us consider the Hanoi-Tower-Puzzle.

The graph of this puzzle is shown in Fig. 3.1.

In this Fig. 3.1, we have shown:

1. The sets $R^{*\bar{n}}{}_i$ and $G^{*\bar{n}}{}_f$, with $\bar{n}$ equal to the minimum value j, such that $H_j \neq \phi$.
2. The elements belonging to $H_{\bar{n}}$.
3. The elements belonging to $\bar{H}$.

We shall, now, illustrate a new algorithm which yields, with an expansion technique, the optimum solution. The algorithm is of bidirectional nature. It is structured into three phases, which cooperate at each level.

PHASE A is related to the generation, with the Dijkstra method, of the path of minimum cost, starting from i.

PHASE B is related to the generation of $G^n_f$, starting from f.

PHASE C is related to the expansion, inside $G^n{}_f$, with a modification of the Dijkstra method.

**Algorithm 3.4.3** Construction of the optimum solution.
**PHASE A.**

STEP A.1. Put the node i into al list called OPEN, and let:

$$h(i) = 0 \tag{3.4.105}$$

STEP A.2. If list OPEN is empty, exit with failure.

STEP A.3. Take from list OPEN the node which has the minimum value for the cost function h.
Put such a node into a list called CLOSED.
Call n such a node.
If more than one node has the minimum value for h, take arbitrarily anyone of them.

STEP A.4. If n is a goal node, exit with the solution obtained by tracing back the pointers, starting from n.

STEP A.5. If n belongs to the list NGN or to the list GN, go to STEP C.1.

STEP A.6. Expand node n by generating all its successor nodes (if there are no successor nodes, go to STEP A.2). For each successor node $n_i$ of n, let:

$$h(n_i) = h(n) + c(n, n_i) \qquad (3.4.106)$$

where $c(n, n_i)$ is the cost of the arc of the graph from n to $n_i$.

STEP A.7. For eachone of the successor nodes $n_i$ of n, which does not belong already either to list OPEN or to list CLOSED, let us associate the value $h(n_i)$ computed according relation (3.4.106).
Put eachone of these successor nodes $n_i$ of n into the list OPEN and direct backward a pointer to n.

STEP A.8. For eachone of the successor nodes $n_i$ of n, which does already belong either to list OPEN or to list CLOSED, let us associate the minimum between the old value of $h(n_i)$ and the new value of $h(n_i)$, computed according relation (3:4.106). Put again in list OPEN eachone of the successor nodes $n_i$ of n, which was in list CLOSED and whose value of $h(n_i)$ was diminuished.
In this case, redirect backward its pointer to n.

STEP A.9. Go to STEP B.1.

**PHASE B.**

STEP B.1. Let the lists G, GN, and NGN, have the following initial values:

$$G = \phi \;, \; GN = \phi \;, \; NGN = \{f\} \qquad (3.4.107)$$

STEP B.2. Put the nodes of list GN into list G and let GN = $\phi$ .

STEP B.3. Put the nodes of list NGN into list GN and let NGN = $\phi$.

STEP B.4. Put into list NGN all the ancestor nodes for eachone of the nodes of list GN.
Go to STEP A.2.

**PHASE C.**

STEP C.1. Put both the nodes of list NGN and of list GN into list G.

STEP C.2. Expand node n by generating only those nodes, among its successor nodes, which belong to list G.

STEP C.3. For eachone of these successor nodes $n_i$ of n, let:

$$h(n_i) = h(n) + c(n,n_i) \qquad (3.4.108)$$

where $c(n,n_i)$ is the cost of the arc of the graph from n to $n_i$.

STEP C.4. It is the same as STEP A.7.

STEP C.5. It is the same as STEP A.8.

STEP C.6. It is the same as STEP A.2.

STEP C.7. It is the same as STEP A.3.

STEP C.8. It is the same as STEP A.4.

STEP C.9. If n belong to list G, go to STEP C.2.
Otherwise, go to STEP A.6.

□

Algorithm 3.4.3 has the typical characteristic of expanding a number of nodes n, for which h has to be computed, less or equal than the corresponding number of nodes in the Dijkstra Algorithm.

In fact, Algorithm 3.4.3 expands, starting from ertain point, only those nodes which belong to $G_f$, while the Dijkstra Algorithm may expand, in principle, also nodes which do not belong to $G_f$.

In the present Chapter 3, we have illustrated a theoretical formalization, called syntactic description of the SSPS.

We have shown that, by utilizing the notion of solution set H, it is possible to derive algebraic properties of H which are helpful in order to provide algorithms for the generation of H, and for the search of the optimum solution.

The results which have been obtained suggest, moreover, the investigation of a certain number of new directions where it seems useful to continue our research effort.

Such directions, suggesting further research work, are the following ones:

1. Determination of an algorithm for the heuristically guided search of the optimum solution.
   We suspect that the lattice oriented algebraic structure of H may allow, in a natural way, to compute the estimate, which embodies the heuristic information.
2. Formalization of the problem-reduction approach and of the logic-formal approach to problem solving.
3. Critical confront among the three different approaches in order to evaluate the adequacy of their representations and the efficiency of their corresponding search strategies, with respect to the task of solving automatically a same problem.
4. Study of automatic programming for a problem, characterized by a structure providing its decomposition into subproblems, subsubproblems, etc.

## Chapter 4

# SSPS SEMANTIC DESCRIPTION

In the previous Chapter 3, we have deeply investigated the SSPS syntactic description.

This formalization clearly presents a great deal of limitation mainly because it considers only that particular informations related with the real problem, which is centered on the existence of states and on transformations between states. On the other hand, all the informations which are related with the nature of a state are not taken into account.

Namely the knowledge, from the real problem domain, about the "structure" of a state is ignored ; the notion of state is itself of atomic nature, since, it is represented by the mathematical concept of the element of a set.

Thus both the meaning of states and operators cannot anymore be related to the real description of the problem, but can only be considered on their algebraic nature.

More specifically, in the description that we have presented, we have not taken in account the particular "meaning" (i.e., structure) of the sets S and $\Gamma$.

As we pointed out in Chapter 2, the most efficient search strategy in SSPS can be considered the Hart-Nilsson-Raphael method, which utilizes some information, which is additional with respect to the SSPS syntactic description.

This information, which is called **heuristic information**, is used in order to guide the search in an efficient way, by using the evaluation function.

Usually this additional knowledge requires human ingenuity based on an appropriate inspection and processing of the semantic domain of the problem.

Therefore, the goal of a **complete automatization** of the problem-solving procedure is incompatible with the use of an heuristic information, which is not contained inside the computer, and which thus implies invention from the man.

For the above considerations, it seems important to develop new techniques which enable in some way the computer to obtain, within an automatic procedure, the heuristic information itself.

This task requires the availability to the computer of new information, outside the SSPS representation, from which with an extraction process, the evaluation function can be computed.

A new way of conceiving the SSPS is therefore required, which we shall call **SSPS semantic description**, in order to distinguish it from the SSPS syntactic description which has been previously described in Chapter 4.

The richer information, which is proper of the SSPS semantic description, is embedded on the SSPS representation, by exploding the notion of state, and by associating to each state a structure in which the new information is inserted.

We shall describe how to utilize the semantic description in order to obtain the computation of the evaluation function, which efficiently guides the search. This technique, which shall be exposed in Section 4, constitutes a new progress in the direction of automatic problem solving.

This Chapter 4 is divided in three Subchapters, namely :

- Subchapter 4.1, where the SSPS semantic description is presented and its equivalence with the SSPS syntactic description is illustrated ;
- Subchapter 4.2, where the examples of the Eight-Puzzle and of the Hanoi-Tower-Puzzle are exposed ;
- Subchapter 4.3, where the implications of the SSPS semantic description on the notion and on the algebraic characterization of auxiliary problem, together with the new approach to the automatization of the problem-solving process, are presented.

## 4.1. Fundamental Notions of SSPS Semantic Description

In this Subchapter we will expose a new formal framework in which it is possible to arrange the new information necessary for the computation of the evaluation function.

Since this new formalization is always related to the SSPS, we will illustrate it with the two following goals :

1) it is sufficient for describing a problem in SSPS ;
2) it is equivalent to the SSPS syntactic description.

The main idea on which the SSPS semantic description is based, is to associate to a state a structure which contains the new information.

Therefore, we will expose the formal schema which is apted to describe the structure of states in SSPS.

This formal schema is designed with the purpose of providing these properties :

1) it is sufficiently powerful in order to contain a great amount of information from the real problem domain, i.e., the semantics of the problem :

2) it presents great flexibility in order to be utilized for the description of a wide class of problems, arising from very different semantic domains ;
3) it is a fruitful basis on which efficient procedures can operate in order to reach the goal of computing the evaluation function, and, in general, the fundamental goals of automatic problem solving.

The schema that is proposed here for a formal structure of a state, is a sequence of attribute-and-value couples. For this reason, we shall call the problems, whose structure can be settled up in this way, **attribute-value problems** (AV problems).

More precisely, we may now introduce the following definitions and properties.

**Definition 4.1.1.** In a problem, we identify a set A of elements called **attributes** :

(4.1.1) $$A = \{A_1, A_2, \ldots, A_i, \ldots A_n\}$$

□

**Definition 4.1.2.** Each attribute $A_i$ is associated with a **value set** $V_i$ , i.e. :

(4.1.2) $$V_i = \{v^i_1, v^i_2, \ldots, v^i_j, \ldots, v^i_{n_i}\}$$

where each $v^i_j$ is called **value** for the attribute $A_i$ .

□

**Definition 4.1.3.** An **attribute-value couple** (AVC) for an attribute $A_i$ is a couple $c_i = (A_i, v^i_j)$ where $A_i$ is an attribute, and $v^i_j$ is a value for the attribute $A_i$ .

□

**Theorem 4.1.1.** An attribute $A_i$ individuates a set $C_i$ of AVC's, called **AVC set** for $A_i$ .

**Proof.** By definitions 4.1.1, 4.1.2, and 4.1.3, we construct $C_i$ in the following way :

(4.1.3) $$C_i = \{c_i | (c_i = (A_i, v^i_j)) \wedge (v^i_j \in V_i)\}$$

□

We arrive now to the main definition in which the notion of structure of a state is introduced.

**Definition 4.1.4.** A **structured state** (SS) $\bar{s}$ (i.e., a state with structure), is an n-tuple of AVC's, s.t. :

(4.1.4) $$\bar{s} = \langle c_1, c_2, \ldots, c_i, \ldots, c_n \rangle$$

where each $c_i$ is an AVC for each attribute $A_i$ of A, i.e. :

(4.1.5) $$(\forall A_i)((A_i \epsilon A) \wedge (c_i = (A_i , v_j^i)))$$

□

We may now introduce the notion of state space (structured).

**Theorem 4.1.2.** The SS set (i.e., the set of structured states) $\bar{S}$ is the cartesian product of the AVC sets for all the attributes $A_i$ of A, i.e. :

(4.1.6) $$\bar{S} = C_1 \times C_2 \times \ldots \times C_i \times \ldots \times C_n$$

**Proof.** From the definition of cartesian product, an element $\bar{s}$ of $\bar{S}$ is, because of (4.1.6), an n-tuple, made up with elements of each AVC set $C_i$ .
From (4.1.3) we obtain therefore the SS set $\bar{S}$, s.t., the (4.1.4) holds.

□

Please note that, within this description, we can clearly understand what does it means that two states $\bar{s}'$ and $\bar{s}''$ are different : it means that they have some AVC's (e.g., $c_i'$ and $c_i''$ ) which are different, i.e., some attribute $A_i$ takes two different values (e.g., $v'^i_j$ and $v''^i_j$ ). Now, in order to set up the notion of problem, we have to introduce somehow the notion of transformations from an SS $\bar{s}'$ to another SS $\bar{s}''$ (which in the SSPS syntactic description were formalized with the operators of $\Gamma$ ). If any transformation between any two states would be possible, we would be faced by a very trivial situation in which any problem (i.e., any choice of initial and final states) would be solved with just an one-step solution.
Problems of this nature, called **universal problems,** would be represented by a **complete graph,** because all the transformations are possible, i.e., any two vertices are connected by an arc.
In this case, the set of the operators, in the SSPS syntactic description, would be represented by the set of all the functions on S, i.e. :

(4.1.7) $$\Gamma_u = \{f | f : S \rightarrow S\}$$

where $\Gamma_u$ is the **universal operator set.**
In a real problem, on the other hand, we are faced with some restrictions with respect to the possible transformations ; therefore, the graph associated with the problem is an **incomplete graph,** and the set of operators would be less powerful than $\Gamma_u$ .

The idea which is embedded in the semantic description is practically this one : to describe in the formal way, the constraints which are imposed either on the possible transformations between two SS's or on the attainable SS's.

More precisely, it will be exposed how to describe, with expressions which deal with attributes and values, i.e., with the structure of a state, the limitations which make up a real problem (i.e., an incomplete graph) starting from an universal problem (i.e., a complete graph).

It is interesting to observe that these expressions will present two different mathematical aspects, namely, the algebraic one, and the logical one.

More precisely, we may now introduce the following definitions and properties.

**Definition 4.1.5.** A legal condition (LC) $L_i$ is a binary relation on $\bar{S}$, i.e. :

$$L_i \subset \bar{S} \times \bar{S} \tag{4.1.8}$$

or :

$$L_i = \{(\bar{s}', \bar{s}'') \mid P_i(\bar{s}', \bar{s}'')\} \tag{4.1.9}$$

where $P_i$ is a predicate, i.e. :

$$P_i(\bar{s}', \bar{s}'') : \bar{S} \times \bar{S} \rightarrow \{T, F\} \tag{4.1.10}$$

(T and F stand for true and false).

□

**Definition 4.1.6.** A set of legal states $\tilde{\bar{S}}_j$ is a subset of $\bar{S}$, s.t. :

$$\tilde{\bar{S}}_j = \{\tilde{\bar{s}} \mid (\tilde{\bar{s}} \in \bar{S}) \wedge \tilde{P}_j(\tilde{\bar{s}})\} \tag{4.1.11}$$

where $\tilde{P}_j$ is a predicate, i.e. :

$$\tilde{P}_j(\tilde{\bar{s}}) : \bar{S} \rightarrow \{T, F\} \tag{4.1.12}$$

□

**Definition 4.1.7.** An induced legal condition (ILC) $\tilde{L}_j$ is a binary relation on $\bar{S}$, i.e. :

$$\tilde{L}_j = \tilde{\bar{S}}_j \times \tilde{\bar{S}}_j \subseteq \bar{S} \times \bar{S} \tag{4.1.13}$$

or :

$$\tilde{L}_j = \{(\tilde{\bar{s}}', \tilde{\bar{s}}') \mid \tilde{P}_j(\tilde{\bar{s}}') \wedge \tilde{P}_j(\tilde{\bar{s}}'')\} . \tag{4.1.14}$$

□

Please note that in Definitions 4.1.5. and 4.1.7., while (4.1.8) and (4.1.13) imply the algebraic nature of a legal condition or of an induced legal condition, while (4.1.9), (4.1.10), (4.1.11), (4.1.12), and (4.1.14) illustrate their logical aspect : in particular, the predicates $P_i$ and $\tilde{P}_j$ can be expressed within some logical calculus (e.g., the first-order predicate calculus) operating on the attributes and the values as variables and constants.

A legal condition or an induced legal condition are therefore mathematical expressions, drawn from the intuitive notion of a problem, which enable one to describe some of the limitations existing on the transformations between SS's.

Therefore, a problem can be made up with a certain number of these expressions.

**Definition 4.1.8. An LC set L is the set :**

(4.1.15) $$L = \{L_0, L_1, L_2, \ldots, L_i, \ldots, L_r\}$$

where :

(4.1.16) $$L_0 = \overline{S} \times \overline{S}$$

and $L_i$, $1 \leqslant i \leqslant r$ are all the LC's.

□

**Definition 4.1.9. An ILC set $\tilde{L}$ is the set :**

(4.1.17) $$\tilde{L} = \{\tilde{L}_1, \tilde{L}_2, \ldots, \tilde{L}_j, \ldots, \tilde{L}_s\}$$

where $\tilde{L}_j$, $1 \leqslant j \leqslant s$ are all the ILC's.

□

When there are not LC's and ILC's, we absume the existence of the special LC $L_0$ which yields the universal problem.

With the next definition we introduce an important notion which takes, in the SSPS semantic description, a place equivalent that one of $\Gamma$ in the SSPS syntactic description.

**Definition 4.1.10.** The constraint C of a problem is a binary relation on $\overline{S}$ (i.e., $C \subset \overline{S} \times \overline{S}$), s.t. :

(4.1.18) $$C = (\bigcap_{i=0}^{r} L_i) \cap (\bigcap_{j=1}^{s} \tilde{L}_j)$$

□

The constraint C is therefore the unification of all the formalized informations which make up a real problem from an universal problem.

This concept provides a new way of defining the notion of problem which is equivalent to that one given in the SSPS syntactic description.

**Definition 4.1.11.** An AV problem schema $\overline{M}$ is a couple $\overline{M} = (\overline{S}, C)$ where $\overline{S}$ is an SS set, and C is a constraint.

□

**Definition 4.1.12.** An AV problem $\overline{P}$ is a triple $\overline{P} = (\overline{M}, \overline{i}, \overline{f})$ (or $\overline{P} = (\overline{M}, \overline{i}, \overline{K})$) where $\overline{M}$ is an AV problem schema, $\overline{i}$ is an initial SS, and $\overline{f}$ is a final SS (or $\overline{K}$ is a set of final SS's).

□

We can now illustrate the main result, which shows, essentially, the equivalence between the SSPS semantic description and the SSPS syntactic description.

**Theorem 4.1.3.** The set of operators $\Gamma$ and the constraint C are equivalent.

**Proof.** First of all, we recall from algebra that, given a function f on a set Q, i.e.:

(4.1.19) $$f : Q \rightarrow Q$$

(4.1.20) $$f : q' \mapsto q''$$

we can associate f, with a binary relation G(f) on Q, called the **graph** of f, s.t. :

(4.1.21) $$G(f) = \{(q', q'') | (q', q'' \in Q) \wedge (q'' = f\ (q'))\}$$

□

It exists clearly an equivalence between S and $\overline{S}$, i.e., between s and $\overline{s}$, because each SS $\overline{s}$ (i.e., each *n*-tuple of AVC's) constitutes the formal structure of each state s. Now, if we consider the set of operators $\Gamma$, because of Definitions 3.1.1, 4.1.18, and (4.1.21), we may obtain the constraint C, in this way :

(4.1.22) $$C = \bigcup_{\gamma_i \in \Gamma} G(\gamma_i)$$

Please not that the C, which is obtained from $\Gamma$, is unique.

On the other hand, if we consider the constraint C, which is a binary relation, we may set up a set of operators in this way :

(4.1.23) $$\Gamma = \{\gamma_i | (\gamma_i : A_i \rightarrow S, A_i \subset S) \wedge (\bigcup_{\gamma_i \in \Gamma} G(\gamma_i) = C)\}$$

In this case, the choice of the operators $\gamma_i$ of $\Gamma$ consists in the covering of a binary relation with functions (i.e., the operators $\gamma_i$ ), which may be done in many different ways, all equivalent to eachother.

□

We may therefore state these two final results.

**Theorem 4.1.4.** An AV problem schema $\overline{M}$ is equivalent with a problem schema M.

**Proof.** From Theorem 4.1.3., we obtain directly that $\overline{S}$ is equivalent to S, and C is equivalent to $\Gamma$.
Therefore, from Definitions 3.1.1. and 4.1.11, we obtain that $\overline{M}$ is equivalent to M.

□

**Theorem 4.1.5.** An AV problem $\overline{P}$ is equivalent with a problem P.

**Proof.** From Theorem 4.1.4 we derive that $\overline{M}$ is equivalent to M. Moreover, from Theorem 4.1.3., since $\overline{S}$ is equivalent to S, we have also that $\overline{i}$ is equivalent to i, and $\overline{f}$ is equivalent to f (or $\overline{K}$ is equivalent to K).
Therefore, from Definitions 3.1.9 and 4.1.12, we conclude that $\overline{P}$ is equivalent to P.

□

### 4.2. Examples

In this Subchapter, two examples of SSPS semantic descriptions are considered. In Chapter 2, two well known puzzles, namely the Eight-Puzzle and the Hanoi-Tower-Puzzle, have been described and an SSPS "naive" description has been presented.

The same puzzles are now described as AV problems.

#### 4.2.1. The Eight-Puzzle

In this problem, we identify, according to Definition 4.1.1, a set A of nine elements, namely :

$$A = \{A_0, A_1, \ldots, A_i, \ldots, A_8\} \tag{4.2.1}$$

where $A_0$ is the empty tile and $A_i$ is the i-th tile. The associated value set, $V_i$, is the set of all the possible positions of the i-th tile.

Recalling the SSPS naive description of the puzzle, it is trivial to observe that the value sets associated to every tile are all equal, namely :

(4.2.2) $$V_i = \bar{3} \times \bar{3} \qquad i = 0, 1, 2, \ldots, 8$$

where $\bar{3}$ is the set of the first three natural numbers, i.e. :

(4.2.3) $$\bar{3} = \{1, 2, 3\}$$

All the value sets $V_i$, associated with each tile are equal. Every element $v_j^i$ of $V_i$ will be indicated in this way :

(4.2.4) $$v_j^i = (x_j^i, y_j^i)$$

The first element, $x_j^i$, of each couple belonging to $V_i$, is the row occupied by the tile, while the second element, $y_j^i$, is the column occupied by the tile.

Then, the structured state corresponding to Fig. 2.1, is given by :

(4.2.5) $$\bar{s}_i = <(A_o, (1, 2)), (A_1, (2, 1)), (A_2, (1, 1)), (A_3, (1, 3)), (A_4, (2, 3)), (A_5, (3, 3)), (A_6, (3, 2)), (A_7, (3, 1)), (A_8, (2, 2))>$$

In order to complete the SSPS semantic description of the puzzle, the legal conditions, $\underline{L}_i$, and the induced legal conditions, $\tilde{\underline{L}}_j$, have to be individuated.

In particular, we individuate the predicates, which specify the legal conditions and the induced legal conditions, according to Definitions 4.1.5 and 4.1.7.

According to the SSPS naive description, we have to formalize that only two tiles can be moved at the same time.

Thus, we have the following predicate $P_1$ :

(4.2.6) $$P_1(\bar{s}', \bar{s}'') = (\exists!\, i)(\exists!\, h)\ ((i \neq h) \wedge (v'^i_j \neq v''^i_j) \wedge (v'^h_j \neq v''^h_j))$$

The predicate $P_2$ is related to the fact that one of the moved tiles has to be the empty tile :

(4.2.7) $$P_2(\bar{s}', \bar{s}'') = P_1(\bar{s}', \bar{s}'') \supset (v'^o_j \neq v''^o_j)$$

Another fact, which is indicated by the predicate $P_3$, expresses that the exchange can be done if the two tiles are on the same row or on the same column :

(4.2.8) $$P_3(\bar{s}', \bar{s}'') = P_1(\bar{s}', \bar{s}'') \supset (\forall i)\ ((v'^i_j \neq v''^i_j) \supset ((x'^i_j = x''^i_j) \vee (y'^i_j = y''^i_j)))$$

The last predicate $P_4$ is related to the fact that the two tiles have to be adjacent to each other :

(4.2.9) $$P_4(\bar{s}', \bar{s}'') = P_1(\bar{s}', \bar{s}'') \supset (\forall i) \; ((v'^i_j \neq v''^i_j) \supset (((x'^i_j - x''^i_j) \in \{-1,0,1\}) \wedge \wedge ((y'^i_j - y''^i_j) \in \{-1,0,1\})))$$

Because of Definition 4.1.5, to eachone of the previous four predicates $P_i(\bar{s}', \bar{s}'')$ corresponds a legal condition $\underline{L}_i$ .

We have also to define the legal states ; therefore,we have to individuate the predicates $\tilde{P}_j$ , according to Definition 4.1.6.

In this puzzle the only condition to be fulfilled is that two tiles are not allowed to occupy the same position.
Therefore, we introduce the following predicate $\tilde{P}_1$ :

(4.2.10) $$\tilde{P}_1(\bar{\bar{s}}) = (\forall i) \; (\forall h) \; ((i \neq h) \wedge (\bar{v}^i_j \neq \bar{v}^h_j))$$

Because of Definition 4.1.7, to the predicate $\tilde{P}_1$ corresponds the induced legal condition $\tilde{\underline{L}}_1$ .
Because of Definition 4.1.10, therefore, the constraint C is obtained.

It has to be noted that the previously expressed predicates can be given in many different ways. However, the constraint C is always the same one.

### 4.2.2. The Hanoi-Tower-Puzzle

In this problem, we identify according to Definition 4.1.1, a set A of three elements, namely :

(4.2.11) $$A = \{A_1 , A_2 , A_3\}$$

where $A_1$ is the largest disk, $A_2$ is the medium one, and $A_3$ is the smallest one.

Recalling the SSPS naive description of the puzzle, it is trivial to observe that the value sets associated to every disk are all equal, namely :

(4.2.12) $$V_i = \bar{3} \times \bar{3} \qquad i = 1, 2, 3$$

where $\bar{3}$ is illustrated in (4.2.3).

All the value sets $V_i$ , associated with each disk, are equal.

Every element $v^i_j$ of $V_i$ will be indicated in this way :

(4.2.13) $$v^i_j = (x^i_j , y^i_j)$$

The first element, $x_j^i$, of each couple belonging to $V_i$, individuates the peg on which the disk is put, while the second element, $y_j^i$, individuates the height of the disk on the peg, i.e., $y_j^i = 1, 2, 3$ respectively, specifies that the disk is in the lowest, middle, and highest position on the peg.

As an example, let us consider Fig. 4.1.

Then, the structured state corresponding to Fig. 4.1, is given by :

(4.2.14) $$\bar{s}_i = \langle (A_1, (1,2)),\ (A_2, (2,1)),\ (A_3, (1,1)) \rangle$$

In order to complete the SSPS semantic description of the puzzle, the legal conditions, $\underline{L}_i$, and the induced legal conditions $\tilde{\underline{L}}_j$, have to be individuaded.

In particular, we individuate the predicates, which specify the legal conditions and the induced conditions, according to Definitions 4.1.5 and 4.1.7.

The first predicate specifies that only one disk can be moved at the same time :

(4.2.15) $$P_1(\bar{s}', \bar{s}'') = (\exists !\ i)\ (v'^i_j \neq v''^i_j)$$

In order to simplify the formalization of the second predicate, we introduce an auxiliary predicate $\bar{P}$. $\bar{P}$ is true when the i-disk $(A_i)$ is on the top, i.e., when no other disk is put on it :

(4.2.16) $$\bar{P}(\bar{\bar{s}}, \bar{A}_i) = (\sim(\exists h))\ ((\bar{x}_j^i = \bar{x}_j^h) \wedge (\bar{y}_j^i < \bar{y}_j^h)) \quad i = 1, 2, 3$$

The second predicate, which specifies another legal condition, requires that only disks on the top can be moved :

(4.2.17) $$P_2(\bar{\bar{s}}', \bar{s}'') = P_1(\bar{\bar{s}}', \bar{s}'') \supset (\forall i)\ ((\bar{v}'^i_j \neq v''^i_j) \supset \bar{P}(\bar{\bar{s}}', \bar{A}_i))$$

Moreover, a third predicate specifies that the moved disk can be put only on the top of another peg.

(4.2.18) $$P_3(\bar{s}', \bar{\bar{s}}'') = P_1(\bar{s}', \bar{\bar{s}}'') \supset (\forall i)\ ((v'^i_i \neq \bar{v}''^i_i) \supset \bar{P}(\bar{\bar{s}}'', \bar{A}_i))$$

Because of Definitions 4.1.5, to eachone of the previous three predicates $P_i(\bar{s}', \bar{s}'')$ corresponds a legal condition $\underline{L}_i$.

We have also to define the legal states; therefore, we have to individuate the predicates $\tilde{P}_j$, according to Definition 4.1.6.

In this puzzle, the first condition to be fulfilled is that two disks are not allowed to occupy the same position :

(4.2.19) $$\tilde{P}_1(\bar{\bar{s}}) = (\forall i) \quad (\forall h) \quad ((i \neq h) \wedge (\bar{v}_h^i \neq \bar{v}_j^h))$$

Moreover, the second condition to be fulfilled, is that a smaller disk cannot be put over a larger one :

(4.2.20) $\tilde{P}_2(\tilde{\bar{s}}) = (\forall i)(\forall h)(((\tilde{x}_j^i = \tilde{x}_j^h) \wedge (i < h)) \supset (\tilde{y}_j^i < \tilde{y}_j^h))$.

Finally, the third condition to be fulfilled is that a disk cannot be "hanging" on a peg :

(4.2.21) $\tilde{P}_3(\tilde{\bar{s}}) = (\forall i)((\tilde{y}_j^i = 1) \vee (\exists h)((\tilde{x}_j^i = \tilde{x}_j^h) \wedge (\tilde{y}_j^i = \tilde{y}_j^h \pm 1)))$

Because of Definition 4.1.7, to eachone of the previous three predicates $\tilde{P}_j$ corresponds an induced legal condition $\tilde{L}_j$.
Because of Definition 4.1.10, therefore, the constraint C is obtained.

In the following Subchapter 4.3, the influence of the predicate choice on the computation of the evaluation function will be illustrated.

### 4.3. The Computation of the Evaluation Function

We will outline a method, based on the SSPS semantic description, which provides the computation of the evaluation function $f(\bar{s})$.

This technique is based on the idea of computing the estimate $\hat{h}(\bar{s})$, by solving an auxiliary problem in which $\bar{s}$ is the initial state, and the solution is easy to be found.

The solution of the auxiliary problem shall provide a lower bound of the cost $h(\bar{s})$ of the optimum solution for a problem which has $\bar{s}$ as initial state and which has the same problem schema and final state of the main problem.

Since all the auxiliary problems share the same goal problem, we shall introduce the notion of auxiliary goal problem.

**Definition 4.3.1.** Let $\bar{F} = (\bar{S}, C, \bar{f})$ (or $\bar{F} = (\bar{S}, C, \bar{K})$) be an **AV goal problem**, obtained from an AV problem $\bar{P}$, $\bar{F}' = (\bar{S}', C', \bar{f}')$ (or $\bar{F}' = (\bar{S}', C', \bar{K}')$) is called an **auxiliary AV goal problem** for $\bar{F}$ if :

(4.3.1) (i) $\bar{S} = \bar{S}'$

(4.3.2) (ii) $\bar{f} = \bar{f}'$ (or $\bar{K} = \bar{K}'$)

(4.3.3) (iii) $L' \subseteq L$, $\tilde{L}' \subseteq \tilde{L}$

where, $L'$ and $\tilde{L}'$, $L$ and $\tilde{L}$, are the LC set and the ILC set, from which, respectively, $C'$ and $C$ are obtained, according to Definition 4.1.10.

We shall indicate :

$$(4.3.4)\qquad \bar{F}' \sqsubseteq \bar{F}$$

□

In other words, we say that $\bar{F}' \sqsubseteq \bar{F}$, if they have the same initial and final SS's, and if the LC set L′ and the ILC set $\tilde{L}'$ are, respectively, subsets of the LC set L and of the ILC set $\tilde{L}$.

**Theorem 4.3.1.** If $\bar{F}' \sqsubseteq \bar{F}$, then :

$$(4.3.5)\qquad C' \supseteq C$$

**Proof.** The proof is obtained directly by Definition 4.1.10, and because of relation (4.3.3), because of the property of set intersection.

□

If we indicate as $\bar{\mathfrak{F}}'$ the set of auxiliary AV goal problems, s.t. :

$$(4.3.6)\qquad \bar{\mathfrak{F}}' = \{\bar{F}' \mid \bar{F}' \sqsubseteq \bar{F}\}$$

where $\bar{F}$ is an AV goal problem, then the following algebraic properties hold.

**Theorem 4.3.2.** Given an AV goal problem $\bar{F}$, $\bar{\mathcal{R}}_F = (\bar{\mathfrak{F}}', \sqsubseteq)$ is a poset.

**Proof.** By Definition 4.4.1, and because of relation 4.3.6, $\sqsubseteq$ is a binary relation, i.e. :

$$(4.3.7)\qquad \sqsubseteq\ \subseteq \bar{\mathfrak{F}}' \times \bar{\mathfrak{F}}'$$

Moreover, $\sqsubseteq$ satisfies the partial order properties, i.e., $\sqsubseteq$ satisfies the reflexive, antisymmetric, and transitive properties.

1. **Reflexive property.**
We have to prove that, for each $\bar{F}' \in \bar{\mathfrak{F}}'$:

$$(4.3.8)\qquad \bar{F}' \sqsubseteq \bar{F}'\ .$$

In fact, because of set properties, we have that :

$$(4.3.9)\qquad C' \supseteq C'$$

Therefore, by Definition 4.3.1 and Theorem 4.3.1, relation (4.3.8) holds .

**2. Antisymmetric property.**

We have to prove that, for each $\overline{F}'_1 \in \overline{\mathfrak{F}}'$ and, for each $\overline{F}'_2 \in \overline{\mathfrak{F}}'$, if :

(4.3.10) $$\overline{F}'_1 \sqsubseteq \overline{F}'_2$$

and if :

(4.3.11) $$\overline{F}'_2 \sqsubseteq \overline{F}'_1$$

then, the following relation holds :

(4.3.12) $$\overline{F}'_1 = \overline{F}'_2$$

In fact, by Theorem 4.3.1, we have that :

(4.3.13) $$C'_1 \supseteq C'_2$$

and that :

(4.3.14) $$C'_2 \supseteq C'_1$$

Then, because of inclusion property, we have that :

(4.3.15) $$C'_1 = C'_2$$

Therefore, by Definition 4.3.1 and Theorem 4.3.1, relation (4.3.12) holds.

**3. Transitive property.**

We have to prove that $\sqsubseteq$ satisfies the transitive property, i.e., for each $\overline{F}'_1 \in \overline{\mathfrak{F}}'$, $\overline{F}'_2 \in \overline{\mathfrak{F}}'$, and $\overline{F}'_3 \in \overline{\mathfrak{F}}'$, if :

(4.3.16) $$\overline{F}'_1 \sqsubseteq \overline{F}'_2$$

and if :

(4.3.17) $$\overline{F}'_2 \sqsubseteq \overline{F}'_3$$

then :

(4.3.18) $$\overline{F}'_1 \sqsubseteq \overline{F}'_3$$

In fact, by Theorem 4.3.1, we have that :

(4.3.19) $$C'_1 \supseteq C'_2$$

and that :

(4.3.20) $$C'_2 \supseteq C'_3$$

Then, because of inclusion property, we have that :

(4.3.21) $$C'_1 \supseteq C'_3$$

Therefore, by Definition 4.3.1 and Theorem 4.3.1, relation (4.3.18) holds. The theorem has been proved.

□

**Theorem 4.3.3.** The poset $\bar{\mathcal{R}}_F = (\bar{\mathfrak{F}}', \sqsubseteq)$ is a distributive lattice.

Proof. Because of Theorem 4.3.2, $\sqsubseteq$ is a partial ordering relation on $\bar{\mathfrak{F}}'$.

Therefore, we have to prove that for every couple $\bar{F}'_1 \in \bar{\mathfrak{F}}'$ and $\bar{F}'_2 \in \bar{\mathfrak{F}}'$, it is possible to define a binary operation of meet :

(4.3.22) $$\sqcap : \bar{\mathfrak{F}}' \times \bar{\mathfrak{F}}' \rightarrow \bar{\mathfrak{F}}'$$

and a binary operation of join :

(4.3.23) $$\sqcup : \bar{\mathfrak{F}}' \times \bar{\mathfrak{F}}' \rightarrow \bar{\mathfrak{F}}'$$

i.e., we have to prove the two following relations :

(4.3.24) $$(\bar{F}'_1, \bar{F}'_2) \overset{\sqcap}{\mapsto} \bar{F}'_p = \bar{F}'_1 \sqcap \bar{F}'_2$$

(4.3.25) $$(\bar{F}'_1, \bar{F}'_2) \overset{\sqcup}{\mapsto} \bar{F}'_q = \bar{F}'_1 \sqcup \bar{F}'_2$$

It has to be recalled that the meet operation individuates the greatest lower bound of any two elements of a poset.

In this particular case, the meet $\bar{F}'_p$ has the following definition :

(4.3.26) $$\bar{F}'_p = \bar{F}'_1 \sqcap \bar{F}'_2 = \max_i \{\bar{F}'_i | \bar{F}'_i \sqsubseteq \bar{F}'_1 \wedge \bar{F}'_i \sqsubseteq \bar{F}'_2\}$$

i.e., for each $\bar{F}'_i$ satisfying :

(4.3.27) $$\bar{F}'_i \sqsubseteq \bar{F}'_1$$

and satisfying :

(4.3.28) $$\bar{F}'_i \sqsubseteq \bar{F}'_2$$

we have that :

(4.3.29) $$\overline{F}'_i \sqsubseteq \overline{F}'_p$$

Therefore, by Definition 4.3.1 and Theorem 4.3.1, we have that :

(4.3.30) $$\overline{F}'_p = (\overline{S}, C'_p, \overline{f}) \quad (\text{or } \overline{F}'_p = (\overline{S}, C'_p, \overline{K}))$$

where :

(4.3.31) $$C'_p = C'_1 \cup C'_2$$

It has to be recalled also that the join operation individuates the lowest upper bound of any two elements of a poset.

In this particular case, the join $\overline{F}'_q$ has the following definition :

(4.3.32) $$\overline{F}'_q = \overline{F}'_1 \sqcup \overline{F}'_2 = \min_i \{\overline{F}'_i \mid \overline{F}'_1 \sqsubseteq \overline{F}'_i \wedge \overline{F}'_2 \sqsubseteq \overline{F}'_i\}$$

i.e., for each $\overline{F}_i$ satisfying :

(4.3.33) $$\overline{F}'_1 \sqsubseteq \overline{F}'_i$$

and satisfying :

(4.3.34) $$\overline{F}'_2 \sqsubseteq \overline{F}'_i$$

we have that :

(4.3.35) $$\overline{F}'_q \sqsubseteq \overline{F}'_i$$

Therefore, by Definition 4.3.1 and Theorem 4.3.1, we have that :

(4.3.36) $$\overline{F}'_q = (\overline{S}, C'_q, \overline{f}) \quad (\text{or } \overline{F}'_q = (\overline{S}, C'_q, \overline{K}))$$

where :

(4.3.37) $$C'_q = C'_1 \cap C'_2$$

The operations introduced in this way are always defined because, for every $\overline{F}'_1$ and $\overline{F}'_2$, it holds that :

(4.3.38) $$\overline{F}_o \sqsubseteq \overline{F}'_1, \; \overline{F}_o \sqsubseteq \overline{F}'_2$$

where :

(4.3.39) $$\overline{F}_o = (\overline{S}, L_o, \overline{f}) \quad (\text{or } \overline{F}_o = \overline{S}, L_o, \overline{K}))$$

and where :

$$L_o = \bar{S} \times \bar{S} \tag{4.3.40}$$

Therefore, $\bar{F}_o$ is the universal lower bound of $\bar{\mathcal{R}}_F$ .
Moreover, for every $\bar{F}'_1$ and $\bar{F}'_2$ , it holds that :

$$\bar{F}'_1 \sqsubseteq \bar{F}, \qquad \bar{F}'_2 \sqsubseteq \bar{F} \tag{4.3.41}$$

where :

$$\bar{F} = (\bar{S}, C, \bar{f}) \quad (\text{or } \bar{F} = (\bar{S}, C, \bar{K})) \tag{4.3.42}$$

Therefore, $\bar{F}$ is the universal upper bound of $\bar{\mathcal{R}}_F$ .

It has to be noted that in the particular case, when, for every $\bar{F}'_1$ and $\bar{F}'_2$ , it holds that :

$$\bar{F}'_1 \sqsubseteq \bar{F}'_2 \tag{4.3.43}$$

then, it holds that :

$$\bar{F}'_p = \bar{F}'_1 \sqcap \bar{F}'_2 = \bar{F}'_1 \tag{4.3.44}$$

$$\bar{F}'_q = \bar{F}'_1 \sqcup \bar{F}'_2 = \bar{F}'_2 \tag{4.3.45}$$

Finally, because of relations (4.3.26), (4.3.31), (4.3.32), and (4.3.37), we have that the meet $\bar{F}'_p$ and the join $\bar{F}'_q$ are distributive operations.

The theorem has been proved.

□

All the results obtained up to this point, are focused on the goal of obtaining a computation of the estimate $\hat{h}(\bar{s})$ associated to an SS $\bar{s}$.

We can now illustrate our main result, by means of the following theorem.

Theorem 4.3.4. If $\bar{F}' \sqsubseteq \bar{F}$, then for any SS $\bar{s} \in \bar{S}$, the optimum cost $\bar{C}'(\bar{\mathcal{G}}^{\prime \bar{n}'})$ of the optimum solution $\bar{\mathcal{G}}^{\prime \bar{n}'}$ of the AV problem $\bar{P}' = (\bar{F}', \bar{s}) = (\bar{S}, C', \bar{s}, \bar{f})$ (or $\bar{P}' = (\bar{S}, C', \bar{s}, \bar{K})$), is a lower bound with respect to the optimum cost $\bar{C}(\bar{\mathcal{G}}^{\bar{n}})$ of the optimum solution $\bar{\mathcal{G}}^{\bar{n}}$ of the AV problem $\bar{P} = (\bar{S}, C, \bar{s}, \bar{f})$ (or $\bar{P} = (\bar{S}, C, \bar{s}, \bar{K})$).

Therefore, it holds that :

$$\hat{h}(\bar{s}) = \bar{C}'(\bar{\mathcal{G}}^{\prime \bar{n}'}) \leqslant h(\bar{s}) = \bar{C}(\bar{\mathcal{G}}^{\bar{n}}) \tag{4.3.46}$$

**Proof.** By Theorem 4.3.1, we have that :

(4.3.47) $$\overline{C}' \supseteq C$$

Therefore, the graph $\overline{G} = (\overline{S}, A)$ and the graph $\overline{G}' = (\overline{S}, A')$, respectively associated to the AV problem schema $\overline{M} = (\overline{S}, C)$ and to the AV problem schema $\overline{M}' = (\overline{S}, C')$, are such that the set of arcs A is a subset of the set of arcs A′ (see Definition 4.1.10 and Theorem 4.1.3).

Then, it holds that :

(4.3.48) $$A' \supseteq A$$

Therefore, if $\overline{\xi}^{\bar{n}}$ is an optimum solution of the problem $\overline{P}$(i.e., it is a path in $\overline{G}$ of optimum cost $\overline{C}(\overline{\xi}^{\bar{n}})$, from $\bar{s}$ to $\bar{f}$ (or from $\bar{s}$ to any $\bar{f} \in \overline{K}$)), then $\overline{\xi}^{\bar{n}}$ is also one solution $\overline{\xi}'^{\bar{n}'}$ of the problem $\overline{P}'$(i.e., it is also a path in $\overline{G}'$, from $\bar{s}$ to $\bar{f}$ (or from $\bar{s}$ to any $\bar{f} \in \overline{K}$)).

On the other hand, the solution $\overline{\xi}^{\bar{n}}$ is not necessarily an optimum solution $\overline{\xi}'^{\bar{n}'}$ of the problem $\overline{P}'$(i.e., it is not necessarily a path in $\overline{G}'$ of optimum cost $\overline{C}'(\overline{\xi}'^{\bar{n}'})$ from $\bar{s}$ to $\bar{f}$ (or from $\bar{s}$ to any $\bar{f} \in \overline{K}$)).

Therefore, it holds that :

(4.3.49) $$\overline{C}'(\overline{\xi}'^{\bar{n}'}) \leq \overline{C}(\overline{\xi}^{\bar{n}})$$

Since $h(\bar{s})$, is, by its definition, the optimum cost of the optimum solution of $\overline{P}$, i.e. :

(4.3.50) $$h(\bar{s}) = \overline{C}(\overline{\xi}^{\bar{n}})$$

we can conclude, because of relation (4.3.49), that :

(4.3.51) $$\overline{C}'(\overline{\xi}'^{\bar{n}'}) = \hat{h}(\bar{s})$$

i.e., $\overline{C}'(\overline{\xi}'^{\bar{n}'})$ yields an estimate $\hat{h}(\bar{s})$ for any SS $\bar{s} \in \overline{S}$.

The theorem has been proved.

□

Theorem 4.3.4 constitutes the basis for the computation of the estimate. In fact, in STEP 5 of the Hart-Nilsson-Raphael method, described in Chapter 2, we can obtain the value of $\hat{h}(\bar{s}_j)$ (i.e., the value of $\hat{h}(n_j)$, where $n_j$ is the node corresponding to the SS $\bar{s}_j$), by means of solving the auxiliary AV problem $\overline{P}' = (\overline{F}', \bar{s}_j)$, where $\overline{F}'$ satisfies the conditions of Theorem 4.3.4.

Now, an important question arises : how to choose the auxiliary AV goal problem $\overline{F}'$.

In fact, it is possible to build up a great number of different auxiliary AV goal problems, by relaxing the legal conditions in all the possible ways. A criterion for guiding the selection of the auxiliary AV problem $\overline{F}'$ is related to the "goodness" of the corresponding estimate $\hat{h}(\bar{s}_j)$, which is obtained by computation.

The following theorem will provide some guidance in considering the "goodness" of such estimate.

**Theorem 4.3.5.** Let $\overline{F}'_1$ and $\overline{F}'_2$ be two auxiliary AV goal problems for an AV goal problem $\overline{F}$.
If :

(4.3.52) $$\overline{F}'_2 \sqsubseteq \overline{F}'_1$$

then, for every SS $\bar{s}$, the estimates $\hat{h}_1(\bar{s})$ and $\hat{h}_2(\bar{s})$, computed by solving, respectively, the auxiliary AV problems $\overline{P}'_1 = (\overline{F}'_1, \bar{s})$ and $\overline{P}'_2 = (\overline{F}'_2, \bar{s})$, satisfy the following condition :

(4.3.53) $$(\forall \bar{s})\ ((\bar{s} \in \overline{S}) \wedge (\hat{h}_2(\bar{s}) \leqslant \hat{h}_1(\bar{s})))$$

**Proof.** The proof is easily obtained by Theorems 4.3.1, 4.3.2, 4.3.3, and 4.3.4.

□

According to the Hart-Nilsson-Raphael method, we can therefore conclude that $\hat{h}_1(\bar{s})$ is "better" (i.e., "more informed") than $\hat{h}_2(\bar{s})$; thus, the estimate is "more precise".

Then, the search based on $\hat{h}_1(\bar{s})$ expands at most the nodes expanded by the search based on $\hat{h}_2(\bar{s})$.

However, in order to evaluate the overall complexity of the search process, we have to take into account also the computational effort needed to compute $\hat{h}(\bar{s})$.

If the search of the auxiliary AV problem $\overline{P}' = (\overline{F}', \bar{s})$ is performed by means of a trial-and-error strategy, which is equal to the strategy followed by the Hart-Nilsson-Raphael method for the solution of the AV problem $\overline{P}$, then, the computational effort required by the solution of the auxiliary AV problem $\overline{P}'$ is essentially the same of that one required by the solution of $\overline{P}$.

In this case, no efficiency can be added by the introduction of an heuristic function.

However, when we freeze some legal conditions, we can change the "nature" of the problem.

In other words, we can create an auxiliary AV problem $\bar{P}'$ which does not require for its solution a trial-and-error strategy, but a less expensive strategy.

In this case, we can call such types of auxiliary AV problems P', as "simple" problems.

Thus, the computational effort needed for solving $\bar{P}'$, and for computing $\hat{h}(\bar{s})$, is by far less than the one required for solving $\bar{P}$, and the overall efficiency of the solution method increases significantly.

Therefore, the selection of an auxiliary AV goal problem $\tilde{\bar{F}}$ has to take into account two distances, measured in the lattice $\mathcal{R}_F$, namely :

(4.3.54) $$d_1 = d(\tilde{\bar{F}}', \bar{F})$$

and :

(4.3.55) $$d_2 = d(\tilde{\bar{F}}', \bar{F}_o)$$

While $d_1$ takes into account the computational effort of solving $\bar{P}$ with the use of the estimate $\hat{h}(\bar{s})$, $d_2$ takes account of the computational effort of computing $\hat{h}(\bar{s})$, i.e., of solving $\tilde{\bar{P}}' = (\tilde{\bar{F}}', \bar{s})$.

A first step for an automatic selection of such a problem is the construction of the lattice $\bar{\mathcal{R}}_F$, as illustrated in Theorem 4.3.3.

We will now propose two different algorithms for generating the lattice $\bar{\mathcal{R}}_F$ , the first one based on a breadth-first strategy, and the second one based on a depth-first strategy.

In order to simplify the description of the algorithms, we shall use the well-known representation of a lattice by means of the associated diagram, corresponding to a graph.

We will first illustrate a breadth-first algorithm for generating the lattice $\bar{\mathcal{R}}_F$ .

STEP 1 – Let $n^{o,o}$ be the node of the graph associated to the universal upper bound of the lattice $\bar{\mathcal{R}}_F$, i.e., $n^{o,o}$ corresponds to the AV goal problem $\bar{F}$, by Theorem 4.3.3.
Let $L^o_o = L \cup \tilde{L}$, where L is the LC set given by Definition 4.1.8, and $\tilde{L}$ is the ILC set given by Definition 4.1.9.
Put the node $n^{o,o}$ on a list called GROW.

STEP 2 – Remove the first node on GROW and put it on a list called LATTICE.

Call suche node $n^{i,k}$, where i is the level index of the node in the lattice $\overline{\mathcal{R}}_F$, and k is the position index of the node in its level.
The node $n^{i,k}$ corresponds to the auxiliary AV goal problem $\overline{F}'^{\,i,k}$.

STEP 3 – Find the successors of $n^{i,k}$.
Every successor of $n^{i,k}$, $n_l^{i+1,k}$ corresponds to a particular auxiliary AV goal problem $\overline{F}'^{\,i+1,k}_l$ of the lattice $\overline{\mathcal{R}}_F$. $L'^{\,i+1}_{k,l}$ corresponding to $\overline{F}'^{\,i+1,k}_l$ is given by either :

(4.3.56) $$L'^{\,i+1}_{k,l} = L'^{\,i+1}_{m_1 m_2 \ldots m_i m_{i+1}} \cup \tilde{L}'^{\,i}_{n_1 n_2 \ldots n_i}$$

or

(4.3.57) $$L'^{\,i+1}_{k,l} = L'^{\,i}_{m_1 m_2 \ldots m_i} \cup \tilde{L}'^{\,i+1}_{n_1 n_2 \ldots n_i n_{i+1}}$$

The LC set $L'^{\,i+1}_{m_1 m_2 \ldots m_i m_{i+1}}$ is obtained from the LC set $L^{i}_{m_1 m_2 \ldots m_i}$, in the following way :

(4.3.58) $$L'^{\,i+1}_{m_1 m_2 \ldots m_i m_{i+1}} = L'^{\,i}_{m_1 m_2 \ldots m_i} - L_{m_{i+1}}$$

where :

(4.3.59) $$L = \{L_0, L_1, L_2, \ldots, L_r\}$$

by Definition 4.1.8, and where :

(4.3.60) $$m_{i+1} \in \{1, 2, \ldots, r\}$$

and :

(4.3.61) $$m_{i+1} \neq m_j, \quad j = 1, 2, \ldots, i$$

The ILC set $\tilde{L}'^{\,i+1}_{n_1 n_2 \ldots n_i n_{i+1}}$ is obtained from the ILC set $\tilde{L}'^{\,i}_{n_1 n_2 \ldots n_i}$, in the following way :

(4.3.62) $$\tilde{L}'^{\,i+1}_{n_1 n_2 \ldots n_i n_{i+1}} = \tilde{L}'^{\,i}_{n_1 n_2 \ldots n_i} - \tilde{L}_{n_{i+1}}$$

where

(4.3.63) $$\tilde{L} = \{\tilde{L}_1, \tilde{L}_2, \ldots, \tilde{L}_s\}$$

by Definition 4.1.9, and where :

(4.3.64) $n_{i+1} \in \{1, 2, \ldots, s\}$

and :

(4.3.65) $n_{i+1} \neq n_j, \quad j = 1, 2, \ldots, i$

STEP 4 – If someone of the generated nodes is already in GROW, associate another pointer to this node and direct it back to $n^{i,k}$.
All the new nodes are put at the end of GROW, in the same order in which they are generated, and pointers are provided from these successors back to $n^{i,k}$.

STEP 5 – If GROW is empty, the algorithm ends, and the lattice $\bar{\mathcal{R}}_F$ is obtained by inspection of the list LATTICE.
Otherwise, go to STEP 2.

□

The algorithm which has been now presented, builds the lattice according to a breadth-first method.

Obviously it is also possible to build up the lattice by means of a depth-first method.

A depth-first algorithm for generating the lattice $\bar{\mathcal{R}}_F$ can be obtained by changing the definition of STEP 4 of the breadth-first algorithm previously presented, in the following way :

STEP 4′ – If someone of the generated nodes is already in GROW, associate another pointer to this node and direct it back to $n^{i,k}$.
All the new nodes are put at the beginning of GROW, in the same order in which they are generated, and pointers are provided from these successors back to $n^{i,k}$.

□

Given a certain AV problem $\bar{P}$, the corresponding lattice $\bar{\mathcal{R}}_F$ contains exactly $2^{r+s}$ auxiliary AV goal problems $\bar{F}'$, where r and s are given in relations (4.3.59) and (4.3.63).

Therefore, the amount of memory necessary for storing $\bar{\mathcal{R}}_F$ is very large.

However, we are not interested in the construction of the complete lattice $\bar{\mathcal{R}}_F$, but only in the construction of those nodes of the lattice which correspond to problems of simple solution, namely not requiring a trial-and-error method for their solution.

Therefore, we can isolate such nodes, corresponding to problems of simple solution.

Moreover, it is not anymore necessary to expand such nodes, since their solution is assumed to be easily obtained by some direct method, and not by a trial-and-error method.

On the other hand, the remaining nodes, corresponding to problems which require a trial-and-error method for their solution, need not to be permanently stored ; thus, the list LATTICE, which was considered by the two algorithms previously described, can now be ignored.

We can now modify the breadth-first algorithm by changing STEP 2, in the following way :

STEP $\bar{2}$ – Remove the first node on GROW.
Call such node $n^{i,k}$ , where i is the level index of the node in the lattice $\bar{\mathcal{R}}_F$ , and k is the position index of the node in its level.
The node $n^{i,k}$ corresponds to the auxiliary AV goal problem $\bar{F}'^{i,k}$.

□

Also, STEP 4 is changed, in the following way :

STEP $\bar{4}$ – If someone of the generated nodes corresponds to a problem of simple solution, put it on a list called NTEP.
All the other new nodes are put at the end of GROW, in the same order in which they are generated, and pointers are provided from these successors back to $n^i_k$.

□

At last, STEP 5 is changed, in the following way :

STEP $\bar{5}$ – If GROW is empty, the algorithm ends, and the auxiliary AV goal problem, which provides the computation of the estimate, can be selected in NTEP.
Otherwise, go to STEP $\bar{2}$.

□

Moreover, the corresponding modification of the depth-first algorithm can be obtained by changing the definition of STEP $\bar{4}$ of the modified breadth-first algorithm previously presented, in the following way :

STEP $\bar{4}'$ – If someone of the generated nodes corresponds to a problem of simple solution, put it on a list called NTEP.

All the other new nodes are put at the beginning of GROW, in the same order in which they are generated, and pointers are provided from these successors back to $n_k^i$.

□

It has to be noted that the two modified algorithms can, in one point, be considered either as completely automatizable ones, or as requiring human interaction.

In fact, either STEP $\bar{4}$ or STEP $\bar{4}'$ imply that a decision should be made whether a problem requires or does not require a trial-and-error method for its solution.

In the case of a completely automatic procedure, we have to provide the computer with a data base containing the list of the problems of simple solution.

In this evenience, the algorithms have to carry on a matching between every problem generated in STEP 3 and the problems contained in the data base.

In the case of an interactive procedure, the first part of either STEP $\bar{4}$ or STEP $\bar{4}'$ is accomplished by man who decides whether a problem requires or does not require a trial-and-error method for its solution.

It has to be noted that the selection of a particular auxiliary AV goal problem in NTEP is not done by the algorithm. In fact, this selection can be based on many different strategies.

Moreover, in this case, Theorems 4.3.4 and 4.3.5 cannot be of any help in performing such selection, since the relation $\sqsubseteq$ is not satisfied for any couple of auxiliary AV goal problems in NTEP.

Anyhow, such choice can be made according, for instance, to one of the following two criteria :

(i) the complexity, i.e., it is chosen the auxiliary AV goal problem $\bar{F}'_C$ in NTEP, whose computational complexity is the lowest one ;

(ii) the distance, i.e., it is chosen the auxiliary AV goal problem $\bar{F}'_D$ in NTEP, whose distance from $\bar{F}$, measured in the diagram associated to the lattice $\bar{\mathcal{R}}_F$ , is the minimum one.

The criterion (ii) can be applied by changing STEP $\bar{4}$ of the previously described modified version of the breadth-first algorithm, in the following way :

STEP $\bar{\bar{4}}$ – If one of the generated nodes corresponds to a problem of simple solution, select it as auxiliary AV goal problem, and the algorithm ends. Otherwise, all the new nodes are put at the end of GROW, in the same order in which they are generated, and pointers are provided from these successors back to $n^i_k$.

□

Moreover, also STEP 5 is modified, in the following way :

STEP $\bar{\bar{5}}$ – If GROW is empty, the algorithm ends without the selection of an auxiliary AV goal problem.
Otherwise, go to step $\bar{2}$.

□

Also in this case, the corresponding modification of the depth-first algorithm can be obtained by changing the definition of STEP $\bar{\bar{4}}$ of the modified breadth-first algorithm previously presented, in the following way :

STEP $\bar{\bar{4}}'$ – If one of the generated nodes corresponds to a problem of simple solution, select it as auxiliary AV goal problem, and the algorithm ends.
Otherwise, all the new nodes are put at the beginning of GROW, in the same order in which they are generated, and pointers are provided from these successors back to $n^i_k$.

□

In this case, the auxiliary AV goal problem, which is selected, is not, in general, the auxiliary AV goal problem $\bar{F}'_D$, whose distance from $\bar{F}$ is the minimum one.

Another possible criterion is to select an auxiliary AV goal problem from NTEP according to some tests performed on particular reference AV problems $\bar{P}_{R_i}$, which share the same problem schema $\bar{M}$ of the AV problem $\bar{P}$.

However, an human interaction procedure can be followed as well.

In this evenience, the selection of an auxiliary AV goal problem from NTEP is made by man, who decides on the basis of some non formalized considerations.

Now, an example will be presented in order to provide a better understanding of the technique which has been illustrated in this Subchapter.

We will consider, as a problem to be solved, the Eight-Puzzle, which has been formalized as an AV problem $\underline{P}$ in the preceeding Subchapter 4.2.

As we have shown, according to Definitions 4.1.5 and 4.1.8, the LC set $\underline{L}$ for the Eight-Puzzle is the following one :

(4.3.66) $$\underline{L} = \{\underline{L}_0, \underline{L}_1, \underline{L}_2, \underline{L}_3, \underline{L}_4\}$$

where :

- $\underline{L}_0$ is the special legal condition yielding the universal problem, and is expressed by (4.1.16) ;

- $\underline{L}_1$ specifies that only two tiles can be moved in the same time, and is related to the predicate $P_1$ expressed in (4.2.6) ;

- $\underline{L}_2$ specifies that one of the moved tiles has to be the empty tile, and is related to the predicate $P_2$ expressed in (4.2.7) ;

- $\underline{L}_3$ specifies that the exchange can be done if the two tiles are on the same row or on the same column, and is related to the predicate $P_3$ expressed in (4.2.8) ;

- $\underline{L}_4$ specifies that the two tiles have to be adjacent to each other, and is related to the predicate $P_4$ expressed in (4.2.9).

Moreover, according to Definitions 4.1.6, 4.1.7, and 4.1.10, the ILC set $\underline{\tilde{L}}$ for the Eight-Puzzle is the following one :

(4.3.67) $$\underline{\tilde{L}} = \{\underline{\tilde{L}}_1\}$$

where :

- $\underline{\tilde{L}}_1$ specifies that two tiles are not allowed to occupy the same position, and is related to the predicate $\tilde{P}_1$ expressed in (4.2.10).

Therefore, the lattice $\mathcal{R}_F$ contains exactly 32 auxiliary AV goal problems $\underline{\overline{F}}'$.

Nilsson has proposed as a particular heuristic function or estimate $\underline{\hat{h}}^*(\underline{\tilde{s}})$, for the Eight-Puzzle, the number of misplaced tiles in the frame.

It is easy to observe that the value of $\hat{h}^*(\underline{\tilde{s}})$, for eachone of the states $\underline{\tilde{s}}$ of the SS $\underline{\tilde{S}}$, can be computed by solving a particular auxiliary AV problem $\underline{\tilde{\overline{P}}}'^* = (\underline{\overline{F}}'^*, \underline{\tilde{s}})$.

According to Definitions 4.1.8, 4.1.9, 4.1.10, and 4.3.1, the particular auxiliary AV goal problem $\underline{\overline{F}}'^*$ is related to an LC set $\underline{L}'^*$ and to an ILC set $\underline{\tilde{L}}'^*$ which satisfy (4.3.3).

More precisely, we have that :

(4.3.68) $$\underline{L}'^* = \{\underline{L}_0, \underline{L}_1, \underline{L}_2\} \subseteq \underline{L}$$

and :

(4.3.69) $$\underline{\tilde{L}}'^* = \{\underline{\tilde{L}}_1\} = \underline{\tilde{L}}$$

This means that LC's $\underline{L}_4$ and $\underline{L}_5$ (i.e., $P_4$ and $P_5$) do not hold anymore.

Therefore, eachone of the auxiliary AV problem $\underline{\tilde{\tilde{P}}}'^*$ allows that two tiles which are not adjacent to each other, and which are not on the same row or on the same column, can be exchanged.

It is also clear that eachone of the auxiliary AV problems $\underline{\tilde{\tilde{P}}}'^*$ is a problem of simple solution, namely it does not require a trial-and-error method for its solution.

In fact, the solution of each $\underline{\tilde{\tilde{P}}}'^*$ can be easily obtained by means of simple confrontations between two different configurations of the Eight-Puzzle (corresponding to the initial and final state of $\underline{\tilde{\tilde{P}}}'^*$).

It has to be noted that the particular selection of $\underline{L}'^*$, i.e., the relaxation of $P_3$ and $P_4$, is necessary in order to provide that each particular auxiliary AV problem $\underline{\tilde{\tilde{P}}}'^*$ is a problem of simple solution.

In the present Chapter 4, we have illustrated a new theoretical formalization of the SSPS, which we have called SSPS semantic description.

We have shown that the SSPS semantic description is equivalent to the SSPS syntactic description which has been previously illustrated in Chapter 3.

Moreover, a method has been discussed, which is based on the SSPS semantic description, and which makes possible to extract, by means of an automatic procedure, i.e., by computation, an heuristic function $\hat{h}(\bar{s})$ which is useful for guiding the solution search of the AV problem $\bar{P}$ in the SS.

More precisely, the computation of the heuristic function $\hat{h}(\tilde{\bar{s}})$, for eachone of the states $\tilde{\bar{s}}$ of the SS $\bar{S}$, is equivalent to the solution of an auxiliary AV problem $\tilde{\tilde{P}}'$, i.e., an AV problem which has been obtained by the initial AV problem $\bar{P}$, by means of a relaxation of some of the LC's and ILC's associated to $\bar{P}$.

It has been shown that eachone of the auxiliary AV problems $\tilde{\tilde{P}}'$, corresponding to eachone of the states $\tilde{\bar{s}}$ of the SS $\bar{S}$, share the same auxiliary AV goal problem $\bar{F}'$ (i.e., $\tilde{\tilde{P}}' = (\bar{F}, \tilde{\bar{s}})$).

Moreover, we have proved as well that the set of all the auxiliary AV goal problems $\bar{F}'$, which can be obtained by relaxating in all the possible ways the LC's and the ILC's, constitute a lattice $\bar{\mathcal{R}}_F$.

Therefore, we have exploited the algebraic properties of the lattice $\bar{\mathcal{R}}_F$, in order to design an automatic procedure devoted to the selection of the auxiliary AV goal problem $\bar{F}'$, which is used for defining eachone of the auxiliary AV problems $\tilde{\tilde{P}}' = (\tilde{\bar{s}}, \bar{F}')$ whose solution yields the heuristic function $\hat{h}(\tilde{\bar{s}})$.

The results, which have been presented in Chapter 4, suggest that a certain number of research directions should be investigated in a future work, namely :

1. Study of efficient automatic procedures for the selection of the auxiliary AV goal problem $\bar{F}'$, from the lattice $\bar{\mathcal{R}}_F$ .
2. Investigation of the most appropriate algorithms able to detect whether an auxiliary AV problem $\bar{P}'$ is a problem of simple solution, namely if it does not require a trial-and-error method for its solution.
3. Implementation of a learning procedure which is based on a continuous improvement and augmentation of the data base in which the problems of simple solution are stored.

## Chapter 5

## THE PROBLEM OF AUTOMATIC LEARNING IN PROBLEM SOLVING

In this Chapter, we analyze the basic philosophy of the problem of giving learning capability to an automatic problem solver : thus, some concepts are illustrated which are of general validity in the project of an automatic learning problem solver using the state space (SS) approach ; however, their extension to any other problem solving approach is immediate.

The Chapter is composed of three Subchapters :

In Subchapter 5.1, an informal but precise definition of learning in problem solving is given ; furthermore, a general schema for an automatic learning problem solver is analyzed.

In Subchapter 5.2, some typical learning methodologies and techniques are studied : in this paper, only classical and well-known learning techniques are presented from the SS point of view. The main philosophy of the work is in fact oriented more in the direction of presenting a complete and unitary treatment of the SS approach to problem-solving, rather than in finding new techniques for solving some particular problem.

In Subchapter 5.3, the concepts previously exposed are examplified by means of the familiar Eight-Puzzle.

### 5.1. Learning Classification in Problem Solving

In this Subchapter, a learning–oriented problem–solving system is described. The schema is as general as possible and due to this reason is "informal", in the sense that non-rigorous mathematical definitions will be introduced.

We intend a learning-oriented problem-solving system as a problem-solving system which is able to modify the way it operates in order to improve its "behaviour" after a period of "experience" on problems of the "same" class.

In general, the performances of a problem solver are evaluated with respect to three main points :

1 – When it terminates, has the required solution of the problem been reached ?
2 – Is the solution an optimal solution with respect to given costs ?
3 – Is the computation time, required by the problem solver in order to terminate, low enough ?

The three requirements cannot always be fulfilled. In fact, some very fast problem solvers are not able to find an optimal solution and, sometimes, even a solution (for instance, depth – first search with depth-bound in SS approach to problem solving).

Other problem solvers are able to find an optimal solution but with a tremendous computation effort (for instance, Dijkstra method in SS approach to problem solving).

Moreover, it is very difficult to "put together" the requirements to compare the behaviour of two challenging problem solvers. In fact, it has to be determined how much we can "spend" for computation time in order to have an optimal solution or a solution, and also what is the "cost" of a non-optimal solution or even of not reaching a solution.

A first step to solve this problem, is to define a mathematical measure :

1) for the "distance" of the reached situation, when the problem solver terminates, from the required solution (a typical way of providing such measure consists in giving a metric to the SS).
2) for the cost difference of the solution obtained with respect to the optimal one ;
3) for the computation time required.

Then, we are concerned with a multiple objective evaluation of problem solvers.

It is well known that we are able to state only a partial ordering between problem solvers using this evaluation.

In fact, we can say that a problem solver is non-dominated if no other problem solver has an evaluation in which all the criteria have better values.

The set of non-dominated problem solvers can be composed of a very large number of elements and then, we cannot have the required discrimination between problem solvers.

However, it is possible to follow a particular approach which allows to aggregate the multiple objective evaluation in a single function defining a complete preference order.

In general, it has to be determined a convex functional which is defined on the three objective functions.

The convex functional represents, of course, the choice of a particular policy in compairing and evaluating the coexisting influences of the three objectives in the expression which indicates how well the problem solver performs. It must be intended here in a generalized sense, which is comprehensive of possible "bounds" on the three measures previously defined. If, for instance, the distance between two states exceeds a bound function defined on the SS, then the convex functional must be set to an infinite value.

The complete preference order introduced by the functional compares the problem solvers in a precise way.

Then, a learning-oriented problem-solving system has to change the way in which it operates in order to improve its performance, according to the evaluation functions (or the convex functional).

We shall now propose a general schema for a learning-oriented problem-solving system.

Recall that the two fundamental activities of a problem-solving system are :

(i) representation of the problem ;
(ii) search of a solution.

In general, the first activity is carried on by the man and the second one is carried on, in a mechanical way, by the computer.

In our schema, we consider that a part of the representation is automatically accomplished.

Our learning-oriented system can modify its representation activity as well as its search activity. In the sequel, we consider problem-solving systems devoted to solve a particular class of "similar" problems (e.g., chess problems, checkers problems, Hanoi-Tower-Puzzle, etc.) because we do not investigate the possibility of using informations about different problems in order to improve the performance of the problem solver.

In particualr, the modification capability has been individuated, in Fig. 5.1, in a particular block of the flow-chart which represents the general schema of the learning-oriented problem-solving system.

The input for the system is considered a formalized description of the problem to be solved which contains all the possible informations and can be thought of as supplied by the man. We consider the information as already coded in SS formalism, because we do not want to enter the problem of coding an informal description.

The first block of our schema is the **representation box (RB)**.

The tasks of this box are the two following ones.

1) To give a possibly different meaning to the same structural elements. As an example, consider the different representations of the same problem in SS approach given by Amarel. What has to be noticed, in the example mentioned by Amarel (the Missionaries-and-Cannibals-Problem), is the fact that the same sintactic description of an SS, is associated with different semantics.
In this way, profitable results in drastically reducing the length of a solution and, thus, the search time, are obtained.

2)To "select" a part of the general supplied informations in order to avoid redundancies.
In fact, it is assumed that the man supplies the informations to the problem solver in a completely unordered way : in some sense, without any structure.
It is therefore the task of the RB of eliminating any redundant informations (e.g., the information "it is raining" in the Eight-Puzzle) and even of generating new problems, with different SS structures, which seem to be helpful for the solution of the original problem.
For instance, the "computation of the heuristics", described in Chapter 4 is a typical procedure of this type.
In the example of Subchapter 5.3, an alternative way of operating in this sense will be illustrated.

The two activities are regulated by the inputs supplied to the box by the **interpretation and modification box** (IMB).

These inputs will be called **representation choice functions.** The output is obviously the problem associated with the selected semantics applied to the states of the SS.

The box following in the schema is the **search box** (SB). The tasks of the SB are the three following ones.

1) To evaluate the possible ways of going on from a problem situation to another one toward the solution of the problem ; this is obtained by means of the **expansion rules.**

2) To choose a strategy of examining the possible ways previously individuated ; this is obtained by means of the **evaluation function.**

3) To decide when to terminate its activity ; this is obtained by means of the **termination rules.**

The three activities are guided by the inputs supplied to the box by the IMB. These inputs will be called **searching rules.**

In this way, it is the IMB which exactly supplies, at each requested time, to the SB, the expansion rules, the evaluation function, and the termination rules.

The output is the running situation of the problem ; in particular, when the box terminates, it is the solution of the problem.

The core of the overall system is obviously the IMB.

This box has to supply the rules according which the RB and the SB operate, considering as informations the general representation of the problem, the representation given by the RB, and the running situation of the problem given by the SB. The modifications of the operating ways are decided by this box, having as aim to improve the "behaviour" of the system.

Therefore, its decisions are taken by considering the multiple objective function which evaluates the behaviour of a problem solver.

In particular, this box can be considered as an algorithm which tries to find a solution for a multiple criteria decision problem.

The algorithm is able to do a step toward the optimization after evaluating the performance of the problem solver on a particular set of problems or even during the solution of a particular problem.

From another point of view, we can consider the IMB as a meta-algorithm.

If we allowed a change, in the criteria according which the box decides its output, for instance by means of another box which judges the performance of the described system, we could interpret this new box as a meta-meta-algorithm. Anyway, we can think that this change can be executed by means of a man-machine interaction.

### 5.2. Automatic Learning Methodologies and Techniques

In this Subchapter, two typical and opposite learning methods, performed by the general schema previously described, are introduced.

In particular, some general techniques for designing a learning system are illustrated.

Then, some classical learning systems like the Samuel's program for checkers are interpreted according to these general techniques related to the learning-oriented system previously introduced.

The learning methods consist mainly in fixing the rules of action for the IMB, and are concerned with the dynamical behaviour of the overall system.

If we consider that the time variable t belongs to the set of integers, a learning machine can be considered as a discrete dynamical system.

Then, the first method is such that at the initial time $t_o$, the outputs of the IMB are supplied by the man.

At time $t_1$, the general representation of the particular problem is given to the system.

At time $t_2$, the RB terminates its first action and gives the problem representation to the SB. At time $t_3$, the SB terminates its search and a final problem situation (it may be also a non-solution) is supplied.

At this time the IMB has all its inputs determined and is ready to change its outputs.

Then, the system can accept another problem (obviously of the same class) and the performed operations will follow in the same order.

Therefore, the system operates in a cyclic way.

The learning activity is performed every cycle and the system learns , after having solved a problem and successively used the received informations.

This learning method is called **block learning (BL)**.

In BL, the IMB is on only at the end of the problem-solver activity on a particular problem, but it is possible to make its activity more "frequent".

In particular, the IMB can operate during the search activity of the system on the problem.

Due to the stepwise characteristic of the solution procedure of the usual problem-solving systems, we can think that the IMB operates at every step of the computation.

In other words, the IMB changes its outputs at every step receiving as informations the problem representation at that moment and the problem situation which is being explored by the SB.

In particular, this second method can be described as follows.

At time $t_o$, the outputs of IMB are given by the man. At time $t_1$, the general representation of the particular problem to be solved is supplied by the man.

At time $t_2$, the RB gives a particular formalization of the problem ar ` the SB operates on this representation with a precise search strategy.

At time $t_3$, the IMB changes its outputs on the basis of the informations given by the RB and the SB at time $t_2$ ; the RB and the SB operate as the new inputs require.

In general, at time $t_i$, the IMB changes its outputs according to the outputs of the other blocks of the system at time $t_{i-1}$.

In some sense, the learning system uses the informations obtained during the previous activity on the same problem in order to improve its performance.

It has to be noted that when the SB definitively terminates its search on the given problem (at time $t_g$ ), the informations achieved during the solution of this particular problem are "coded" in the outputs of the IMB at the subsequent time $t_{g+1}$.

Therefore, these informations are used by the system to solve another problem of the same class, given by the man at time $t_{g+1}$ or successively.

This methodology is called step-by-step learning (SBSL).

Now, some typical learning techniques introduced by Samuel in his classical checkers program, will be interpreted in the terms of the above given classification.

The simplest learning technique was called by Samuel rote learning (RL). This strategy consists simply in recording, for every solved problem P= (M, i, F), which corresponds to the solution :

$$(5.1) \qquad < s_0 = i, \quad s_1, \ldots, s_i, \ldots, s_n = s_f > \quad (s_f \in F)$$

the (possibly optimal) solution sequence :

$$(5.2) \qquad i = s_0 \overset{a_1}{\longmapsto} s_1 \overset{a_2}{\longmapsto} s_2 \ldots s_{n-1} \overset{a_n}{\longmapsto} s_n = s_f$$

If during the solution of another problem P′ = (M, i′, F) a state $s_i$. belonging to P, is reached, then a (possibly optimal) solution of P′is already :

$$(5.3) \qquad < s'_0 = i', \quad s'_1, \ldots, s'_i = s_i, \quad s_{i+1}, \ldots, s_n = s_f >$$

It is quite simple to recognize this technique as a BL method : in fact, the IMB can improve the performance of the system by copying previously obtained solutions.

Another technique implemented by Samuel is the $\beta$ procedure ($\beta$P).

The searching rules consist mainly in an evaluation function which specifies a precedence among the states to be expanded.

This evaluation function has a parametric expression and the parameters are fixed at time $t_o$ by the man.

It is obvious that a "perfect" evaluation function would assign to each state s the real cost of an optimal path from s to $s_g$ (if only a solution (not necessarily an optimum one) is desired, we can utilize the previous exposed method, by simply setting $c(s_i, s_j) = 0$ for each arc, i.e., for each couple of connected states).

Therefore, in order to check the "goodness" of the evaluation function at time $t_i$, the IMB verifies along the pathes of n steps (n fixed) in the SS whether the evaluation function has the same value in the "ancestors" and in the "sons". The word "same" must be intended in a generalized sense : in fact, if the costs of the arcs are different from 0, then, the evaluation function $\hat{h}(s)$ is considered to be the "same", when it satisfies the following relation :

$$\hat{h}(s_i) = \hat{h}(s_j) + c(s_i, s_j) \tag{5.4}$$

where $c(s_i, s_j)$ is the cost of an n-step optimal path from $s_i$ to $s_j$.

In the Subchapter 5.3, we shall completely illustrate, by means of an example, this philosophy.

If the answer is yes, the parameters are unchanged.

If not, the IMB modifies the parameters in such a way that the previously illustrated property holds.

It has to be noted that this procedure is an SBSL one; in fact,the searching rules are modified at every step on the basis of the informations obtained by the SB.

The program developed by Samuel considers also a procedure called $\alpha$ - $\beta$ procedure ( $\alpha\,\beta$ P). This method consists in comparing the performances of the $\beta$ P, previously described, with a BL which has an evaluation function with fixed parameters. The comparison is made considering the results obtained by "$\alpha$ against $\beta$"; if $\alpha$ is worse, it copies the final evaluation function of $\beta$ , otherwise, its evaluation function does not change. It has to be noted that this methodology can be interpreted only by adding a new level of learning.

In fact, it is able to compare two learning procedures at a lower level and then to modify a learning activity.

We can introduce this methodology in our schema by considering an "higher level" block which is able to modify the IMB on the basis of the informations obtained by the overall system.

It is also possible to introduce a generalization from this point of view. In fact, a meta-IMB can compare any BL procedure with any SBSL and, consequently, can change both the procedures in order to improve the learning activity.

This generalization, together with other classical learning techniques, constitutes a direction for further research work.

### 5.3. An Example

In this Subchapter, we present an example of a learning-oriented problem-solver system in order to evidentiate the focal points introduced in the previous Subchapters and in order to indicate new possible research directions.

For sake of simplicity, we consider a particular problem which has been already introduced in the previous Chapters 2 and 4, namely the Eight-Puzzle.

The general states of the Eight-Puzzle, as it has been already seen, can be described as an n-tuple of AVC's :

$$\bar{s} = \langle c_0, c_1, \ldots, c_8 \rangle \tag{5.5}$$

where:

$$c_i = (A_i, v_j^i) \tag{5.6}$$

where $A_i$ is an attribute and $v_j^i$ is the value of $A_i$ (see Chapter 4). In our problem, $A_i$ can be considered as the position of the i-th tile and $v_j^i$ the cartesian coordinates in our problem. We can consider a slight modification of our problem, i.e., let us assume that also the colour of the i-th tile has to be taken into account as another attribute, $A_i^c$, and let us suppose that particular colours (green, red, etc.) are the possible values of such attribute $A_i^c$ .

The operators are defined as the shifts of the blank tile from a position in the vertical or in the horizontal direction, as previously seen, and another operator can be considered as the colouring operator which defines what are the changes of colour that we have allowed (e.g., from red to green).

The goal state can be considered as a well defined position and colour of the tiles in the square.

First of all, we have to introduce the functions which rank the performance of a problem solver.

As previously done, we shall indicate by $\tilde{\mathfrak{C}}$ a solution of the problem.

A search strategy can terminate without finding the goal state. The state reached, when the search procedure terminates, is called final state.

The sequence $\mathfrak{C}$ from the initial state to the final state can be called a "pseudo-solution". It is quite obvious that a pseudo-solution is not satisfying, if the "distance", in the complete graph of the problem, of the final state from the goal state, is excessive.

Then, the "cost" of having a pseudo-solution can be considered as proportioned with respect to the distance of the final state from the goal state.

Now, we must define in a rigorous way the distance between the final state and the goal state in such a way that the the intuitive meaning of "goodness" of a pseudo-solution is respected.

In general, we shall try to define a metric on the whole SS, i.e., a function $d : S \times S \rightarrow R$ (the real numbers) such that the usual axioms of the distance are fullfilled. A first attempt could be to define the distance $d(s_1, s_2)$ as equal to the length of an optimal path from $s_1$ to $s_2$.

But in order to compute such a distance, it would be necessary to solve completely the problem.

Furthermore, it could happen that two quite "similar" configurations of our problem have even an infinite distance. Therefore, we prefer to define more semantically, the distance $d(s_1, s_2)$ as equal to the number of tiles which have different position in $s_1$ and $s_2$.

For a sequence $\mathcal{G}$ we define :

$$d(\mathcal{G}) = \min_{s_g \in F} d(s_f, s_g) \qquad (5.7)$$

where $s_f$ is the final state of $\mathcal{G}$ and $s_g$ belongs to the set of final states F.

Such a function satisfies indeed the distance property.

Therefore, if a problem solver, after computing a solution $\mathcal{G}$, is able to find another solution $\mathcal{G}'$,such that $d(\mathcal{G}') < d(\mathcal{G})$, then we can say that it improves its own performance.

This constitutes the first criterion for problem-solvers ranking.

In general, we can be interested in finding an optimal solution with respect to a given cost associated to each operator.

In the Eight-Puzzle the optimality is represented, as it has been already seen, by the minimum number of elements in the solution $\mathcal{G}^o$ , i.e., a solution $\mathcal{G}^o$ is optimal if it "requires" the minimum number of moves.

In general, we can assume that the cost of not reaching an optimal solution is proportional to the "distance" of a solution $\mathcal{G}$ from the optimal solution $\mathcal{G}^o$ .

Thus, for two generical solutions $\mathcal{G}_1$ and $\mathcal{G}_2$ , we define:

(5.8) $$D(\xi_1, \xi_2) = \frac{|c(\xi_1) - c(\xi_2)|}{\max\{c(\xi_1), c(\xi_2)\}}$$

In particular, for any solution $\xi$, we define :

(5.9) $$D(\xi) = D(\xi, \xi^o)$$

where $\xi^o$ is an optimal solution.

In general $c^o = c(\xi^o)$ is not available, but we can find a bound for it. Therefore, $c^o$ is an estimate of the cost of the optimal solution.

In our problem $c = c(\xi)$ is the number of steps required by $\xi$, and $c^o$ is the number of steps required by $\xi^o$, in order to reach the final state from the initial state.

The third criterion for problem-solvers ranking is related to the computational effort required to compute $\xi$.

In SS representation, a measure of the computational effort can be given by the number of nodes "expanded" before the search algorithm terminates.

Then, this measure of the computational effort required for a solution $\xi$, can be defined as :

(5.10) $$\phi(\xi) = \frac{n}{n_p}$$

where n is the number of nodes expanded and $n_p$ is the number of nodes between the initial state and the final state.

We can therefore observe that, in order to rank the performance of a problem solver, the three previously described criteria can be taken into account.

More precisely, we can say that, in order to improve its own performance, by means of a learning behaviour, a problem solver should diminuish the value of a "performance functional", which takes, as its own arguments, three objective functions, which correspond to the three criteria for problem-solvers ranking.

Now, we will show how could operate a good learning problem solver in order to improve its behaviour (our attention is principally focused on the third objective function, which is, in this Eight-Puzzle, the most interesting, maintaining uneffected the two other ones).

From the point of view of the representation, a good IMB ought to "understand" that the "colour" attribute is completely independent from the "position" attribute ; it could, therefore, give to the RB the "order" of "splitting" the original problem into two distinct subproblems :

1) the position problem (which is indeed the classical Eight-Puzzle) ;
2) the colour problem, which consists in making the tiles of the desired colour.

Furthermore, the IMB could generate some other problems of the lattice of problems of the Eight-Puzzle in order to compute a good evaluation function for the originary problem (see Chapter 4).

It is obvious that the complexity of the two distinct subproblems is drastically reduced with respect to the complexity of the original problem.

From the searching point of view, we can first observe that the heuristic function which approximates the length of a path from a generical state to the goal state is a typical ordering function; thus, the task of the IMB is that of changing it in order to decrease the number of expanded nodes in searching the solution. It is useful to recall that, if we accept to find a suboptimal solution instead of an optimal one, or even a pseudo-solution instead of a solution, it is possible to use heuristic functions which improve the third objective function much more than the ones guaranteeing the optimality of the solution.

The learning techniques, exposed in the previous Subchapter 5.2, can supply some tools which can be used in order to reach this objective.

Suppose that, as a first step, the search algorithm for the Eight-Puzzle is the Dijkstra algorithm which has no heuristic information ; for a given problem (initial and goal state : i,g), it shall find an optimal solution. Therefore, for all the nodes n belonging to the optimal path between i and g, it shall be known the exact value of the length of an optimal path between n and g.

Let us now change the problem by changing only the initial state i ; the IMB can therefore define an heuristic function $\hat{h}(n)$ approximating the length of an optimal path between n and g in the following way :

$\hat{h}(n)$ = 0 if n does not belong to the preceeding optimal solution;

$\hat{h}(n)$ = the computed value, if n belongs to the preceeding optimal solution.

Therefore, if the SB is an Hart-Nilsson-Raphael-type algorithm with variable heuristic function $\hat{h}$, certainly its behaviour shall be improved for every new problem.

Notice also that the function $\hat{h}$ previously defined does meet the admissibility and optimality criterion of the Hart-Nilsson-Raphael algorithm which has been previously exposed. This is a typical example of RL.

On the other hand RL (in this case and in other ones) is a quite simple but also quite poor automatic learning technique; in fact, generally, it is only a part of a learning system.

A more sophisticated technique consists in an application of the Samuel's $\beta P$ to the Eight-Puzzle.

Let us define a parametric function $\hat{h}$, on the nodes of the graph representing the problem, depending on some significative characteristics of the state (e.g., $\hat{h}$ could be a polynomial function, with parametric coefficients of the variables: number of tiles with different position with respect to the goal state, number of consecutive tiles in the same order, vertical or horizontal, as in the goal state, etc.).

Let us consider now Fig. 5.2, which represents a portion of a generical SS.

Then, $\hat{h}$ is a "good" heuristic function if the following relation holds:

(5.11) $$\min \hat{h}(n_i) + 2 = \hat{h}(n_o)$$

In fact, if $n_i'$ is s.t. :

(5.12) $$\hat{h}(n_i') = \min_i \hat{h}(n_i)$$

then, it is **probable** that $n_i'$ belongs to an optimal path from $n_o$ to a goal state; carrying on the reasoning to a limit point, a "perfect" heuristic function h is a function s.t., we obtain an optimal path, as shown in Fig. 5.3, where :

(5.13) $$h(n_i') = s - i$$

Thus, if the IMB rearranges the coefficients in the polynomial function $\hat{h}$ in such a way that relation (5.11) holds, then it is **probable** that the new heuristic function $\hat{h}'$ is better than $\hat{h}$. On the other hand, it must be noticed that nothing is known about the admissibility and the optimality of the function obtained in this way. We can intuitively conjecture that such a system learns in some way; it is an interesting open problem to state necessary and/or sufficient conditions for the convergence of this method.

In this Chapter, we have exposed some concepts on the problem of studying and designing automatic learning problem solvers in the SS approach. This is obviously only a first step toward the goal of generating a theory of learning in SS approach to problem solving (or, more generally, in problem solving).
Therefore, we have only attempted to embed some well known and general ideas into an unified theory of learning in SS approach to problem solving.

After having presented, in an informal way, some basic definitions, we have analized a general schema of a learning-oriented problem solver; finally, we have outlined some designing criteria and we have exemplified them by means of a very simple example.

Obviously, a greater research effort has still to be done in order to achieve the goal of developing a learning-oriented problem solver.

First of all, it is certainly useful to examine, from our point of view, other ideas on learning in problem solving, which have been presented in the known literature.

It can be interesting to observe, as it has been already said, that our "computation of an evaluation function" is indeed a learning process in the sense specified by the third objective function.

Finally, it has to be noted that, in correspondence of every learning idea, it is quite important to state if the Hart-Nilsson-Raphael method's admissibility and optimality criteria are fullfilled.

## Chapter 6

## CONCLUSIONS

The concepts presented in this paper constitute a progress for the development of a theory of problem solving.

The goal of this theory is the understanding of the problem-solving activity toward the design of automatic problem solvers intended as the interpreters of the representation languages.

The results here exposed have been obtained, within the Milan Polytechnic Artificial Intelligence Project (MP-AI Project), by the authors in developing such a theory of problem solving, in the last two years.

The notions which have been presented, can be briefly sketched as follows :

- naive description of problem solving ;
- algebraic framework for the illustration of the main notions and properties involved both in problem representation and in solution search ;
- extended formalization for the description of a more informed problem representation ;
- automatic evaluation and use of heuristic information for improving the efficiency of the solution search ;
- generalization and development of a learning ability during the problem-solving activity.

The research directions, which are considered as promising for future investigation, can be briefly summarized as follows :

- implementation of efficient heuristically guided search algorithms, based on the techniques which have been here presented ;
- precise characterization of the proposed structure of an automatic problem solver ;
- unitary formalization of both the state space and the problem reduction approaches to problem solving ;
- definition of complexity measures for both problem representation and solution search ;
- development of more advanced learning techniques embedded in the illustrated general approach ;
- design of automatic problem solvers, i.e., representation-languages interpreters,

with the choice of a special semantic domain for evaluating the obtained performance and characteristics.

## AKNOWLEDGMENTS

The authors desire to express their gratitude for the stimulating discussions held with the researchers of the MP-AI Project.

In particular, the suggestions and observations of Drs. Giovanni Guida, Amedeo Paci, and Enrico Pagello have been valuable and helpful.

The continuous attention and efficient effort of Mrs. Mariangela Rodolfi Pileri, in typing the manuscript, is sincerely acknowledged with grateful appreciation.

## REFERENCES


[1] Banerii, R.B. "Theory of Problem Solving, An Approach to Artificial Intelligence". American Elsevier Publishing Company, Inc. New York. 1969.

[2] Berge, C. "Théorie des Graphes et Ses Applications". Dunod. Paris. 1958.

[3] Bobrow, D.G. and Raphael, B. "New Programming Languages for AI Research". Tutorial Lecture Presented at the Third International Joint Conference on Artificial Intelligence. Stanford University. Stanford, California. August, 1973.

[4] Coray, G. "Additive Features in Positional Games". ORME–IP–IRIA–NATO, Nato Advanced Study Institute on "Computer-Oriented Learning Processes, Procédures Informatique d'Apprentissage". Bonas (Gers), France. August-September, 1974. Imprimé en France, IRIA, Domaine de Voluceau.

[5] Ginzburg, A. "Algebraic Theory of Automata". Academic Press, Inc. New York. 1968.

[6] Hartmanis, J. and Stearns, R.E. "Algebraic Structure Theory of Sequential Machines". Prentice-Hall, Inc. Englewood Cliffs, New York. 1966.

[7] Mac Lane, S. and Birkhoff, G. "Algebra". The MacMillan Company. New York. 1967.

[8] Nilsson, N.J. "Problem-Solving Methods in Artificial Intelligence". Mac Graw-Hill Book Company. New York. 1971.

[9] Pohl, I. "Bi-Directional and Heuristic Search in Path Problems". SLAC Report N. 104. Stanford Linear Accelerator Center. Stanford University. Stanford, California. May, 1969.

[10] Sangiovanni Vincentelli, A. and Somalvico, M. "Formulazione Teorica del Metodo dello Spazio degli Stati per la Risoluzione Automatica dei Problemi". Politecnico di Milano. Istituto di Elettrotecnica ed Elettronica. Laboratorio di Calcolatori. Relazione Interna n. 72-74. MEMO MP–AIM–6. October, 1972.

[11] Sangiovanni Vincentelli, A. and Somalvico, M. "State-Space Approach in Problem-Solving Optimization". Politecnico di Milano. Istituto di Elettrotecnica ed Elettronica. Laboratorio di Calcolatori. Relazione Interna n. 73-15. MEMO MP–AIM–12. May, 1973.

[12] Sangiovanni Vincentelli, A. and Somalvico, M. "Theoretical Aspects of State-Space Approach to Problem Solving". Politecnico di Milano. Istituto di Elettrotecnica ed Elettronica. Laboratorio di Calcolatori. Relazione Interna No. 73-16. MEMO MP-AIM-16. August, 1973.

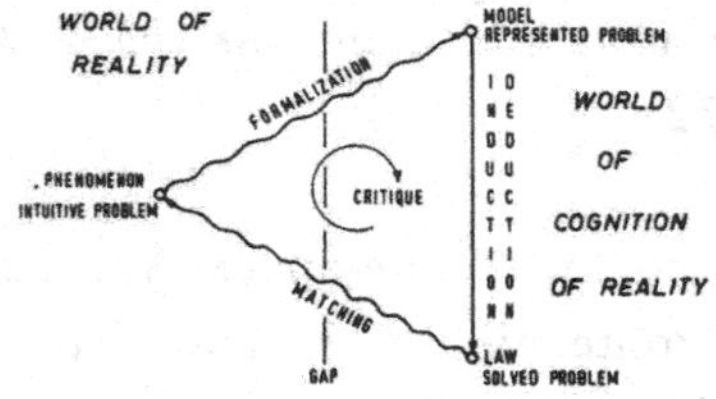


Fig. 1.1 The Galileian inductive-deductive experimental method.

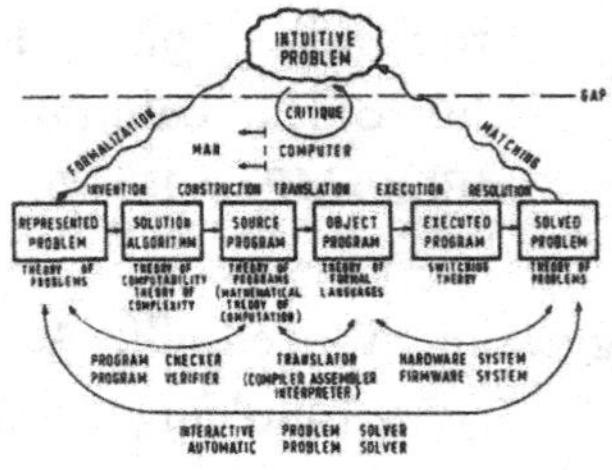


Fig. 1.2 Present state of art in man-computer interaction in solving problems.

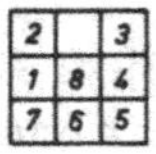


Fig. 2.1 One configuration of the Eight Puzzle.

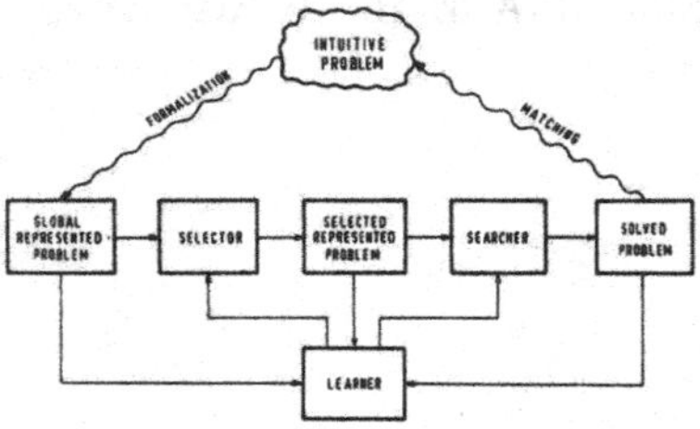


Fig. 1.3 Structure of an automatic problem solver.

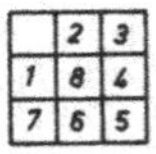


Fig. 2.2 Another configuration of the Eight Puzzle.

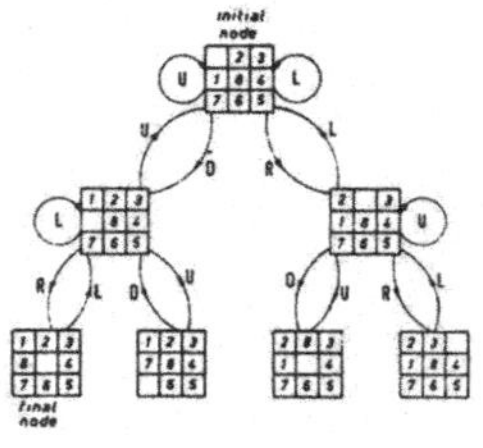


Fig. 2.3 Partial graph of the Eight Puzzle.

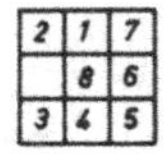


Fig. 2.4 One unreachable state from the initial state.

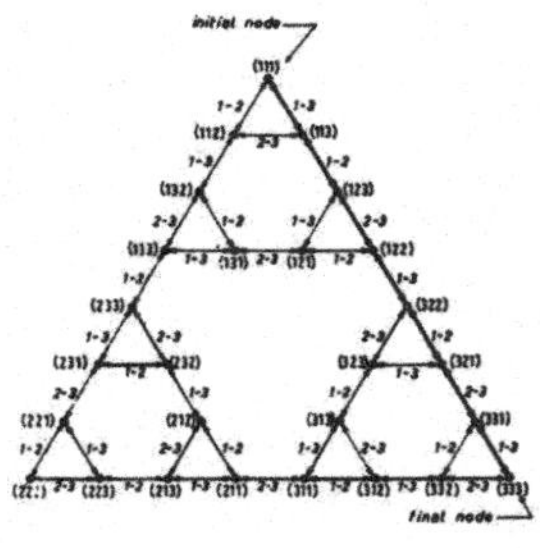


Fig. 2.5 Graph of the Hanoi Tower Puzzle.

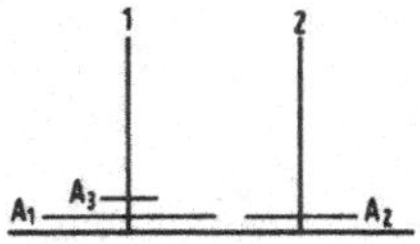


Fig. 4.1 One configuration of the Hanoi Tower Puzzle.

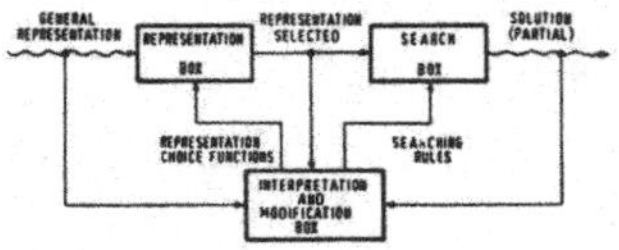


Fig. 5.1 General schema of the learning oriented problem solving system.

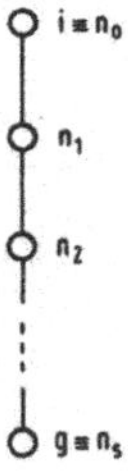


Fig. 5.3 An optimal path.

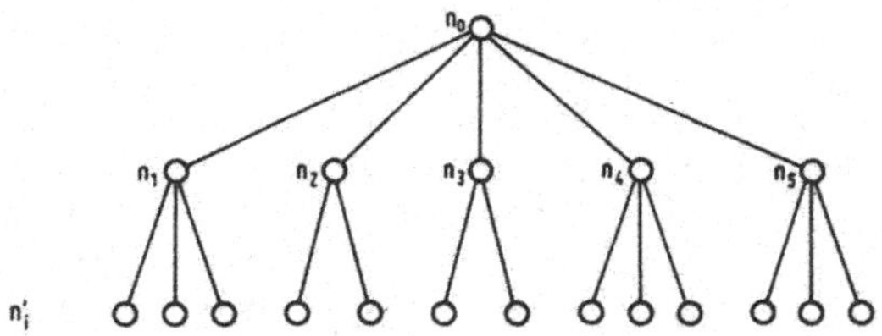


Fig. 5.2 Portion of a generical SS.

Y.L. KULIKOWSKI (*)

# RECOGNITION OF COMPOSITE PATTERNS

(*) Institute of Applied Cybernetics of the Polish Academy of Sciences, Warsaw.

## BASIC SYMBOLS

a) **General**

| | |
|---|---|
| $\{a_1, a_2, \ldots, a_n\}$ | – unordered set consisting of the elements $a_1, a_2, \ldots, a_n$ ; |
| $a \in A$ | – inclusion ("a belongs to A"); |
| $A \subset B$ | – inclusion ("A is a subset of the set B"); |
| a family | – a set of some sets; |
| a class | – a set of some functions or operators; |
| $\{u : u(a)\}$ | – the set of all elements a satisfying to the condition u(a); an ordered set consisting of the elements $a_1, a_2, \ldots, a_n$ ; |
| $[\overline{a, b}]$ | – an interval/an ordered set with a as the first and b as the last element; |
| $\emptyset$ | – an empty set; |
| $f : B \to C$ | – a function f prescribing to any element from the set B some element from the set C; |
| $\vert A \vert$ | – the cardinal number of the set A (the number of the elements in the set A) |
| $A \times B \times \ldots \times C$ | – a cartesian product of the sets A,B,...,C (a set of all possible ordered sets a,b,...,c such that $a \in A, b \in B, \ldots, c \in C$); |
| $A \cup B$ | – a disjunction of the sets A and B (a set consisting of all the elements belonging to A even /or to B) ; |
| $A \cap B$ | – a conjunction of the sets A and B (a set consisting of all the elements belonging both to A and to B); |
| $A \setminus B$ | – an asymmetrical difference of the sets A and B (a set of all the elements belonging to A not belonging to B); |
| $P\{\ \}$ | – the probability of the event given in the brackets; |
| $X, x$ | – a random variable and its realization; |
| $H_X$ | – the entropy of the random variable X; |
| $H_{X\vert Y}$ | – the conditional entropy of the random variable X given Y; |
| $F\{\ \}$ | – the Fourier transformation of the function given in the brackets; |
| $F^{-1}\{\ \}$ | – the inverse Fourier transformation of the function given in the brackets |
| $\neg u$ | – logical negation of the proposition u ("not u"); |
| $u \vee v$ | – logical sum of the propositions u and v ("u even) or v"; |
| $u \wedge v$ | – logical alternative of the propositions u and v ("u and v"); |
| $u \Rightarrow v$ | – logical implication ("v or not u"); |
| $u \equiv v$ | – logical equivalence ("u is equivalent to v"); |
| $\exists(s(v) s)$ | – a particular quantifier ("there exists such an s that v(s)"); |
| $\forall(s(v) s)$ | – a general quantifier ("for all s v(s)"); |

b) **Special**

R – a two-dimensional cadre;
k – an address of an element belonging to the cadre;
$X_k$ – an ordered set of the values of a picture in the point addressed by k;
$\underline{x}$ – a picture (a K-dimensional vector of the local values of the picture);
$x_k$ – the k-th component of $\underline{x}$;
$\Omega_R$ – a set of all possible pictures on the cadre R;
$\Omega_R^*$ – a subset of all possible pictures satisfying to some formal properties (a planar code);
A – an alphabet;
$a^i$ – the i-th symbol of the alphabet A;
L – the set of all possible finite strings made of symbols belonging to A;
$L^*$ – a subset of L containing the strings satisfying to some formal properties (a linear code);
S – a set of all possible elementary senses of the pictures (a semantical field)
s – an elementary sense belonging to S;
$\sigma$ – a subset of the set S (a pattern);
$B_S$ – a family of patterns defined on S;
$\mathcal{L}$ – a graphical language;
$\mathcal{L}^*$ – a linear language.

## I. General Aspects of Pattern Recognition

There exists a class of real objects like graphical pictures, schemas, diagrams, photographs, microscopic images, fingerprints, etc., which we shall in general call pictures and which play an important role in many areas of technology and investigations. Our attention will be paid to some aspects of computer processing of the pictures.

Let R be a finite set on a two-dimensional plane and let $X_k, k \in [\overline{1,K}]$, K being a natural number, denote some linearly ordered sets of the values of some measurable photooptical parameters. The set R will be called a discrete cadre and it will be assumed that its cardinal number $|R|$ is equal K. Any vector

$$\underline{x} = [x_1, x_2, \dots, x_K] \quad , \quad x_k \in X_k \quad , \quad k \in [\overline{1,K}] \tag{1}$$

will be called a picture. The set of all possible pictures on the given cadre R can be represented by a cartesian product

$$\Omega_R = X_1 \times X_2 \times \dots \times X_K \ . \tag{2}$$

Any subset

$$\Omega'_R \subset \Omega_R \tag{3}$$

in a formal sense can be interpreted as a relation described on the ordered family of sets $X_k, k \in [\overline{1,K}]$. From another point of view $\Omega'_R$ is a code expressed in the terms of the values of the photooptical parameters. So as the symbols of the code are connected with some geometrical points on the plane, it will be called a planar code. However, while considering pictures something more than the simple code properties should be taken into account. Picture are, in particular, carrying some statistical information, some semantical sense and some useful value. That is why our formal model should be completed.

Let us suppose that a given level of abstraction that is a set of S of some elementary meanings, properties of features of the pictures can be specified. S will be also called a semantical field, its elements will be denoted by s. Usually, we shall not discriminate between the meanings of the pictures but within some subsets $\sigma \subset S$.

The subsets $\sigma$ will be called the patterns. Thus, it will be assumed that a family

(4) $$B_S = \{\sigma_i\}$$

of patterns is defined on the semantical field S. $B_S$ will be called a semantical space. Any function

(5) $$g : \Omega'_R \rightarrow B_S$$

assigning some patterns to the expressions of the planar code $\Omega'_R$ will be called the semantics of the code. It is clear that the semantical space $B_S$ can be always completed by adding a pattern $\sigma_0$, interpreted as "no meaning", assigned to all the pictures not belonging to $\Omega'_R$. Therefore, it can be assumed that g projects all the set $\Omega_R$ on $B_S$. The ordered four elements

(6) $$G = [[X_k], \Omega_R, B_S, g]$$

will be called a planar language. Otherwise speaking, a planar language will here be considered as a planar (graphical) code with semantics. Computing the value

(7) $$\sigma = g(\underline{x}), \ \underline{x} \in \Omega_R, \sigma \in B_S ,$$

will be called the recognition of the pattern represented by the picture $\underline{x}$.

By some practical reasons (such as sequential action of the commonly used digital computers) it is desirable to use some auxiliary language for representing the pictures before recognition of patterns.

Let A be a finite set of symbols called an alphabet. The symbols from the set A can be arranged into some linearly ordered sets called the strings of symbols

(8) $$\underline{a} = [a_1, a_2, \ldots, a_n],$$

n being a natural number. Let L denote a set of all possible strings of finite length and let L* be a subset of L. L* can be interpreted as a linear code expressed in the terms of the alphabet A.

We shall suppose that there is given a function

$$h : \Omega_R \to L^* \tag{9}$$

assigning some linear code expression to any picture $\underline{x}$. The function h will be sometimes called an indexing function and the expression

$$\underline{a} = h(\underline{x}), \; \underline{x} \in \Omega_R, \; \underline{a} \in L^* \tag{10}$$

will be called an index assigned to the picture $\underline{x}$.

Let us suppose that another class of subsets

$$B_S^* = \{\sigma_j^*\}, \; \sigma_j^* \subset S, \tag{11}$$

can be defined in such a way that there exists a function

$$f : L^* \to B_S^*. \tag{12}$$

Otherwise speaking, the subsets $\sigma_j^*$ are some patterns that can be specified by the terms of the language L*. Thus, if a composite function

$$g^* = fh : \Omega_R \to B_S^* \tag{13}$$

is considered, it can be interpreted as a new semantics of a planar language

$$G^* \cdot = [[X_k], \Omega_R, B_S^*, g^*] \tag{14}$$

Both language G and G* are coupled on the lowest, graphical level. It is also desirable to have them coupled on the highest, semantical level in order to make them semantically equivalent. However, it is necessary to make it clear, what should be meant by semantical equivalence or similarity of two languages like G and G*. The problem will be solved here under some additional restrictive assumptions.

Let us take into account the disjunction of the families of subsets

$$B = B_S \cup B_S^*. \tag{15}$$

It will be taken into account the minimum Borel's family of subsets of the set S containing the family of sets B. This can be obtained in the following manner. There is taken into account the family of subsets of the set S defined as all possible disjunctions, conjunctions and asymmetrical differences of the subsets belonging to the family B completed by the set S; we denote it by $B^1$. Then, the family of subsets of S obtained by taking all possible disjunctions, conjunctions or asymmetrical differences of the subsets belonging to the family $B^1$ are taken into account and we denote it by $B^2$. The families of subsets of the set S denoted by $B^3$, $B^4$ etc. can be obtained by repeating the above described procedure. The minimum Borel's family of subsets of the set S can be defined as a set $B^n$ for n going to infinity. Let us denote it by Q and let us use the symbol q for the subsets belonging to this family. It is clear that the qs are some new patterns which can be formally represented by some algebraical combinations of the patterns belonging to $B_S$ as well as to $B_S^*$. In particular, any $\sigma$ and any $\sigma^*$ is an element of Q.

Let us suppose that a probability measure P can be described on the family of subsets Q, the patterns q being considered as some random events. Otherwise speaking, to any pattern $q_r \in Q$ its probability

(16) $$p_r = P(q_r), \quad 0 \leqslant p_r \leqslant 1, \quad \sum_r p_r = 1,$$

can be assigned. The conditional probabilities

(17) $$p_{i|j} = \frac{P\{\sigma_i \cap \sigma_j^*\}}{P\{\sigma_j^*\}}$$

will be also of interest.

Now, the entropy of the set of original patterns can be defined

(18) $$H_B = - \sum_{\sigma_i \in B_S} p_i \cdot \log_2 p_i \quad , \quad p_i = P\{\sigma_i\} .$$

In similar way, the conditional entropy of the original pattern given the indexed (recognized) patterns can be obtained from the formula

(19) $$H_{B|B^*} = - \sum_{\sigma_i \in B_S} \sum_{\sigma_j^* \in B_S^*} p_{ij} \cdot \log_2 p_{i|j} \quad , \quad p_{ij} = P\{\sigma_i \cap \sigma_j^*\} .$$

The difference

$$\Delta H = H_B - H_{B|B*} \tag{20}$$

according to the general rules of the theory of communication gives us a mean statistical value of the information contained in a recognized pattern about the original one. However, if the similarity of the planar (graphical) languages G and G* is to be defined, it seems reasonable to use a normalized figure

$$\gamma = \frac{\Delta H}{H_B} . \tag{21}$$

Our aim is thus to obtain a machine-computable indexing function g, may be satisfying some additional conditions, such that a planar language G* obtained on the basis of the function g is similar semantically in a given sense as far as possible. It is to be stressed out at once, that we can not solve this kind of problem exactly. Nevertheless, one of possible approaches to the above given problem will be given here.

It will be supposed that we have a set of particular indexing functions

$$h_n : \Omega_R \rightarrow A_n , \quad A_n \subset A, \quad n \in [\overline{1,N}] , \tag{22}$$

$A_n$ being a sub-alphabet (a set of all possible results of applying the n-th test to a picture).

The set of all possible pictures indexed in the same way by the function $h_n$:

$$X_{nm} = \{\underline{x} : h_n(\underline{x}) = a^m , \underline{x} \in \Omega_R, a^m \in A_n\} \tag{23}$$

will be called the nm-th decision area. The recognized pattern corresponding to $X_{nm}$ in the g* projection will be now denoted by $\sigma^*_{nm}$. It is clear that $\sigma^*_{nm} \in Q$.

Let us assign a cost $c_n$, $n \in [\overline{1,N}]$ to the function $h_n$ when computed in an automized system. It is clear that from the total costs of indexing minimization point of view we would like to choose the sets of tests as close as possible to the original semantics but mutually rather different semantically. Let us thus remark that the figure (21) can be used for measuring the semantical similarity of the tests as well. If, for example, two indexing functions $h_{n_1}$ and $h_{n_2}$ are considered,

(24) $$\pi_{\mu,\nu} = P\{h_{n_1} = a^{\mu}, h_{n_2} = a^{\nu}\}, \quad a^{\mu} \epsilon A_{n_1}, \quad a^{\nu} \epsilon A_{n_2},$$

(25) $$\pi_{\mu} = P\{h_{n_1} = a^{\mu}\}, \quad a^{\mu} \epsilon A_{n_1},$$

(26) $$\pi^*_{\nu} = P\{h_{n_2} = a^{\nu}\}, \quad a^{\nu} \epsilon A_{n_2},$$

(27) $$\pi_{\mu|\nu} = P\{h_{n_1} = a^{\mu} \mid h_{n_2} = a^{\nu}\}$$

being the corresponding probabilities, then the entropies $H_{B_1}$ and $H_{B_1 | B_2}$ can be obtained in the usual way and we get the figure of similarity of both tests

(28) $$\gamma_{n_1,n_2} = \frac{H_{B_1} - H_{B_1 | B_2}}{H_{B_1} + H_{B_2}} .$$

It should also be remarked that

(29) $$\gamma_{n_1,n_2} = \gamma_{n_2,n_1} .$$

Now, let us suppose that we want to choose a subset of the first- level indexing functions. An auxiliary variable is defined

(30) $$z_n^{(1)} = \begin{cases} 1, \text{if the function } h_n \text{ is included into the subset of the first-level indexing tests,} \\ 0, \text{otherwise.} \end{cases}$$

The costs of the first-level indexing are given by a formula

(31) $$Z' = \sum_{n=1}^{N} c_n \cdot z_n^{(1)} + \lambda' \cdot \sum_{n_1=1}^{N} \sum_{n_2=1}^{N} \gamma_{n_1,n_2} \cdot z_{n_1}^{(1)} \cdot z_{n_2}^{(1)}$$

$\lambda'$ being here an arbitrary real positive coefficient. Before minimizing the costs of the first-level indexing by an appropriate choosing the values of the $z_n^{(1)}$ - s we shall find the second-level indexing costs. Let us denote by

$$A' = A_1^{z_1^{(1)}} \times A_2^{z_2^{(1)}} \times \ldots \times A_N^{z_N^{(1)}} \qquad (32)$$

the set of all possible results $\underline{a}'$ of the first-level indexing of the pictures.

We shall define the following additional auxiliary variables:

$$z^{(2)}_{n'',\underline{a}'} = \begin{cases} 1, \text{if the function } h_{n''} \text{ is included into the set of test functions} \\ \text{used for the pictures indexed at the first-level by } \underline{a}', \\ 0, \text{otherwise.} \end{cases} \qquad (33)$$

Let us denote by $\pi(\underline{a}')$ the probability of obtaining $\underline{a}'$ as a result of the first-level indexing of the pictures. Thus, an additional cost of the second-level indexing will be given by the formula

$$Z'' = \sum_{\underline{a}' \in A'} \pi(\underline{a}') \sum_{n=1}^{N} z^{(2)}_{n,\underline{a}'} c_n + \lambda'' \sum_{n'=1}^{N} \sum_{n''=1}^{N} \gamma_{n',n''}(\underline{a}') \cdot z^{(2)}_{n',\underline{a}'} \cdot z^{(2)}_{n'',\underline{a}'} \qquad (34)$$

where $\lambda''$ is a real positive arbitrary coefficient and $\gamma_{n',n''}(\underline{a}')$ is a conditional semantical similarity figure defined as follows.

There will be considered a conditional family of subsets of S when the pattern $\sigma(\underline{a}') \in Q$ corresponding to the first-order index $\underline{a}'$ is fixed:

$$Q(\underline{a}') = \{\sigma_i \cap \sigma(\underline{a}')\}. \qquad (35)$$

The conditional probabilities

$$\pi_{\mu,\nu}(\underline{a}') = \frac{\pi_{\mu,\nu}}{\pi(\underline{a}')}, \qquad (36)$$

$$\pi_{\mu}(\underline{a}') = \frac{\pi_{\mu}}{\pi(\underline{a}')}, \qquad (37)$$

$$\pi^*_{\nu}(\underline{a}') = \frac{\pi^*_{\nu}}{\pi(\underline{a}')}, \qquad (38)$$

$$\pi_{\mu|\nu}(\underline{a}') = \frac{\pi_{\mu|\nu}}{\pi(\underline{a}')} \qquad (39)$$

instead of the $\pi_{\nu,\mu}$ $\pi_{\mu}$ , $\pi^{*}_{\nu}$ , and $\pi_{\mu|\nu}$ will be used and the conditional entropies $H_{B_1}(a')$ and $H_{B_1|B_2}(a')$ instead of the $H_{B_1}$ and $H_{B_1|B_2}$, correspondingly. will be computed.

Thus, we can define

$$(40) \qquad \gamma_{n',n''}(\underline{a}') = \frac{H_{B_1}(\underline{a}') - H_{B_1|B_2}(\underline{a}')}{H_{B_1}(\underline{a}') + H_{B_2}(\underline{a}')}$$

and we can use it in the formula (34).

Thus, in order to have an optimum set of tests for the two-level indexing of the pictures it is necessary to choose the values of the variables $z^{(1)}_{n'}$ , $z^{(2)}_{n'',\underline{a}'}$ for $n'n'' \in [\overline{1,N}]$ and $\underline{a}' \in A'$ minimizing the total cost

$$(41) \qquad Z = Z' + Z''$$

and taken from the binary set $\{0,1\}$. The solution should satisfy to the condition that the tests should give a sufficient quantity of information about the original patterns. Therefore, we put

$$(42) \qquad \sum_{n'=1}^{N} z^{(1)}_{n'} \gamma_{n'} + \sum_{n''=1}^{N} z^{(2)}_{n'',\underline{a}'} \gamma_{n''} \geq b(\underline{a}') , \quad \text{for } \underline{a}' \in A'$$

as a set of additional conditions, the $b(\underline{a}')$-s being some positive real constants.

However, it is evident that if a test $h_n$ is included into the subset of the first-level tests, there is no reason for including it into the subset of the second-level tests. It seems also clear, that if some test $h_n$ is included into the subsets of the tests corresponding to all first-level indexes $\underline{a}'$, it should be rather included into the subset of the first-level tests. Thus, the additional conditions can be formulated:

$$(43) \qquad z^{(1)}_{n} + z^{(2)}_{n,\underline{a}'} \leq 1 \quad \text{for} \quad n \in [\overline{1,N}] \text{ and } \underline{a}' \in A' .$$

The restrictions (43) are not necessary from the computational point of view, so as they would be satisfied automatically as a result of minimization of the cost function Z. Nevertheless, they can accelerate the computational process.

The problem of optimization of the set of indexing functions used for the recognition of pattern leads thus to a binary-programming problem with nonlinear cost function and nonlinear constraints. This kind of problems can be solved for not too large a number of variables using some standard techniques like a so called branch-and-bound method.

Let us also remark, that the two-level indexing schema, as well as those ones based on more levels of indexing (which can be optimized by a similar manner), contains some elements of a programmed experiment. There is meant by that the dependence of the second-level (as well as eventually the higher-level) sets of indexing functions on the result $\underline{a}'$ already reached on the lower-levels of indexing the pictures.

## II. Formal Properties of Discrete Pictures

The following additional assumptions will be made:

(1) $$R = R_I \times R_J ,$$

where

(2a) $$R_I = [1,2,\dots,I] ,$$

(2b) $$R_J = [1,2,\dots,J] ,$$

(3) $$X_k = X = \{0,1\} \text{ for } k \in [\overline{1,K}] ,$$

I,J and K being some natural numbers. Thus, the white-black discrete pictures will be considered.

To any point $\rho_{ij} \in R$ the following metric coordinates will also be preassigned

(4a) $$\xi_i = i.\Delta_\xi , \quad i \in R_I ,$$

(4b) $$\eta_j = j.\Delta_\eta , \quad j \in R_J ,$$

for some fixed real and positive $\Delta_\xi$ , $\Delta_\eta$ . Therefore, the discrete cadre R forms a periodic rectangular net plunged into an euclidean plane $E^2$ . The number I.J represents a maximum quantity of information in bits that may be delivered by a picture.

So as the discrete pictures are some representations of the general (also continuous) geometrical objects in $E^2$, the problem arises of giving some general characteristics of the continuous objects that can be assigned to the discrete pictures in an unique manner. Otherwise speaking, we would try to find the recognized semantical sense (within the field S containing the continuous and discrete objects in $E^2$ ) of the pictures $\underline{x}$, given by a function $g^*$.

The result depends mostly on the model of a photelectronic transformer of images, so as the cadre-points $\rho_{ij}$ represent the photosensitive cells. There is a lot of possible models of this type, one of them is the following.

1° .The discrete pictures will be represented by the matrices

$$\underline{x} = [x_{ij}] \quad , x_{ij} \in X, \; i \in R_I \; , j \in R_J \; . \tag{5}$$

2° . It will be supposed that

$$x_{ij} = 1$$

if and only if

$$u_\sigma \cap \pi_{ij} \neq \emptyset \tag{6}$$

where $u_\sigma$ is a geometrical object under consideration in the plane $E^2$, $\pi_{ij}$ is a set of points

$$\rho = (\xi, \eta) \in E^2 \tag{7}$$

satisfying to the following conditions:

$$\pi_{ij} = \left\{ (\xi,\eta) \; : \; \xi = \xi_i \, , \eta_j - \frac{\Delta_\eta}{2} < \eta \leqslant \eta_j + \frac{\Delta_\eta}{2} \quad \text{even/or} \atop \xi_i - \frac{\Delta_\xi}{2} < \xi \leqslant \xi_i + \frac{\Delta_\xi}{2} \, , \; \eta = \eta_j \right\} \tag{8}$$

The principle of picture discretization satisfying to the above- given formula is shown in the Fig. 1. As a consequence, the subset of all geometrical objects in $E^2$ that can be assigned to the same discrete picture $\underline{x}$ can be easily obtained; it is shown in Fig. 2.

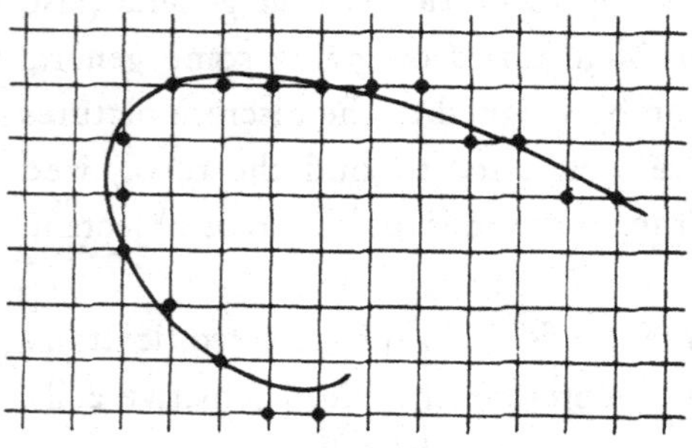
Fig. 1

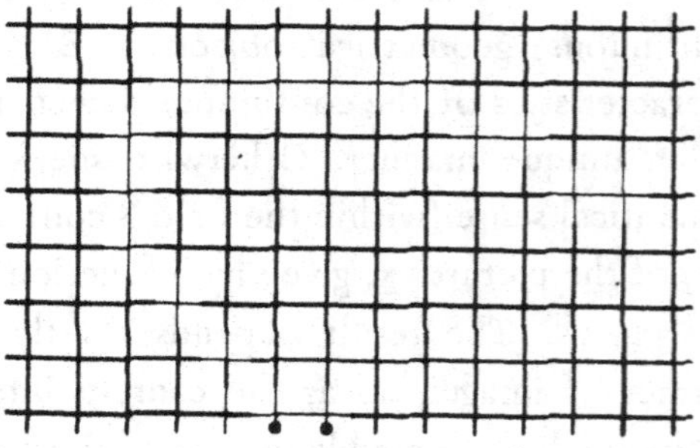
Fig. 2

Formally, it can be described as follows.

Let us define the subset of the cadre R consisting of all the "black" points belonging to the discrete picture $\underline{x}$:

$$r(\underline{x}) = \{\rho_{ij} : x_{ij} = 1,\ x_{ij} \in \underline{x}\} . \tag{9a}$$

Let us also define the set

$$\Pi_{ij} = \left\{ (\xi,\eta) : (0 < |\xi - \xi_i| < \Delta_\xi) \wedge (0 < |\eta - \eta_j| < \Delta_\eta) \vee (\xi,\eta) \in \pi_{ij} \right\} \tag{9b}$$

Now, it can be defined a family of subsets of $E^2$

$$G(\underline{x}) = \left\{ u(\underline{x}) : u(\underline{x}) \subset \bigcup_{\rho_{ij} \in r(\underline{x})} \Pi_{ij} ,\ \forall(\rho_{ij}) [\rho_{ij} \in r(\underline{x}),\ u(\underline{x}) \cap \pi_{ij} \neq \emptyset] \right\} \tag{10}$$

which is the solution of the above formulated problem.

Therefore, if a geometrical object $u \subset E^2$ is given, the discrete picture $\underline{x}$ and the corresponding discrete geometrical representation $r(\underline{x})$ can be obtained in the above described way. On the other hand, when some discrete picture $\underline{x}$ is given, a family $G(\underline{x})$ of the geometrical objects $u(\underline{x})$ can be found and

$$u \in G(\underline{x}) .$$

Any geometrical relation in the periodic rectangular net R thus can be interpreted in the corresponding classes of geometrical objects in the space $E^2$ sense.

There are several kinds of metrices commonly used in the discrete geometrical objects considerations. For example,

$$d'(\rho_{ij}, \rho_{kl}) = |i-k| + |j-l| , \tag{11a}$$

$$d''(\rho_{ij}, \rho_{kl}) = \max(|i-k|, |j-l|) . \tag{11b}$$

$$d'''(\rho_{ij}, \rho_{kl}) = \sqrt{(i-k)^2 + (j-l)^2} , \tag{11c}$$

etc.

The consequences of the different geometrical assumptions can be illustrated when a discrete circle with a fixed radius is considered. Let us take, for example, the radius $r = 4$ into account:

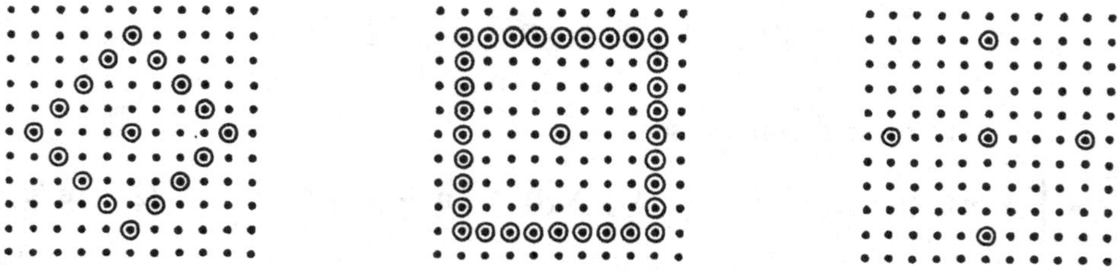

d′ d″ d‴

It becomes clear that there may be no similarity between the discrete and the continuous geometrical constructions even if based on similar formal assumptions. On the other hand, the constructions based on the d' or d"- metrices have some advantages from the computational point of view. We are particularly interested in the geometrical properties of the original objects that can be revealed by investigating their discrete representations using the computer techniques.

Let us define the weight of a discrete picture $\underline{x}$

$$w(\underline{x}) = \sum_{i \in I} \sum_{j \in J} x_{ij} \quad . \tag{12}$$

For a given discrete geometrical object $u(\underline{x})$ a category of a given point $\rho \in u(\underline{x})$ will be defined as follows

$$k(\rho) = w(\underline{x} . c_1(\rho)) \tag{13}$$

where $c_1(\rho)$ is a picture corresponding to the circle with the center in the point $\rho$ and with the radius $= 1$ and the multiplication of the vectors is taken in a logical sense:

$$\underline{x} . \underline{y} = [x_{ij} \cdot y_{ij}] \quad , \; i \in R_I \quad , \; j \in R_J \quad . \tag{13a}$$

Thus, the category of a point belonging to the given discrete geometrical object $u(\underline{x})$ is the number of all discrete points of the object located at the distance of the given point equal to 1. It is evident, that the category depends, in general, on the metrics.

Discrete objects u(x) consisting only of the points of the category equal to 0 will be called point-objects. The examples corresponding to the metrices d' and d" are given below:

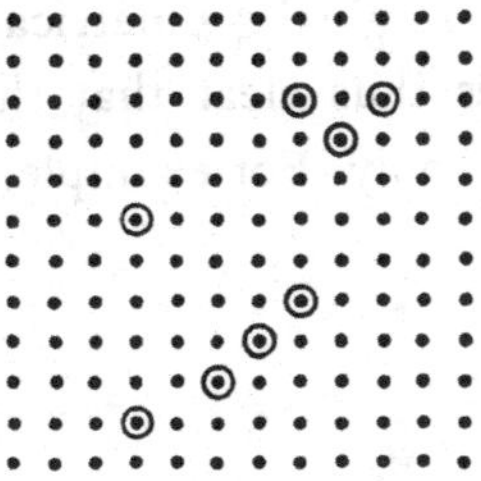

d'

d"

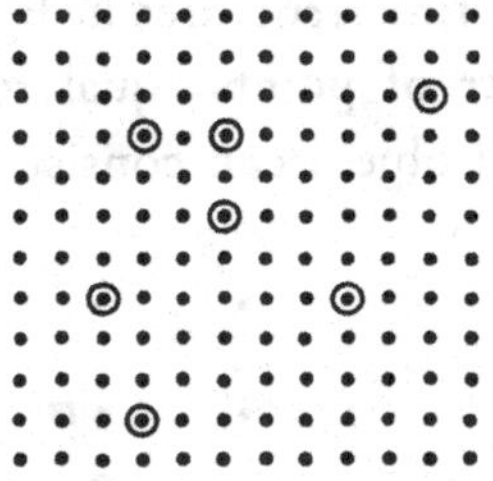

Let us suppose that a discrete picture has been recognized as a point-object. The problem arises, what can be told about the properties of the original picture in $E^2$ . It is evident (see Fig. 2) that if the discrete metrics d' is used, a continuous skew line can be discretized in such a way that a point-object is obtained. On the other hand, if the d" metrics is used the "kernels" $\pi_{ij}$ arrounding any two points are disjoint:

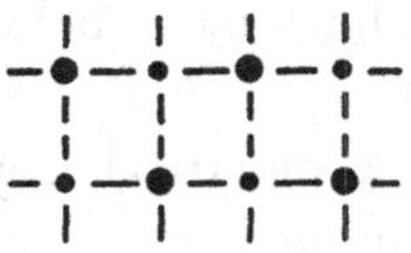

where $\pi_{ij}$ = 

However, the original picture may consist of several mutually disjoint subsets in $E^2$ fully contained by the corresponding "environments" $\Pi_{ij}$ of the kernels $\pi_{ij}$ .

Discrete objects u(x) consisting of the points of the category 1 or 2 only will be called line-objects. The examples corresponding to the metrices d' and d" are given below:

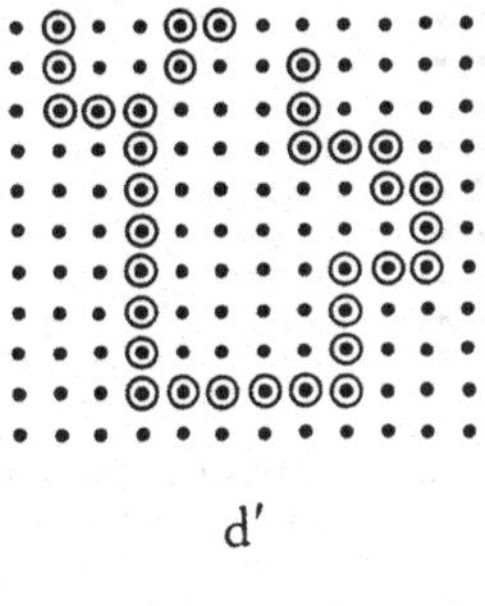

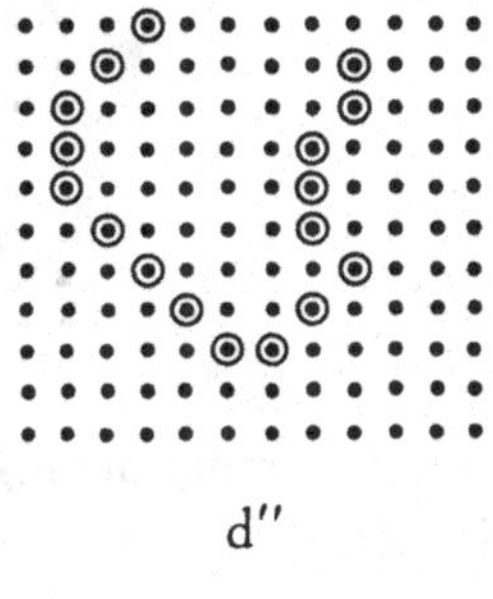

d'

d"

The question arises, what conclusions concerning the class of possible original geometrical objects can be made when a discrete line-object is identified. For both the metrices d' and d'' the kernels corresponding to the discrete picture $\underline{x}$ form some fine structures in $E^2$ that must intersect the original geometrical object in the number of points equal to the weight $w(\underline{x})$. It is thus clear that the original geometrical object can consist of a finite set of points only. For example, an object

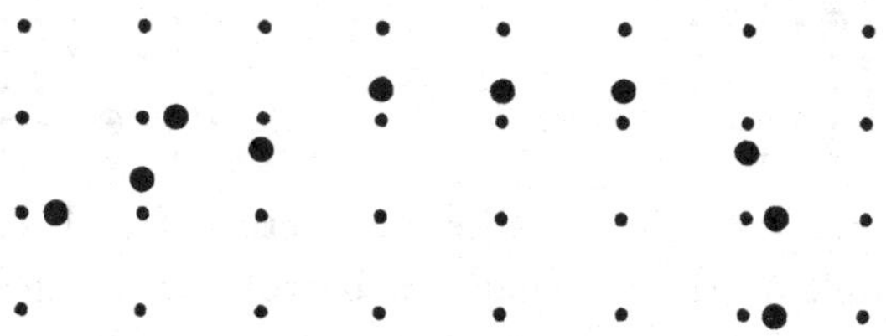

will be identified as a discrete line-object in the d'-metrics sense.

A discrete geometrical object $u(\underline{x})$ corresponding to a given discrete picture $\underline{x}$ will be called compact if it is a point of category 0 or if for any two points $\rho'$, $\rho'' \in u(\underline{x})$ it can be found a discrete line-object belonging to $u(\underline{x})$ and containing both $\rho'$ and $\rho''$.

It will be called that a discrete geometrical object $u(\underline{x})$ contains $\nu$ compact components if it can be represented in the form

$$u(\underline{x}) = \bigcup_{n=1}^{\nu} u_n \tag{14}$$

where $u_n$ are some mutually disjoint compact discrete geometrical objects and $\nu$ is the minimum natural number that admits this kind of decomposition of $u(\underline{x})$. For example, the following object

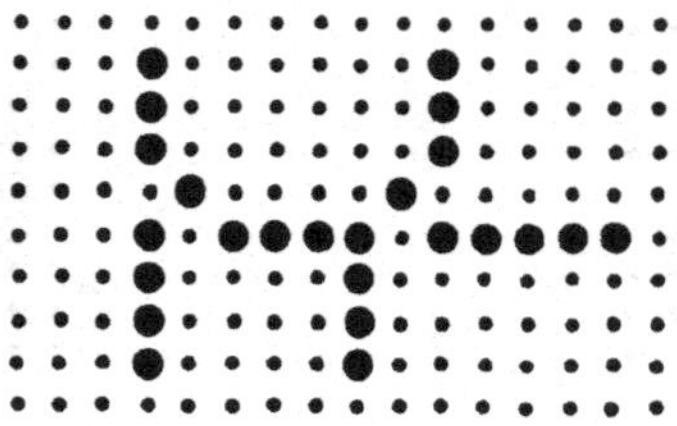

contains 8 compact components in the d'-metrics sense and one component only in the d''-metrics sense.

The decomposition (14) is unique. If not, there would be two possible families of subsets: $\{u_n\}$ and $\{u'_m\}$ both satisfying to the formula (14) and such that at least one of the components $u_n$ can be fully covered by some components $u'_m$ or, otherwise, one of the components $u'_m$ can be fully covered by some components $u_n$ . In any case this would mean that at least one of the decompositions is not minimum.

So as the sufficient condition for an original geometrical object in $E^2$ to have a non-empty discrete representation in R is that it has the diameter at least equal to max $(\Delta_\xi , \Delta_\eta)$ (it must then intersect the kernel of at least one discrete point $\rho_{ij}$ in this case), the corresponding sufficient conditions for the compactness of a geometrical object to be detected can be formulated. The compactness cannot be detected but using the d''-metrics approach to the original objects having the diameter at least equal to max $(\Delta_\xi , \Delta_\eta)$. On the other hand, if a discrete representation of a geometrical object is compact it does not guarantee that the original object in $E^2$ is also compact.

A discrete geometrical object u consisting of the points of the category not greater than 3 will be called a fine geometrical object. Two examples (with the numbers indicating the categories of the points) are given below:

```
. . . . . . . . . .        . . . . . . . . . .
. 1 . . 2 2 3 2 2 .        . 1 . . 2 2 . 3 2 .
. 2 2 2 3 . 1 . 2 .        . 2 3 3 . . 2 . 3 .
. . . . 2 . . . 2 .        . . . . 2 . . . 2 .
. . . . 3 2 2 2 2 .        . . . . . 3 2 2 . .
. 1 . . 2 . . . . .        . 1 . . 3 . . . . .
. 3 2 2 3 2 1 . . .        . . 3 2 . 2 1 . . .
. 2 . . . . . . 1 .        . 2 . . . . . . 1 .
. 2 2 2 2 2 2 2 2 .        . 2 2 2 2 2 2 3 2 .
. . . . . . . . . .        . . . . . . . . . .
        d'                         d''
```

It should be remarked that the first object cannot be identified as a fine geometrical object in the d''-metrics sense so as it contains some points of the category 4. The d'-metrics has some advantages with respect to the d'' one in this case, because the category of a point in the d'-metrics sense indicates the number of line-objects going out of the given point, if the category does not overpass the number 3.

An ordered pair of points on the discrete cadre R:

$$\underline{v} = [\rho_{ij} , \rho_{kl}] \tag{15}$$

such that

(16) $$d(\rho_{ij}, \rho_{kl}) = 1$$

will be called a unity vector and the ordered pair

(17) $$p = [k-i\ ,\ l-j]$$

will be called its direction.

It is clear that there are no more than four unity vectors going out of a point in the d'-metrics sense and no more than eight unity vectors in d''- metrics sense. The number of possible directions on the discrete plane R is also 4 and 8, correspondingly.

The ordered pair of points $\underline{v}$ given by (15) will be called a vector going out of the point $\rho_{ij}$, having the length l and the direction [b,c] where

(18a) $$l \in [1,2,3,...]$$

(18b) $$b,c \in \{-1,0,1\}\ ,$$

if there exists a series of l + 1 points on the cadre R:

$$[\rho_{ij}, \rho_{\alpha\beta}, \rho_{\gamma\delta}, ..., \rho_{\mu\nu}, \rho_{kl}]$$

such that any two consecutive points of this series form a unity vector of the same direction [ b,c ] on R. It seems also reasonable to include the ordered pairs

(19) $$\underline{0} = [\rho_{ij}, \rho_{ij}], \rho_{ij} \in R$$

into the set of all possible vectors going out of the point $\rho_{ij}$ and to call it a zero-length vector with undefined direction.

The set $\lambda$ (b,c; $\rho_{ij}$ ) of all possible points on the cadre R that can end the vectors of any length (including zero) and of the directions [b,c] or [-b,-c] going out of the point $\rho_{ij}$ will be called a discrete straight line of the direction [ b,c ] going through the point $\rho_{ij}$. It is clear that the number of discrete straight lines going through a given point $\rho_{ij}$ is the same as the number of all possible unity vectors in the given metrics sense.

Any discrete straight line can be interpreted as a representation of a class of original geometrical objects in $E^2$ in the sense of the general expression (10). This class also contains the continuous straight line in $E^2$ containing all the points of the discrete straight line if the discrete cadre R is plunged into $E^2$.

However, not any continuous straight line in $E^2$ has its discrete representation in the form of a discrete straight line. A more general class of discrete representants of straight lines can be defined as follows.

For any direction [b,c], $b,c \in \{-1,0,1\}$, b and c being not equal to zero simultaneously and for the metrices d', d" being not both different of zero, the neighbour directions can be defined: $[b_1, c_1]$ and $[b_2, c_2]$ such that

- for the d'-metrics

$$|b - b_1| = |c - c_1| = 1 , \tag{20a}$$

$$|b - b_2| = |c - c_2| = 1 ; \tag{20b}$$

- for the d"-metrics

$$|b - b_1| + |c - c_1| = 1 ,$$

$$|b - b_2| + |c - c_2| = 1 .$$

Thus, for example, for the direction [-1,0] in the d'-metrics sense the two neighbour directions will be [0,1] and [0,-1] while in the d"- sense we obtain the directions [-1,1] and [-1.-1] (the direction [0,0] not being taken into account).

Let us take into account a series of discrete points

$$\ldots \rho^{(2k)}, \rho^{(2k+1)}, \ldots \quad \text{for } k = 1,2,3,\ldots$$

such that any ordered pair $[\rho^{(2k)}, \rho^{(2k+1)}]$ forms a discrete vector of given length 1 and given direction [b,c] and any ordered pair $[\rho^{(2k+1)}, \rho^{(2k+2)}]$ forms a unity vector of a given direction [b',c'] neighbour to the direction [b,c]. Any subseries obtained as an intersection of the cadre R with the given series of points can be considered as a representant of a continuous straight line in the space $E^2$.

**III. Distinctive Relations in the Image Space**

In the lectures given by the author during the CISM Summer School in 1971, attention was paid to a concept of an algebra of relations as an appropriate tool for the description of deterministic patterns. However, this tool becomes inadequate for the patterns that cannot be defined in a deterministic manner. On the other hand, a probabilistic approach needs sometimes too much of prior knowledge about the probability densities describing the classes of images. That is why there will be given here some suggestions about a more general approach that will have some advantages with respect to the former ones. The approach is based on a well known idea of semi-ordered sets.

If there is given a set

(1) $$Z = \{z_1, z_2, \ldots, z_k, \ldots\} ,$$

then any binary relation $\approx$ satisfying to the condition of:

- reciprocity, i.e. for any $z_i \in Z$,

(2a) $$z_i \approx z_i ,$$

- symmetricity, i.e. for any $z_i , z_j \in Z$, if

(2b) $$z_i \approx z_j , \text{ then also } z_j \approx z_i ,$$

- transitivity, i.e. for any $z_i , z_j , z_k \in Z$, if

(2c) $$z_i \approx z_j \text{ and } z_j \approx z_k , \text{ then } z_i \approx z_k ,$$

will be called an equivalence in Z.

Any subset $Z' \subset Z$ of the elements such that for any $z_i , z_j \in Z'$ it is $z_i \approx z_j$,
will be called a class of equivalence in Z.

The classes of equivalence in Z do not overlap each with the other one. The set Z thus can be presented in the form of a disjunction of mutually disjoint classes of equivalence.

Any binary relation $<$ (read "before") described in the set Z and satisfying to the conditions of reciprocity, transitivity and to the following condition of asymmetricity:

- for any $z_i , z_j \in Z$ if $z_i < z_j$, then

$$z_j < z_i \text{ if and only if } z_i \approx z_j , \tag{3}$$

will be called a semi-ordering in the set Z.

**Example 1**

Let us consider a set X and a sigma-algebra $B_x$ of the subsets of the set (i.e. a family of subsets of the set X closed with respect to any countable combination of disjunctions or asymmetrical differencies of the subsets). Any probability measure (nonnegative, additive and normalized to 1 on the set X) P described on $B_x$ introduces there a semi-ordering. Really,

1° for any $\omega \in B_x$ ,

$$P(\omega) \leqslant P(\omega) ; \tag{4a}$$

2° for any $\omega_i , \omega_j \in B_x$ if

$$P(\omega_i) \leqslant P(\omega_j) \text{ and } P(\omega_j) \leqslant P(\omega_i), \text{ then } P(\omega_i) = P(\omega_j); \tag{4b}$$

3° for any $\omega_i , \omega_j , \omega_k \in B_x$ if

$$P(\omega_i) \leqslant P(\omega_j) \text{ and } P(\omega_j) \leqslant P(\omega_k), \text{ then } P(\omega_i) \leqslant P(\omega_k). \tag{4c}$$

Thus, $\omega_i < \omega_j$ can be read as "$\omega_i$ goes before $\omega_j$ in the sense of increasing probabilities" while the meaning of $\omega_i \approx \omega_j$ is that of an equivalence in the sense of the corresponding probabilities equality.

It is also clear that not any semi-ordering can be characterized by a corresponding probability measure. This, in particular, concerns the pairs of subsets $\omega_i , \omega_j \in B_x$ such that neither $\omega_i < \omega_j$ nor $\omega_j < \omega_i$ holds. The subsets will be called mutually irrelative in this case and the notation

$$\omega_i \not\approx \omega_j \tag{5}$$

will be used for this case. Irrelativeness is neither reciprocal nor transitive, therefore, the irrelative elements form no class of equivalence.

As a consequence of the above-given example it should be remarked that any subset $Z' \subset Z$ generates a semi-ordering in a natural way. Really, we can put

$$z_i \approx z_j \text{ if and only if } z_i \in Z' \text{ and } z_j \in Z' \tag{6a}$$

as well as

(6b) $$z_i < z_j \text{ if } z_i \notin Z' \text{ and } z_j \in Z'.$$

The semi-ordering described on the set Z will be called trivial if it generates only one class of equivalence identical with Z and is called insufficient if for any pair of elements $z_i, z_j \in Z$ there is $z_i \not\approx z_j$.

There will be considered now a linearly ordered family of sets $[X_{ij}]$ for which

(7) $$\Omega = \underset{(i,j)\in R_I \times R_J}{\text{X}} X_{ij}$$

and a sigma-algebra $B_\Omega$ of subsets of the set $\Omega$. We shall take into account a semi-ordering $\pi$ described on $B_\Omega$ and satisfying to the following condition:

for any $\omega \in B_\Omega$ there is

(8) $$\emptyset < \omega < \Omega$$

where $\emptyset$ stands for an empty set;

- for any $\omega_i, \omega_j \in B_\Omega$ there is

(9) $$\omega_i, \omega_j < \omega_i \cup \omega_j .$$

**Definition 1**

The ordered three elements

(10) $$r_\pi = [[X_{ij}], B_\Omega, \pi]$$

will be called a distinctive relation described on the family of sets $[X_{ij}]$.

In particular, the subsets $\omega \subset \Omega$ can be semi-ordered in a natural way by inclusion i.e.

(11) $$\omega_i < \omega_j \text{ if and only if } \omega_i \subset \omega_j ;$$

the distinctive relation will be called a natural one in this case.

**Example 2.**

Any given element $\underline{x}^o \in \Omega$ generates a distinctive relation in $[X_{ij}]$ for any $\omega \in B_\Omega$ we can put

$$\omega < \{\underline{x}^o\} \,, \tag{12a}$$

$$\{\underline{x}^o\} < \omega \text{ if and only if } \underline{x}^o \in \omega \,. \tag{12b}$$

It thus can be seen that all the subsets $\omega \subset \Omega$ such that $\underline{x}^o \in \omega$ form a class of equivalence $Q_{\underline{x}^o}$ and

$$\omega \approx \Omega \text{ for any } \omega \in Q_{\underline{x}^o} \,. \tag{13}$$

**Example 3**

The last example can be easily generalized if we take a subset $\omega^o \subset \Omega$ instead of the one-element subset $\{\underline{x}^o\}$. Then for any $\omega \in B_\Omega$ we can put

$$\omega < \omega^o \,, \tag{14a}$$

$$\omega^o < \omega \text{ if and only if } \omega^o \subset \omega \tag{14b}$$

All the subsets $\omega \subset \Omega$ such that $\omega^o \subset \omega$ thus form a class of $Q_{\omega^o}$ of equivalence and (13) holds also for any $\omega \in Q_{\omega^o}$.

**Example 4**

Let us suppose that there is given a probability measure P described on the sigma-algebra $B_\Omega$. It generates a distinctive relation. Really, all the assumptions of the Definition 1 are fulfilled if we put that for any $\omega_i , \omega_j \in B_\Omega$ there is

$$\omega_i < \omega_j \text{ if and only if } P(\omega_i) \leqslant P(\omega_j) \,. \tag{15}$$

It is also clear that the distinctive relation concept is a more general one, because no additive and normalized measure is here supposed to exist and to be known. In pattern recognition we often deal with the objects which cannot be but sometimes mutually compared and relatively preferred. While stimulating a source of images to produce a "learning series" of images corresponding to a given pattern we cannot assert that the frequencies of representants give us any information about their probability distribution, so as the stimulated conditions differ from the natural ones. Nevertheless, a representant that has been observed should be preferred in some sense with respect to the other ones which are at most potentially possible. The distinctive relation gives us the possibility of introducing the preferences without probabilities.

The following interpretation, based on the graphs, can be given for the distinctive relations described on finite sets. To any subset $\omega \in B_\Omega$ there will be assigned a node $0_\omega$ of the graph. Two nodes $0_{\omega_1}$ , $0_{\omega_2}$ of the graph will be linked together by the edge

(16a) $$1_{\omega_1 \omega_2} = [0_{\omega_1}, 0_{\omega_2}]$$

if and only if

(16b) $$\omega_1 < \omega_2$$

and no other subset $\omega_3 \subset \Omega$ exists such that

(16c) $$\omega_1 < \omega_3 < \omega_2$$

(excepting $\omega_1 \approx \omega_3$ or $\omega_2 \approx \omega_3$). So as for finite sets $X_{ij}$ the sigma algebra $B_\Omega$ is also finite, a graph-representation of any distinctive relation described on any finite number of finite sets can be, in general, obtained.

However, the main disadvantage of this kind of representation is the enormous order of the graph: if the cardinal number of the set $\Omega$ is $|\Omega|$ then the cardinal number of $B_\Omega$ is $2^{|\Omega|}$ and so is the cardinal number of the set of the graph-nodes. This can be reduced if only one node is assigned to any class of equivalence in the set $B_\Omega$ .

**Example 5**

Let us consider a family of sets $[X_{ij}]$ , $i \in \{1,2,3\}$, $j \in \{1,2,3\}$.

(17) $$X_{ij} = \{0,1\}$$

The cadre-points corresponding to the sets $X_{ij}$ will be arranged on the cadre R as illustrated below:

$$\begin{matrix} \rho_{11} & \rho_{12} & \rho_{13} \\ \rho_{21} & \rho_{22} & \rho_{23} \\ \rho_{31} & \rho_{32} & \rho_{33} \end{matrix}$$

For the sake of shortness the elements $\underline{x} \in \Omega$ will be denoted by the indices obtained as the decimal representation of the binary numbers ordered in the way given below:

$$i = [x_{11}, x_{12}, x_{13}, \ldots, x_{33}]_{10} .$$

Thus, for example, the element

$$\underline{x} = \begin{bmatrix} 1 & 0 & 0 \\ 0 & 1 & 0 \\ 0 & 0 & 1 \end{bmatrix}$$

will be denoted by $\underline{x}_i$ where

$$i = 1.2^8 + 0.2^7 + 0.2^6 + 0.2^5 + 1.2^4 + 0.2^3 + 0.2^2 + 0.2^1 + 1.2^0 =$$
$$= 256 + 16 + 1 = 273.$$

The subsets of the elements will be represented by the subsets of the corresponding indices.

We shall describe a distinctive relation corresponding to a vertical line going through the given fragment of the cadre. First of all, the subset consisting of the elements:

$$\underline{x}_{292} = \begin{bmatrix} 1 & 0 & 0 \\ 1 & 0 & 0 \\ 1 & 0 & 0 \end{bmatrix}, \quad \underline{x}_{146} = \begin{bmatrix} 0 & 1 & 0 \\ 0 & 1 & 0 \\ 0 & 1 & 0 \end{bmatrix}, \quad \underline{x}_{73} = \begin{bmatrix} 0 & 0 & 1 \\ 0 & 0 & 1 \\ 0 & 0 & 1 \end{bmatrix},$$

will be checked as a class of equivalence $0' = \{292,146,73\}$ preferred to the other ones.

The next class of equivalence will consist of the elements:

$$\underline{x}_{164} = \begin{bmatrix} 0&1&0 \\ 1&0&0 \\ 1&0&0 \end{bmatrix}, \quad \underline{x}_{276} = \begin{bmatrix} 1&0&0 \\ 0&1&0 \\ 1&0&0 \end{bmatrix}, \quad \underline{x}_{290} = \begin{bmatrix} 1&0&0 \\ 1&0&0 \\ 0&1&0 \end{bmatrix},$$

$$\underline{x}_{274} = \begin{bmatrix} 1&0&0 \\ 0&1&0 \\ 0&1&0 \end{bmatrix}, \quad \underline{x}_{162} = \begin{bmatrix} 0&1&0 \\ 1&0&0 \\ 0&1&0 \end{bmatrix}, \quad \underline{x}_{148} = \begin{bmatrix} 0&1&0 \\ 0&1&0 \\ 1&0&0 \end{bmatrix},$$

$$\underline{x}_{82} = \begin{bmatrix} 0&0&1 \\ 0&1&0 \\ 0&1&0 \end{bmatrix}, \quad \underline{x}_{138} = \begin{bmatrix} 0&1&0 \\ 0&0&1 \\ 0&1&0 \end{bmatrix}, \quad \underline{x}_{145} = \begin{bmatrix} 0&1&0 \\ 0&1&0 \\ 0&0&1 \end{bmatrix},$$

$$\underline{x}_{137} = \begin{bmatrix} 0&1&0 \\ 0&0&1 \\ 0&0&1 \end{bmatrix}, \quad \underline{x}_{81} = \begin{bmatrix} 0&0&1 \\ 0&1&0 \\ 0&0&1 \end{bmatrix}, \quad \underline{x}_{74} = \begin{bmatrix} 0&0&1 \\ 0&0&1 \\ 0&1&0 \end{bmatrix}.$$

The class will be denoted by $0'' = \{290,276,274,164,162,148,145,138,137,82,81,74\}$. The other elements will form the next class of equivalence; let us denote it by $0'''$.

Any class of equivalence can be unfolded into the subclasses. For the first class we shall have, for example:

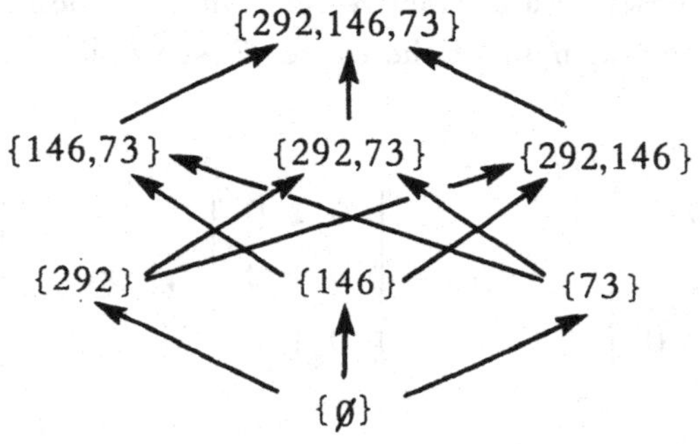

The expanded tree for the second will consist of 13 levels obtained in a similar way. The last class of equivalence, consisting of $2^9 - 12 - 3 = 497$ elements can be unfolded into a tree consisting of 498 levels. Once more it becomes clear that the full graph could not be designed. However, it is not necessary, so as the construction of the graph is rather standard for the natural semi-ordering of subsets. The distinction should be also symmetrical with respect to the subclasses of the elements forming any fixed level of the tree obtained of any given class of equivalence. Let us remind that any set $\Omega$ and a family B of subsets of the set $\Omega$ form a hypergraph

$$\Gamma = [\Omega, B]$$

in the Claude Berge's sense. Thus, any class of equivalence can be also represented by a natural hypergraph with the nodes corresponding to the subclasses of the given class. Graphically it can be represented by a column consisting of the shelves, any shelf corresponding to the subclasses consisting of the given number of elements. The full hypergraph corresponding to the class of equivalence 0' and all its possible subclasses can be thus shortly represented in the form:

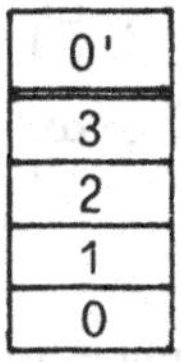


where the shelf denoted by "2" stands, for exanple, for the following subclasses consisting of two elements: {292,146}, {292,73}, {146,73}. However, the hypergraph gives us no information about the relations between the subsets $\omega \in B_\Omega$ excepting the cases when they are naturally ordered by inclusion. That is why we shall represent the distinctive relations by ordered graphs rather using the above-defined columns for short representation of their subgraphs corresponding to the naturally ordered subfamilies of the classes of equivalence. The graph thus will be given in the form

$$\Gamma = [B_\Omega, L] \tag{18}$$

where L is a set of ordered pairs of the subsets $\omega_i$, $\omega_j \in B_\Omega$. It will be given in the form of a disjunction

(19) $$L = L' \cup L'',$$

where L' consists of all the pairs of subsets naturally ordered, that is

(20) $$L' = \{l_{ij} : \omega_i \subset \omega_j , \omega_i , \omega_j \in B_\Omega\} ,$$

and L" consists of the ordered pairs of subsets that satisfy to the relation

(21) $$\omega_i < \omega_j$$

by other purposes. In particular, we shall put

(22) $$L'' = L_1'' \cup L_2''$$

where

(23) $$L_1'' = \{ l_{ij} : \omega_i = 0'' , \omega_j = \{\underline{x}_j\} , \underline{x}_j \in 0' \} ,$$

(24) $$L_2'' = \{ l_{ij} : \omega_i = 0''' , \omega_j = \{\underline{x}_j\} , \underline{x}_j \in 0''\} ,$$

0" and 0"' being the classes of equivalence and 0' being the complementary subset. The last two assumptions thus give us • the rule of semi-ordering of the subsets belonging to the classes 0',0" and 0"', which can be also illustrated by the following schema:

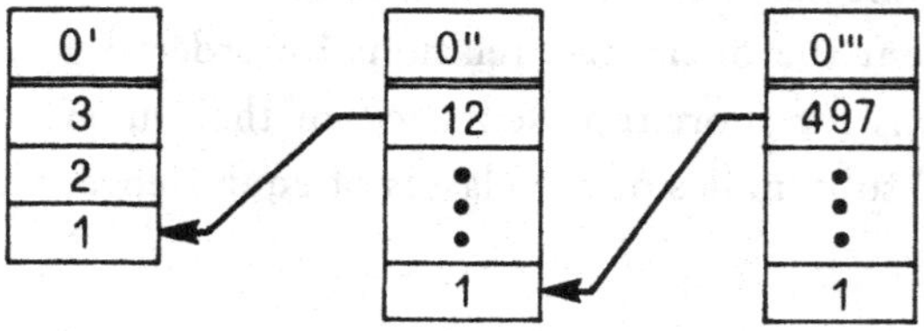

Taking, for example, the subsets:

$\{292,73\}$ and $\{274,162,148,82,74\}$

the first one belonging to the shelf "2" of 0' and the second one - to the shelf "5" of 0" we find easily that

$\{274,162,148,82,74\} < \{292,73\}$

If the distinctive relation is generated by a probability measure, the last statement would be interpreted as

$$P\{\underline{x}_{274}, \underline{x}_{162}, \underline{x}_{148}, \underline{x}_{82}, \underline{x}_{74}\} \leqslant P\{\underline{x}_{292}, \underline{x}_{73}\} .$$

It is clear now, that the main information about the classes of images is given by the set of L" of pairwise relations between the subsets of the images, the relations belonging to L' being possible to be generated automatically on the basis of the inclusions of the subsets.

Let us go back to the distinctive relation $r_\pi$ given by the expression (10). We shall take into account a subset $\omega^o \in B_\Omega$ and a family of subsets

$$B_{\Omega|\omega^o} = \{\omega : \omega = \omega' \cap \omega^o, \omega' \in B_\Omega\} . \tag{25}$$

It is clear that $B_{\Omega|\omega^o} \subset B_\Omega$ and it is a sigma-algebra of subsets of the set $\omega^o$.

**Theorem**

The semi-ordering relation $\pi$ generates also a semi-ordering relation $\pi^o$ in the family of subsets $B_{\Omega|\omega^o}$ satisfying to the conditions (8),(9).

**Proof**

So as for any subsets $\omega_i$, $\omega_j \in B_{\Omega|\omega^o}$ the relations $\omega_i$, $\omega_j \in B_\Omega$ also hold, it becomes clear that the possible relations $\omega_i < \omega_j$ and $\omega_j < \omega_i$, if fulfilled, satisfy to the conditions of reciprocity, asymmetricity and transitivity and thus the subfamily of subsets $B_{\Omega|\omega^o}$ is also semi-ordered.

For any $\omega \in B_{\Omega|\omega^o}$ the relation

$$\omega \subset \omega^o$$

holds and thus

$$\phi < \omega < \omega^{o}. \tag{26}$$

So as for any $\omega_i$ , $\omega_j \in B_\Omega$ the relations

$$\omega_i , \omega_j < \omega_i \cup \omega_j$$

hold, it is also satisfied

$$\omega_i \cap \omega^{o}, \omega_j \cap \omega^{o} < (\omega_i \cap \omega^{o}) \cup (\omega_j \cap \omega^{o}) \tag{27}$$

which completes the theorem.

**Definition 2**

For a semi-ordering relation $r_{\pi^o}$ generated by a fixed subset $\omega^o$ the ordered three elements

$$\pi^{o} = \{[X_{ij}] , B_{\Omega|\omega^o} , r_{\pi^o}\} \tag{28}$$

will be called a conditional distinctive relation described on the family of sets $[X_{ij}]$ for fixed $\omega^o$.

## IV. Composite Distinctive Relations

The formalism of distinctive relations can be used for the description and recognition of composite patterns. The compositeness of the patterns can be considered practically (as a certain level of technical difficulties connected with pictures processing) as well as in a theoretical sense suggesting a certain kind of relations existing in the semantical field S or in the image-space $\Omega$. In any case it means that the algorithms of images processing will consist of several functionally distinguished blocks, as for example:

a) optical transformation images,
b) input discretization and quantization,
c) input filtering,
d) integral parameters measurements,
e) recognition of local features,
f) recognition of higher-order features,
g) total description or recognition

Our attention will be mainly paid to the blocks e) and f) as the most typical ones for the composite patterns recognition.

There will be taken into account a cartesian product

$$\Xi = S \times \Omega \tag{1}$$

S being a semantical field and $\Omega$ being an image-space. There will be supposed that a preliminary analysis of the recognition problem or a series of "learning" experiments gave us some indications making it possible to describe a distinctive relation r in the space $\Xi$ . This means that the space $\Xi$ has been partitioned into a certain number of subclasses of equivalence

$$\Xi = \bigcup_k \Xi^k \tag{2}$$

and there are given also some suggestions concerning the relative preferences between the subclasses. The ordered pairs

$$\xi = [\sigma, \underline{x}] \tag{3}$$

belonging to the first subclass $\Xi^1$ will be supposed to be preferred with respect to the other pairs belonging to other subclasses. The principle of semiordering thus can be illustrated by the schema given below

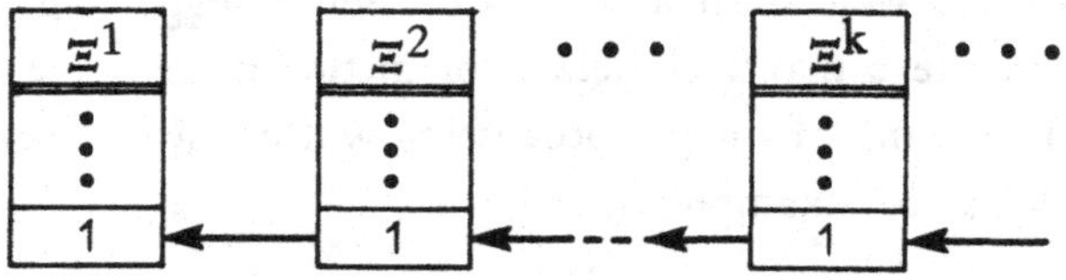


(the principle is here somewhat different of this one presented in the former lecture; as it has been already said, in both cases the semi-ordering relation reflects our state of knowledge about the patterns representants in the image space, thus, it remains in some sense arbitrary).

Suppose, it has been observed that the image is

(4) $$\underline{x} = \underline{x}_i$$

Fixing the second component in (3) we shall take into account a subset

(5) $$\Xi(\underline{x}_i) = \{\xi : \xi = [\sigma, \underline{x}_i], \sigma \in B_S\}$$

Now, the conditional distinctive relation $r(\underline{x}_i)$ (see the Definition 2 in the former lecture) should be taken into account instead of the original relation r. We shall fix the number of elements in the classes of equivalence, for example, we demand to deal with the one-element subsets $\omega$ only. Thus, we shall look for the most preferable subclass of equivalence containing the one-element subsets. Let it be the following one:

$$[\sigma_a, \underline{x}_i], [\sigma_b, \underline{x}_i], \ldots, [\sigma_c, \underline{x}_i].$$

The patterns $\sigma_a, \sigma_b, \ldots, \sigma_c$ are the recognized patterns. So as they belong to the same class of equivalence, no further distinction between them is possible until the distinctive relation r holds.

This general schema of pattern recognition reminds us of the well known principles of statistical inference; we can really reach the likelihood schema or the a posteriori probability one under some additional assumptions concerning the semi- ordering relation based on the corresponding probability measures. However, the main problem consists in the fact that the general method cannot be used directly when the composite patterns are dealt with. Digitial computers which are rather typical tools of picture processing usually operate in a sequential manner. Thus, the image $\underline{x}$ is analysed part by part and its total recognition is a result of a synthesing procedure based on the results of the former stages of analysis.

Let us suppose that R' and R'' are some subareas of the cadre R, not obviously disjoint, as illustrated below:

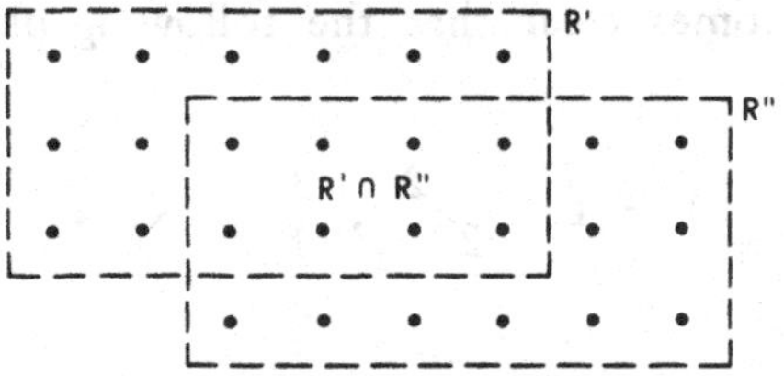


It is clear that the geometrical objects $\underline{x}'$ and $\underline{x}''$ observed independently on R' and R'' should have identical components belonging to the cross-section R' ∩ R''. Thus, whatever is the interpretation of the images observed on R' and R'', the geometrical sense $\sigma'$ assigned to the first and $\sigma''$ assigned to the second one should be consistent. If, for example, R' and R'' are situated as illustrated before and a section of a line from NW toward SE has been detected in R', then the objects being extrapolated out of the SE end of the line-section will be preferred on the R'' sub-area, the next NW-SE line-section being the most preferable one. This simple example thus leads us to a more general principle of concatentation on the plane:

- if $\sigma^{(1)}, \sigma^{(2)}, \dots, \sigma^{(k)}, \dots$ are the geometrical meanings assigned to the images observed on the sub-areas $R^{(1)}, R^{(2)}, \dots, R^{(k)}, \dots \subset R$, then the meanings must be consistent in the sense that they cannot lead to contradictory geometrical statements on the cross-sections of the sub-areas.

This principle seems quite evident, however it has also some linguistic consequence. Suppose, the geometrical patterns can be represented by some planar expressions consisting of the symbols of an alphabet A disposed on the plane in the points corresponding to the centers of the corresponding sub-areas. Suppose, the alphabet A consists of the following symbols (given here with their geometrical interpretation under the assumption that the geometrical objects represent some distinct line-objects):

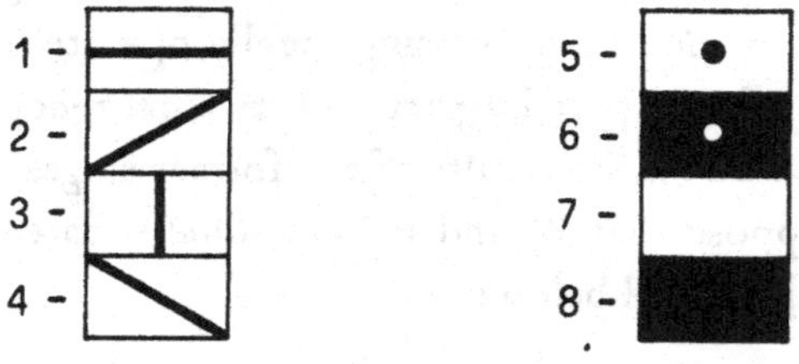


Now, it becomes clear that the following planar concatenations are admissible:

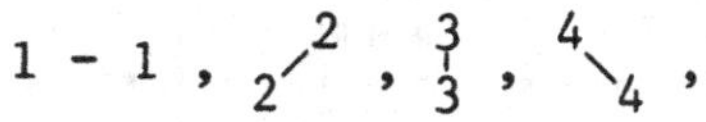


as well as all possible concatenations of 1,2,3 and 4 with 6 and 8 and all possible concatenations of 5 and 7. The concatenations of 1,2,3 and 4 and 5 and 7 are admissible under the assumption that the line is broken off; this means that the symbolical representation is an approximation of a real geometrical object. Other concatenations like, for example:

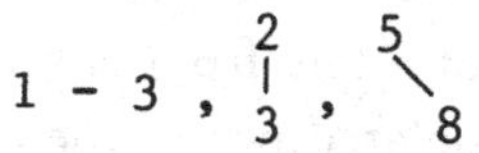


etc. will be prohibited. So as we have four possible mutual dislocations of the sub-areas of rectangular form (partially overlapping) and any one of them can be filled with one of the eight symbols of the alphabet A, we have $4.8^2 = 256$ possible concatenations and the above described rules introduce a distinctive relation into this set of concatenations. Thus, we obtain a sort of grammar governing in the space of planar symbolical expressions corresponding to the semantical field S of fine geometrical structures on the plane. For example, a following geometrical structure will have the corresponding symbolical representation:

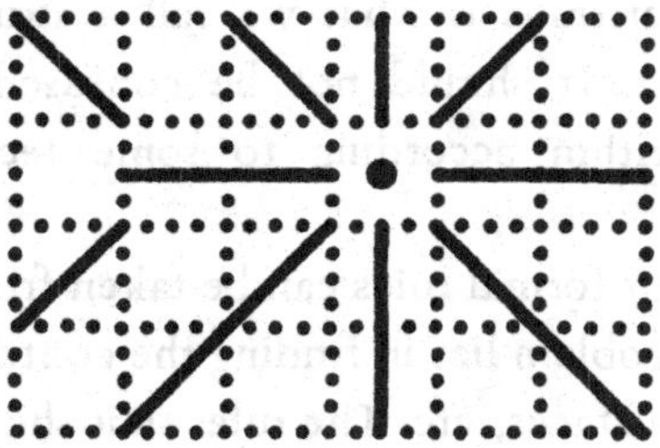

| | | | | | |
|---|---|---|---|---|---|
| 4 | 7 | 4 | 3 | 2 | 7 |
| 7 | 1 | 1 | 5 | 1 | 1 |
| 2 | 7 | 2 | 3 | 4 | 7 |
| 7 | 2 | 7 | 3 | 7 | 4 |

We can neglect now the geometrical interpretation of the symbolical expressions and to consider them as some formal expressions constructed according to some rules. The rules are given here in the form of distinctive relations. They can be specified, if necessary, into some strictly logical or into probabilistic rules. In other situations the principles of semi-ordering may be arbitrary. For example, if there are considered the symbolical expressions of given dimensions and there is given the number n of all possible concatenations between the symbols the expressions consist of, the set of all possible expressions will be partitioned into classes of equivalence as follows:

1°. The lowest class consists of the expressions containing at least one concatenation fully prohibited;

2°. There is prescribed a weight 1 to the concatenations conditionally admissible and the weight 2 to the concatenations fully admissible; any class of equivalence consists of all the symbolical expressions of given dimensions having the same ratio

$$\eta = \frac{w}{n}, \qquad (6)$$

where w is a total weight of concatenations of the given expression. The higher is the ratio $\eta$, the more preferable is the expression in the distinctive relation sense.

There is no reason in limiting our considerations to the concatenations only. It can be supposed that, in general, the elements of $B_S$ satisfy to a set of formal rules which make it possible to introduce a distinctive relation $\pi_S$ into the set of geometrical meanings. The pattern recognition algorithms should reconstruct the rules and relations governing in the semantical field (no other semantical sense of the pictures is being here suspected to exist but the geometrical one, however, this simplification does not change the general approach to the problem presented here). This supposition concerning the parallelism existing between the formal structure of patterns and this one of the recognition algorithms is what we call a structural approach to the pattern recognition problem. It should not be confused with choosing a particular structure of the algorithm according to some technical preassumptions.

A typical example of other kinds of formal rules can be taken from the field of crystallographical investigations. The problem lies in finding the contours of the grains, finding their maximum diameters, surfaces, etc. The rules that should be taken into account are the following:

1° any geometrical object is a contour or it is a line without branchings with the ends laying on the contour of the cadre;

2° the contours and the lines cannot intersect each with each other.

A typical example is given below:

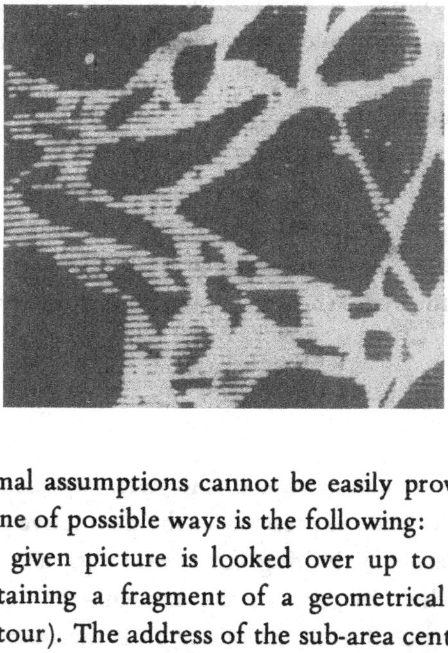

The formal assumptions cannot be easily proven if the above described alphabet A is used. One of possible ways is the following:

1° The given picture is looked over up to finding the first sub-area containing a fragment of a geometrical object (a fragment of a contour). The address of the sub-area center is put down into a list.

2° There are identified, step by step, the other sub-areas containing the extrapolated fragments of the contour under consideration. The addresses of the sub-areas are put down into the list together with the symbols indicating the type of local geometrical structures.

3° The procedure is continued up to reaching the contour of the cadre or up to reaching the address of the first found sub-area crossed by the contour.

4° The procedure is repeated; the addresses of the sub-areas already looked over are omitted while the next contours are analysed.

5° The procedure is ended when no other sub-area remains being not proven.

The main disadvantage of the above-described procedure lies in the fact that full description of the geometrical objects the pattern consists of must be taken in the memory up to the last stage of pattern analysis. A slight modification of the alphabet A makes it possible to prove the formal correctness of the pattern without overloading the memory. This needs introducing several new symbols corresponding to the line-ends of different direction as well as some branching-points:

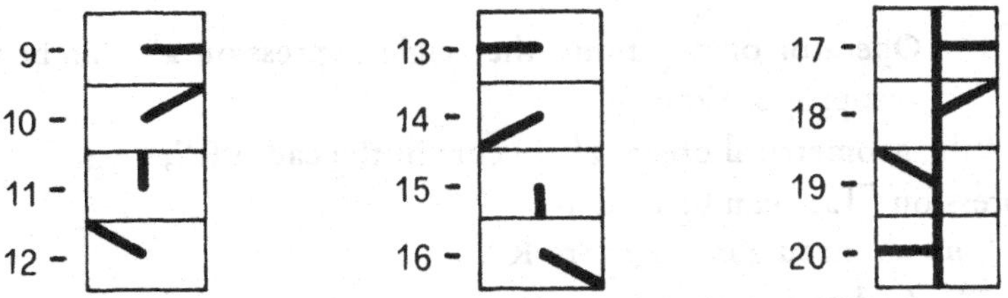


etc. Now, the formal demands are the following:

1° no symbols of the 9,10,11, etc., types are admissible inside the cadre R;

2° the symbols 9,10,...,16 are admissible on the contour of the cadre R only.

The two restrictions can be proven easily all over the cadre R without remembering the symbols belonging to the other sub-areas of the cadre.

Planar symbolical expressions are rather inconvenient for machine-processing. That is why we shall look for a linear language representing the same area of geometrical meanings as the planar one. We shall use the same basic alphabet (can be enlarged) A. However, some new symbols corresponding to the basic relations in the semantical field will be introduced..

The basic fact that a local attribute, say $a^i$, occurs in the sub- area $R^{(k)}$, may be coded as, for example, $a^i(k)$,. Thus, the planar expression can be directly translated into a linear one having the form:

$$a^{i_1}(1),\ a^{i_2}(2),\ a^{i_3}(3),\dots$$

However, this kind of representation is rather tremendous and redundant. The exact position of a geometrical object in the cadre may be of very little importance in comparison with the proper features of the object. On the other hand, an observation that two symbols like $a^{i}(k')$, and $a^{i''}(k'')$ satisfy to the condition of concatenation needs some additional analysis of the total expression: finding out the symbols corresponding to the neighbour addresses and analysing their geometrical meanings. The necessity of a higher-order linear language for the description of geometrical objects seems rather evident.

We shall define a number of geometrical operators that project the set of "simple" geometrical objects represented by the symbols of the alphabet A into a set of higher-order geometrical objects. The operators can be divided into several classes, according to the number of their arguments. Several examples will be given below.

1° Operator of negation: the single expression $a^i$ can be interpreted as a proposition:

"the geometrical object $a^i$ occurs in the cadre R";

thus the expression $\neg a^i$ can be read as:

" no $a^i$ occurs in the cadre R".

2° Addressing operator: $\gamma_k a^i$ can be read as:

"the geometrical object $a^i$ occurs in the k-th sub-area of the cadre R".

The expression $\gamma_k \neg a^i$ as well as $\neg \gamma a^i$ will have the sense that can be obtained immediately from the above-given examples.

3° Logical operators of alternative $\wedge$ and disjunction $\vee$ will have the usually used sense.

4° Mutual position operators:

$b'(a^i, a^j)$ – "$a^i$ on the left side of $a^j$",

$b''(a^i, a^j)$ – "$a^i$ above $a^j$",

$b'''(a^i, a^j)$ – "$a^i$ near $a^j$"

etc. The operators: "on the right side", "beyond", "far" etc. can be defined using the above-given ones and the negation operator.

5° Operator of continuity:

$c(a^i, a^j, \dots, a^p)$ – "$a^i, a^j, \dots, a^p$ belong to the same compact geometrical object".

6° General disposition operators:

$g(a^i, a^j, \ldots, a^p)$ - "$a^i, a^j, \ldots, a^p$ lie on a clock-wise oriented contour",

$g'(a^i, a^j, \ldots, a^p; \alpha, \beta)$ - "$a^i, a^j, \ldots, a^p$ lie along a line characterized by the parameters $\alpha$, $\beta$".

Other possibilities are connected with the properties of some spatially spread geometrical objects. If the symbols $d^i$, $d^j$, ..., $d^q \in A$ are assigned to this kind of geometrical objects, then the following operators will be useful:

7° The half-addressing operators:

$\delta_k d^i$ — "the geometrical object $d^i$ occurs in the k-th part of the cadre R", the "part" being defined as a higher-order sub-area (like the half or the quarter of the cadre).

8° The class of mutual-position operators can be completed now by the one $b(d^p; a^i, \ldots, a^q)$ - "the geometrical objects $a^i$, $a^j$, ..., $a^q$ occur on the background $d^p$".

A typical example is a trychina spiral on the strand background of a microscopic cytological section.

The list will be completed by some auxiliary operators like the operator of denomination: $\overset{d}{=}$. It can be used as follows:

$$f^i \overset{d}{=} Q \tag{7}$$

where Q is a formal expression consisting of the basic symbols of the alphabet A, operators and the proper names of the geometrical objects already defined using the operator of denomination. If the expression Q is formally right, then $f^i$ becomes a proposition read as

"the geometrical object $f^i$ occurs in the cadre R".

Any operator acting on the well-defined geometrical arguments becomes a proposition.

Any expression consisting of the proposition connected by the logical operators becomes a proposition.

These simple rules are the basis of a formal language L suitable for the description of geometrical objects included by the set of patterns $B_S$.

The language has been proposed according to some rather heuristic preassumptions. Till now, no effective method of optimization of the problem-oriented languages exists.

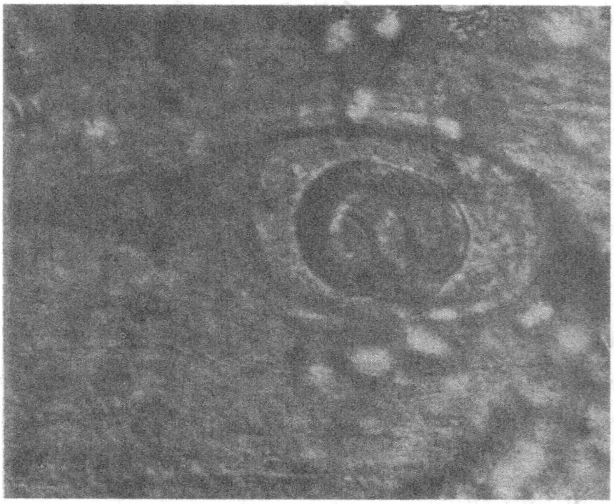

## V. Formal Analysis of Composite Pictures

The linear language L* plays a role of a common tool for the representation of the patterns as well as of the recognized geometrical objects. Two main problems are arising there:

1° the technical problem of pictures indexing in the terms of the language L*;

2° the more basic problem of proving the equivalence of some formal expressions in the language L* possibly describing the same pattern but using different terms.

The standard methods used for the local attributes detection are usually based on the principle of distance or angle measurements in a signal space between the vectors representing the input signals and some standard representants of the patterns. An alternative method consists in performing some arithmetical calculations and logical tests on the input signal components. Both above-mentioned methods have been described many times and they will not be presented here in any more detailed way. In any case an input signal $\underline{x}$ after some first stages of images processing can be represented by a list of addressed attributes:

$$\underline{y} = \left[ a^{i_k}\ (k) \right], \quad a^i \in A, \quad k \in K, \tag{1}$$

K being a linearly ordered set of the indices assigned to the sub-areas $R^{(k)} \subset R$ into which the total cadre R has been partitioned. In order to avoid some difficulties with the unconsistency of the recognized local geometrical attributes the sub-areas $R^{(k)}$ are usually chosen somewhat overlapping, the decisions being made on ther central parts only. being strictly tangent each to each other, as indicated below:

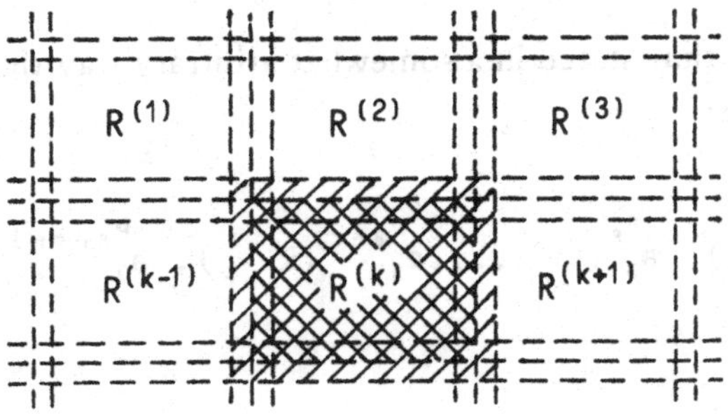


From a computational point of view it seems sometimes reasonable to keep the results (1) in the computer memory in the form of lists:

(2) $$1^{(n)}(\underline{x}) = \left[ a_n^{i_k}(k) \right] \quad a_n^i \in A_n$$

$A_n \subset A$ being a sub-alphabet of the values of the attribute detected by the indexing function $h_n$. This form of representation makes it possible passing to the concatenation of the picture compact fragments.

Let us take, for example, into account a list of the $a_3$ -attributes (the sections of vertical lines) detected in a picture $\underline{x}$:

$$1^{(3)}(\underline{x}) = \left[ a_3^{i_k}(k) \right], \quad a_3^i \in A_3 \ ,$$

where the sub-alphabet $A_3$ contains the symbols of classes of equivalence of the subvectors $\underline{x}' \subset \underline{x}$ having the property of containing a vertical line in the corresponding sub-area $R^{(k)}$ with the given level of certainty, like:

$a_3^3$ - "surely vertical",
$a_3^2$ - "possibly vertical",
$a_3^1$ - "doubtfully vertical".
$a_3^0$ - "evidently not vertical".

The list $1^{(3)}$ $(\underline{x})$ now can be analysed along the columns formed by the sub-areas correspondingly displaced in the cadre R. Let a typical column have the addresses of the sub-areas disposed each over each other one:

$$k_1, k_2, k_3, \ldots, k_m, \ldots$$

It can be thus stated in a somewhat arbitrary way that having a "block" of attribute values like:

$$a_3^{p_{s-1}}(k_{s-1}),\ a_3^{p_s}(k_s),\ \ldots,\ a_3^{p_{s+r}}(k_{s+r}),\ a_3^{p_{s+r+1}}(k_{s+r+1})$$

such that, for example,

$$a_3^{p_{s+t}}(k_{s+t}) \in \{a_3^3, a_3^2\} \text{ for all } 1 \leq t \leq r,$$

$$a_3^{p_s}(k_s),\ a_3^{p_{s+r+1}}(k_{s+r+1}) \in \{a_3^1, a_3^0\},$$

a new attribute of the picture $\underline{x}$ will be put down into a list $1^{(3)^\circ}(\underline{x})$ of all detected sections of vertical lines of any length (let us remark the difference between $1^{(3)^\circ}(\underline{x})$ and the list $1^{(3)}(\underline{x})$ which contained only the local vertical fragments). The new attribute ("containing a vertical fragment of a line between the sub-areas $R^{(k_s)}$ and $R^{(k_{s+r})}$) can be denoted as $a_3(k_s, k_{s+r})$.

After the concatenation the former list $1^{(3)}(\underline{x})$ can be destroyed. Similar technique can be also used for the other local attributes; the original picture $\underline{x}$ is thus represented by several lists of uniform compact geometrical fragments, a proper name (a proper symbol) being assigned to a fragment, if necessary.

The next stage of concatenation consists in a cross-examination of the lists in order to detect the higher-order concatenations between the uniform geometrical fragments. This can be illustrated by the following

**Example 1**

Suppose, there are given the lists of uniform geometrical fragments corresponding to the basic four directions of the lines:

$$1^{(1)^\circ}(\underline{x}) = [\ldots, a_1(k_1, k_2), \ldots, a_1(k_6, k_7), \ldots, a_1(k_{11}, k_{12}), \ldots],$$
$$1^{(2)^\circ}(\underline{x}) = [\ldots, a_2(k_5, k_6), \ldots, a_2(k_{10}, k_9), \ldots],$$
$$1^{(3)^\circ}(\underline{x}) = [\ldots, a_3(k_2, k_3), \ldots, a_3(k_4, k_5), \ldots, a_3(k_9, k_8), \ldots, a_3(k_{11}, k_{10}), \ldots],$$
$$1^{(4)^\circ}(\underline{x}) = [\ldots, a_4(k_3, k_4), \ldots, a_4(k_8, k_7), \ldots]$$

Looking over the lists and comparing the addresses we can detect the higher-order concatenations. They can be illustrated by a schema:

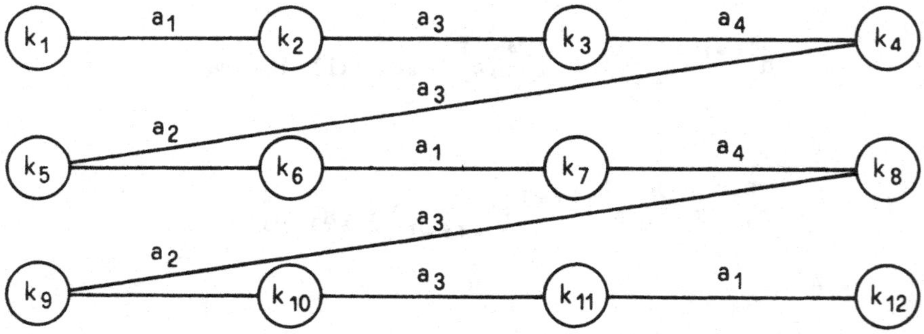


It can be easily proven analytically that there has been obtained an opened compact linear geometrical structure. It can be characterized by the "spectrum" consisting of the orderd names of the attributes:

$$C = [a_1, a_3, a_4, a_3, a_2, a_1, a_4, a_3, a_2, a_3, a_1]$$

This last can be used as a characteristic of the linear geometrical object under some additional assumptions. These are connected with the fact that some short sections of the curve may not be essential from its general shape point of view. Therefore, there will be introduced the relative weights of the sections:

(3) $$w_k = \frac{d_k}{\sum_\mu d_\mu}$$

and the components of the spectrum C having the weights under certain threshold level $w^o$ will be omitted. The modified spectrum thus has the form:

(4) $$C' = \left[ a_{\tilde{\imath}_1}, a_{\tilde{\imath}_2}, \ldots, a_{\tilde{\imath}_{m'}} \right]$$

where $[\tilde{\imath}_1, \tilde{\imath}_2, \ldots, \tilde{\imath}_{m'}]$ is a subset of indices corresponding to the components being accepted. Recognition of the curve-shape can thus be performed on the basis of a standard technique (distance or correlation proof) in a space of spectra. It should be remarked that the recognition will be invariant within a comparatively wide class of topological transformations, as illustrated below :

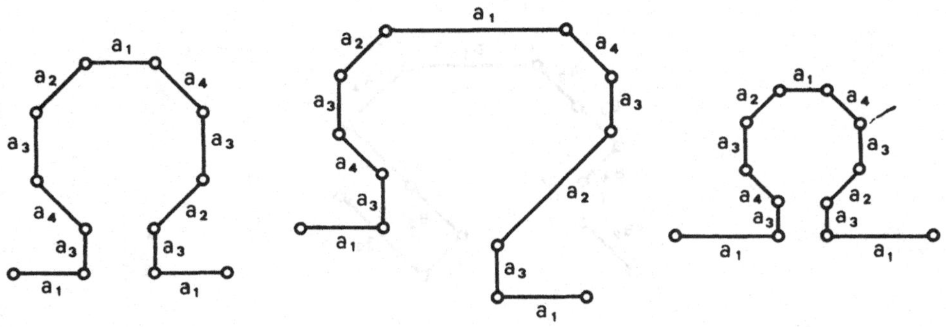

If necessary, the test thus should be completed by some auxiliary (higher-level indexing) tests, for example, taking into account some additional geometrical properties of the curves.

The problem becomes more complicated if the line-slopes cannot be determined exactly because of the influence of random factors (discretization or noise). Instead of a standard spectrum a set of alternative spectra should be taken into account in this case. The situation can be illustrated by a graph:

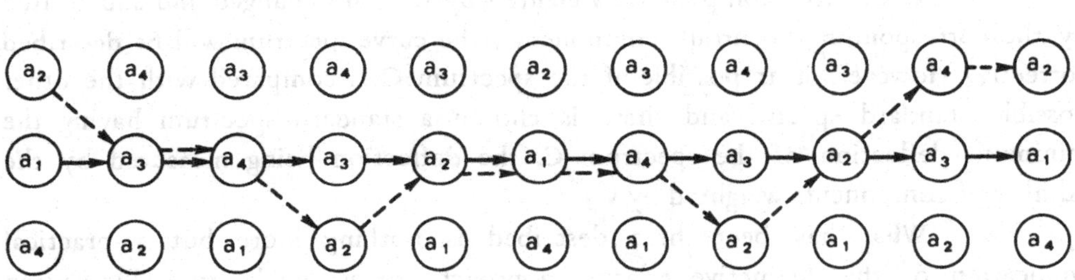


The typical "Ω-looking" curve will be represented by a path going through the central nodes of the graph. The upper and the lower rows of the nodes represent here the local slopes that are deflected of the central one; for example, a spectrum

$$C = [\, a_2 , a_3 , a_4 , a_2 , a_2 , a_1 , a_4 , a_2 , a_2 , a_4 , a_2 \,]$$

represented on the graph by a dotted line, will correspond to a following curve:

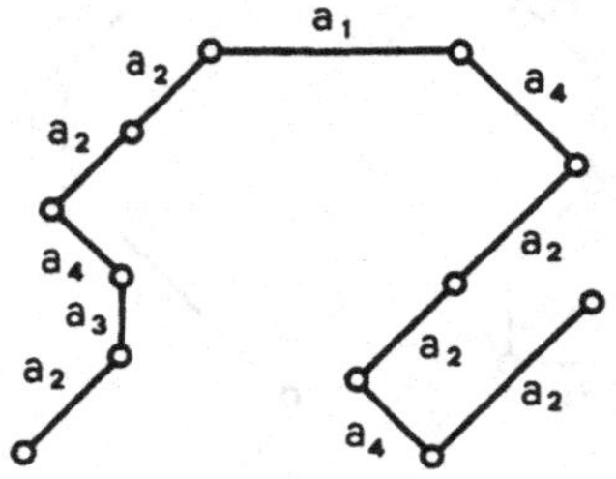


Let us prescribe a weight-coefficient $w_0$ to any node of the central row of the graph and a coefficient $w_1$ to any other node. The spectrum C can thus be weighted as follows:

$$C = \begin{bmatrix} a_2, & a_3, & a_4, & a_2, & a_2, & a_1, & a_4, & a_2, & a_2, & a_4, & a_2 \\ w_1 & w_0 & w_0 & w_1 & w_0 & w_0 & w_0 & w_1 & w_0 & w_1 & w_1 \end{bmatrix}$$

If the five components weighted by $w_1$ are changed and substituted by the corresponding "central" components, the curve-spectrum will be described correctly. However, it is possible if the spectrum C is compared with the other possible standard spectra and there is chosen a standard spectrum having the minimum deflection of the spectrum C, the deflection being measured by the number of components weighted by $w_1$ .

What has been here described is nothing more but a practical application of the distinctive relation approach, so as the heuristically chosen weights define some classes of equivalence in the space $B_S x\, \Omega$ .

Let us go to a somewhat more complicated example of planar symmetrical graphs recognition. The following local attributes are detected on the first level of picture analysis:

$a_1$ - the ends of the lines.

$a_2$ - the higher order ( $\geqslant 3$) nodes,

$a_3$ - the continuous lines (of any shape).

The results of the first-level analysis will be put down into three lists:

$$1^{(1)}(\underline{x}) = [a_1(k_1), a_1(k_2), a_1(k_3), a_1(k_4), a_1(k_5)],$$
$$1^{(2)}(\underline{x}) = [a_2(k_6), a_2(k_7), a_2(k_8)],$$
$$1^{(3)}(\underline{x}) = [a_3(k_1,k_6), a_3(k_2,k_6), a_3(k_3,k_8), a_3(k_4,k_7), a_3(k_5,k_8),$$
$$a_3(k_6,k_7), a_3(k_7,k_8)] \;;$$

The lists are presented here in a rather redundant form. It should be remarked that in general the numerical denotations of the nodes are unessential from the point of view of topological properties of a graph. Therefore, if two graphs are to be compared and the same symbols have been used for denoting their nodes, all possible permutations of the indices of at least one of them should be taken into account, what would lead us to a rather tremendous work.

Therefore, it seems desirable to use a standard method of the graph-nodes denotation. For example, a binary matrix of incidencies of the graph:

$$M = [m_{ij}] \;,$$

$$m_{ij} = \begin{cases} 1, & \text{if the node } 0_i \text{ is directly connected with } 0_j \;, \\ 0, & \text{otherwise} \;, \end{cases} \tag{5}$$

can be rearranged in such a way that a certain functional f(M) is minimized. The order of the rows and columns of the rearranged matrix will also define some standard consecution of the graph-nodes. In this case the algorithm of graph-recognition will contain the following procedures:

1° lower-levels picture processing;

2° finding the incidence-matrix M on the basis of the lists $1^{(1)}(\underline{x})$, $1^{(2)}$, $(\underline{x})$ and $1^{(3)}(\underline{x})$;

3° finding all possible solutions of the numerical problem

$$f(M) = \text{minimum} \tag{6}$$

the minimum being taken over the set of all possible permutations of the matrix rows and columns;

4° remembering of all the equivalent forms M', M'' ,... etc. of the matrix M that minimize the functional f (if the solution is not unique) and comparing the matrices with the standard matrices representing the typical planar graphs of the given order.

The above-given example leads us to a general problem of semantical equivalence of formal expressions of the linear language L*. Even if the indexing function

$$h : \Omega \to L^*$$

is univalued to any fixed pattern $\sigma^*$ there corresponds, usually, a subset $\lambda(\sigma^*)$ of semantically equivalent formally admissible expressions. Therefore, in composite pattern recognition the problem of finding a pattern

$$\sigma^* \in B_S \quad \text{such that}$$
$$h(\underline{x}) \in \lambda(\sigma^*)$$

usually arises, even if the problem of picture indexing has already been solved effectively. From a linguistic point of view two basic approaches to the problem are possible:

1 finding a transformative grammar for the language L* such that for any expression $\underline{a} \in L^*$ all possible formally and semantically equivalent expressions are obtained;

2 finding a generative grammar for the language L* such that for any fixed semantical meaning (a hypothesis about the picture under consideration) the set $\lambda(\sigma^*)$ of the corresponding expressions can be generated in order to be consecutively compared with the given expression $\underline{a}$.

Both approaches are valuable in the practice of pattern recognition. The second one has also a following aspect. So as most of the lower-level recognition algorithms are based on the principle of the received picture comparison with the standard ones, the problem arises of generating the standards dynamically instead of keeping them in the memory of a computer.

Let us take into account the following practical problem. For some biological investigations it was necessary to classify the biological cells visible under the microscope according to the ratio:

$$b = \frac{z_n}{z}$$

where $z_n$ stands for the surface of a nucleus of a given cell and z denotes the total surface of the cell planar projection. In order to have both the surfaces measured (so as their contours are usually rather irregular) it became necessary to reconstruct the cell- and nucleous-contours. Therefore, the problem arised of generating all possible sequences of the symbols:

$$a^{i_1}, a^{i_2}, \dots, a^{i_k}, \dots \in A$$

corresponding to the sub-areas $R^{(k)} \subset R$ of the cadre and satisfying to the following conditions:

1° of concatenation,
2° of representing the line - objects only,
3° of containing no points of the first category,
4° of envelopping the shadows visible on the picture as close as possible.

The experiments with this class of algorithms were made in the Institute of Applied Cybernetics of the Polish Academy of Sciences (Warsaw, Poland).

## APPENDIX

### Several Properties of the Coincidence Matrices

Any finite semi-ordered set $\Omega$ can be represented by a matrix of coincidence:

(1) $$M = [m_{ij}] \ , \quad i,j \in [\overline{1,N}]$$

(2) $$m_{ij} \in \{0,1\} \ ,$$

where

(3) $$(m_{ij} = 1) \Leftrightarrow [\,(x_i < x_j) \wedge \neg \exists (k)\,(x_i < x_k < x_j \ \wedge x_i \not\approx x_k \vee x_j \not\approx x_k)] . \quad i,j \in [\overline{1,N}]$$

The matrices of coincidence should satisfy to the following rules

(4) $$M' + M'' = M = [m_{ij}] \ ,$$

where

(4a) $$m_{ij} = m'_{ij} + m''_{ij} \ ,$$

$m'_{ij}$ and $m''_{ij}$ being the elements of the matrices M' and M'', correspondingly, and the basic operations on them being taken in a logical sense:

(5)

| + | 0 | 1 |
|---|---|---|
| 0 | 0 | 1 |
| 1 | 1 | 1 |

| . | 0 | 1 |
|---|---|---|
| 0 | 0 | 0 |
| 1 | 0 | 1 |

(6) $$M' \cdot M'' = M = [m_{ij}] \ ,$$

where

$$m_{ij} = \sum_{k=1}^{N} m'_{ik} \cdot m''_{kj} , \tag{6a}$$

both summation and multiplication being taken in logical sense.

According to the reciprocity property of semi-ordering it is also clear that in the coincidence matrix

$$m_{ii} = 1 \text{ for any } i \in [\overline{1,N}] \tag{7}$$

For any coincidence matrix M and for any integer n the matrix $M^n$ is also a coincidence matrix. The element

$$m_{ij}^{(n)} = 1$$

corresponds to the pair of nodes $[0_i , 0_j]$ of a graph $\Gamma$ such that $0_i$ is connected with $0_j$ by an oriented path of the length (the number of edges) equal to n. Therefore, the matrix $M^{|\Omega|}$ , where $|\Omega|$ is a cardinal number of the set $\Omega$, represents the semi-ordering relations between all the elements of the set $\Omega$ . In particular,

$$m_{ij}^{(\Omega)} = 0$$

if and only if

$$x_i \not\lessgtr x_j$$

and

$$m_{ij}^{(\Omega)} = 1$$

if

$$x_i < x_j .$$

The matrix $M^{|\Omega|}$ will be called a full-coincidence matrix. The problem arises if given a full-coincidence matrix M' any coincidence matrix M corresponding to M' can be also found. The answer is given by the following

**Theorem**

The necessary and sufficient condition for a binary square matrix M' to be a full-coincidence one is that:

(8) a) $$m'_{ii} = 1 \text{ for all } i \in [\overline{1,N}]$$

N being the dimension of the matrix M',

b) for any $i,j,\dots,k,l \in [\overline{1,N}]$

(9) $$(m_{ij} = 1) \wedge \dots \wedge (m_{kl} = 1) \Rightarrow (m_{il} = 1).$$

**Proof**

The condition a) is evident, so as M' should be a coincidence matrix.

The necessity of the condition b) follows from the fact that if for any coincidence matrix there exists a series of coefficients:

(10) $$m_{i_1 i_2},\ m_{i_2 i_3},\ m_{i_3 i_4},\ \dots,\ m_{i_{k-1} i_k} = 1,$$

then for the second, third and all other powers of this matrix there will be

(11a) $$m^{(2)}_{i_1 i_3} = m^{(2)}_{i_2 i_4} = \dots = m^{(2)}_{i_{k-2} i_k} = 1,$$

(11b) $$m^{(3)}_{i_1 i_4} = m^{(3)}_{i_2 i_5} = \dots = m^{(3)}_{i_{k-3} i_k} = 1,$$

..............................

(11c) $$m^{(n)}_{i_1 i_{n+1}} = \dots = m^{(n)}_{i_{k-n} i_k} = 1 .$$

Therefore, the full-coincidence matrix can be obtained by consecutive multiplication (in logical sense) of a coincidence matrix, for which the left- side of (9) holds. This completes the theorem.

Let M' be a full-coincidence matrix. We shall fix a subset $\omega'$ of its column-indices and we shall take into account a subset $\omega''$ of the rows:

$$\omega'' = \{i : \exists(j)(j \in \omega', m'_{ij} = 1)\}. \tag{12}$$

There will be taken into account a subset of indices

$$\omega = \omega' \cup \omega'' \tag{13}$$

and if M is a coincidence matrix corresponding to the full coincidence matrix M', there will also be taken into account a matrix $M_{\omega'}$ such that

$$M_{\omega'} = [m_{ij} : i,j \in \omega]. \tag{14}$$

$M_{\omega'}$ is a coincidence matrix: it is binary, square and its diagonal coefficients are equal to zero. So as it contains all the rows and columns corresponding to the elements of a set being arranged (in the semi-ordering-rule sense) before the elements of the set of $\omega'$, $M_{\omega'}$ is a coincidence matrix describing the conditional semi-ordering relation for fixed $\omega'$.

Thus, the basic operations of the distinctive relations theory: completing the set of semi-ordering relations between the elements of a set of observed signals as well as describing the conditional relations can easily be represented by the above-described operations on the matrices of coincidence.

W.J.M. LEVELT (*)

# FORMAL GRAMMARS AND THE NATURAL LANGUAGE USER : A REVIEW

(*) Psychologisch Laboratorium Katholieke Universiteit Nijemegen

# 1. INTRODUCTION:

## General review of relations between formal grammar theory, natural linguistics and psycholinguistics.

## 1.1 Origin and basic problems of formal grammar theory

This chapter is introductory to the following three. Its aim is to give an historical outline of the mutual inspiration that we have seen in the last fifteen or so years between formal grammar theory, natural language theory and psycholinguistics. In the following three chapters we will discuss some recent characteristic examples of this interaction.

Fifteen to twenty years are long enough to have almost forgotten how formal grammar theory came into existence. The origin of this theory comes from the study of natural language. A description of natural language is traditionally called a grammar. It specifies construction of sentences, relations between linguistic units, etc.. Formal grammar theory started from the need to give a formal mathematical basis for such descriptions. Initially the creation of these new formal systems was largely the work of Noam Chomsky. His aim was not so much to refine linguistic descriptions, but to construct a formal basis for the discussion of the foundations of linguistics. "What should be the form of a linguistic theory?", "What sort of problems can be expressed by way of different formal means, and what do we take to be a solution?": these were the main issues to be tackled. In short, formal grammars were developed as mathematical models for linguistic structure.

The first developments only concerned the syntax of natural languages, not their semantics. The most successful application of formal grammar theory have been up to now in the area of syntax. All our discussion will therefore be largely limited to syntactic issues.

The first and most obvious use of formal grammar theory in linguistics was to create a variety of more or less restrictive grammars, and to compare their generative power to the empirical requirements of linguistic data. Let us call this the problem of "generative power". In this chapter we will discuss and criticize some historical highlights in the approach to this problem. In the next chapter some important recent results will be discussed.

The explicit use of formal grammars in linguistics also created a more general and more philosophical problem. It is one thing to formalize a linguistic theory, it is quite another thing to formulate the relation between such a theory on the one hand, and empirical linguistic data on the other hand. The problem here consists in clarifying what, exactly, is the empirical domain of the linguistic theory, and what is the empirical interpretation of the elements and relations that figure in the theory. We will call this problem the interpretation problem, after Bar-Hillel. In this chapter we will only make some general points relating to this issue. The third chapter, however, will be devoted to a formal psycholinguistic analysis of the interpretation problem.

The linguistic origin of formal grammar theory, finally, also led to the early development of theories of grammatical inference. There were two reasons for this. Firstly, a main theme in structural linguistics had for a long time been the development of so-called "discovery procedures", i.e. methods to detect structures in linguistic data. Secondly, probably under the influence of the psychologist George Miller, Chomsky had realized the fundamental problem of language acquisition. The description of a language is one thing, but the causation of linguistic structures is another more fundamental issue. Only a solution of this latter problem will give linguistic theory an explanatory dimension. Efforts to write formal systems which are able to infer a grammar from a data corpus can be found as early as 1957. Since then, inference theory has had a considerable development. In the last chapter we will be concerned with some relations between recent inference theory and psycholinguistic models of language acquisition.

## 1.2 Observational adequacy of regular and context-free grammars.

Let us now return to the early developments of formal

grammar theory. We will first very quickly review the variety of grammars that Chomsky developed in the second half of the fifties. Then we will discuss some problems relating to the linguistic adequacy of regular and contex-free grammars.

According to Chomsky, a <u>grammar</u> is defined as a system

$$G = \langle V_N, V_T, P, S \rangle ,$$

where $V_N$ is a finite nonempty set, the nonterminal vocabulary, whose elements are called category symbols or auxiliary variables;

$V_T$ is a finite nonempty set, the terminal vocabulary whose elements are usually called "words" or "morphemes",

S is an element of $V_N$ (the start symbol).

Given a set E of symbols, we denote by $E^*$ the set of all strings of finite length which can be obtained by concatenation of symbols in E; by $E^+$ we shall denote the set $E^* - \{\lambda\}$, where $\lambda$ is the null string (of zero length).

Now P (the set of production rules of the grammar) is a finite set of rules of the form $\alpha \longrightarrow \beta$, with $\alpha \in V^+$ and $\beta \in V^*$, where $V = V_T \cup V_N$.

We shall say that a string $\gamma \in V^+$ directly produces a string $\delta \in V^*$ (in symbols $\gamma \Rightarrow \delta$) if $\gamma = \varphi \eta \psi$, $\delta = \varphi \theta \psi$, for some $\eta, \theta, \varphi, \psi \in V^*$, and $\eta \longrightarrow \theta$ is in P. Finally, we say that $\gamma \in V^+$ derives (directly or not) a string $\delta \in V^*$ (in symbols $\gamma \overset{*}{\Longrightarrow} \delta$) if either $\gamma = \delta$, or there exist strings $\gamma_0, \gamma_1, \ldots, \gamma_n$, for some finite, n, such that

$$\gamma_0 = \gamma, \quad \gamma_i \Longrightarrow \gamma_{i+1}, \text{ for } i = 0, \ldots, n-1,$$

and $\gamma_n = \delta$.

Now the <u>language</u> $L_G$ generated by a grammar G as above is defined as the set

$$L_G = \{ \alpha \mid \alpha \in V_T^*, S \overset{*}{\Longrightarrow} \alpha \}$$

The variety of grammars that Chomsky defined came about by putting more and more restrictive conditions on the format of production rules.

These are:

(0) no restriction: type 0 grammars.

(1) for all rules $\alpha \longrightarrow \beta$ of P, the length of $\beta$ should be not less than the length of $\alpha$ : context-sensitive grammars (type 1)

(2) for all rules $\alpha \longrightarrow \beta$ of P, we must have $\alpha \in V_N, \beta \neq \lambda$ : context-free grammars (type 2).

(3) for all rules $\alpha \longrightarrow \beta$ of P, we must have $\alpha \in V_N$, and either $\beta \in V_T$, or $\beta$ equal to the concatenation of an element of $V_T$ and one of $V_N$, in that order: regular grammars (type 3).

A language is called type-i if it can be generated by a type-i grammar.

There is a strict inclusion relation among the classes of languages defined above: if $C_i$ is the class of langua ges of type i, then $C_{i+1} \subsetneq C_i$. In particular there are not regular (i.e. type 3). These are exactly the languages that are called "self-embedding". A context-free language is self-embedding if all grammars generating it are self-em bedding. A context-free grammar is self-embedding if there is a $B \in V_N$ such that $B \overset{*}{\Longrightarrow} \alpha B \gamma$ , where $\alpha$ and $\gamma$ are non-empty strings.

Chomsky (1956, 1957) rejected regular languages as ade quate models for natural languages. The argument used by Chomsky to conclude that natural languages are at least non-regular had an enormous influence on the development of mo-dern linguistics; this justifies a rather detailed discus-sion of it. It is also the case that the argumentation, as given in Syntactic Structures (1957), is not completely ba lanced (the same is true, to a lesser degree, of Chomsky's treatment of the question in 1956). A consequence of this has been that the same sort of evidence is incorrectly used for the rejection of other types of grammars, and erroneous conclusions have been drawn. The argument of inadequacy advanced in Syntactic Structures is of the following form :

(a) A language with property X cannot be generated by a regular grammar;

(b) Natural language L has property X;

therefore

(c) L is not a regular language.

For property X self-embedding is taken. Then step (a) in the argument is correct. The problem, however, resides in (b). One must now show for (b) that e.g. English is a self-embedding language. This is done by referring to self-embedding subsets of English, such as

- the rat ate the malt
- the rat, the cat killed ate the malt
- the rat the cat the dog chased killed ate the malt, and so on.

It would not be difficult to think of other examples.

Chomsky, in Syntactic Structures, gives this as evidence that English is self-embedding, and therefore is not a regular language. The self-embedding property of English is, however, not demonstrated by the examples above, in spite of appearance of the contrary. The only thing which has been proved is that English has self-embedding subsets. But it by no means follows from this that English is a self-embedding language.

This can easily be seen in the following. Let language L consist of all non-empty strings over a given alphabet $V_T$, i.e. $L_T^+$. A grammar for L is $G = \langle V_N, V_T, P, S \rangle$, where $V_N = \{S\}$ and P contains $S \rightarrow a$, $S \rightarrow aS$ for all a in $V_T$. This is clearly a regular grammar. Since L contains all strings over $V_T$ of positive lengths, it also contains all self-embedding languages over $V_T$. In conclusion, from the existence of self-embedding subsets it does not follow that a language is self-embedding.

Chomsky's original argumentation (1956), in the technical paper which preceded Syntactic Structures, is considera bly more precise. There he explaned that it is not only necessary to show that the language containes self-embedding subsets, but also that a particular change in the sentences of a self-sembedding subset must always he accompanied by a certain other change, on pain of ungrammaticality.

Let us clarify this by a simple example. Take the construct if $s_1$ then $s_2$ in English. There is a self-embedding subset- of--English of the form

$$(*) \quad \{\text{if}^n \ s_1 \ (\text{then} \ \ s_2)^n, \ \ n = 1, \ldots\}$$

In order to show that English is self-embedding, according to Chomsky, one has not only to show that all strings in the subset above are grammatical (i.e. are good, though awkward, English), but also that

$$(**) \quad \text{if}^n \ \ s_1 \ (\text{then} \ s_2)^m$$

is ungrammatical for all cases with $n \neq m$. This reasoning is correct. The interesting thing is, however, that Chomsky in the article quoted (1956) only shows the existence of self-embedding constructs of the form (*), and does not give data to support that all constructs of the form (* *) are ungrammatical. In fact, one might say that the latter condition does not hold at all, since grammatical examples of the form (* *) are

if John sleeps, he snores
John drank coffee, then he left

and so on.

Similar objections may be made to the other examples in Chomsky (1956) and (1957).

Fewer problems occur when the "proof" is stated as follows (this is due to Dr. H. Brandt Corstius, personal communication).

It has been proved by Bar-Hillel (see Hopcroft and Ullman, 1969) that the intersection of two regular languages is regular. So, if L is a language, T is a regular language, and $T \cap L$ is non-regular, then L is non-regular. Assume for L the English language, and construct T as follows:

$$T = \{\text{William (whom William)}^n \text{ succeded}^m \text{ succeded William} \mid n, m \geq 1\}.$$

This is a regular language, because it can be generated by the following grammar

$$G = \langle V_N, V_T, P, S \rangle$$

where $V_N = \{S, A, B, C\}$ , $V_T = \{\text{William, succeded, whom}\}$

$$P = \begin{cases} S \longrightarrow \text{William } A \\ A \longrightarrow \text{whom William } A \\ A \longrightarrow \text{whom William } B \\ B \longrightarrow \text{succeded } B \\ B \longrightarrow \text{succeded } C \\ C \longrightarrow \text{succeded William} \end{cases}$$

G is so-called "right-linear" grammar: such grammars generate regular languages (see Hopcroft and Ullman, 1969).

Let us now have a closer look at English $\cap$ T. Intuitively, the only grammatical sentences in T are those for which $n = m$, though some people have the intuition that one may delete occurrences of <u>succeed</u> so that the grammatical sentences in T are those for which $n \geqslant m$. In both cases ($n = m$, $n \geq m$), however, the intersection is self-embedding. Hence English is not a regular language.

Although this form of proof avoids the formal difficulties, the "proof" remains as weak as the empirical observation on which it is based. We cannot expect more evidence than such weak intuitions. However, it is upon reaching this level of empirical evidence that one can decide in theoretical linguistics to formulate the state of affairs as an axiom: <u>natural languages are non-regular</u>. Given the independent character of a theory, this is a more correct method of work than simply acting as though one were dealing with a <u>theorem</u> which could be proven, as linguists often do. The latter method is an incorrect mixture of theory and observation.

We have discussed at some length the problem of adequacy of regular languages, because a next step in lingui stics has been to examine the observational adequacy of context-free languages. Postal (1964) "proves" the theorem (his term) that the North American Indian language Mohawk is not context-free, by following the argumentation schema of Syntactic Structures, i.e.:

(a) A language with property x is not context-free;
(b) Mohawk has property x
(c) Then Mohawk is not context-free.

As property x he takes the property of "string repetition", as in the language $\{W\ W\}$ , where every sentence consists of a string followed by its repetition. Then (a) is true.

Postal then shows the existence of string-repetition phenomena in Mohawk, i.e. sentences of the form

$$a_1\ a_2\ \dots\ a_n\ b_1\ b_2\ \dots\ b_n$$

where $a_i$ "corresponds" to $b_i$. From this, he concludes that Mohawk is not context-free. This reasoning is as defective as the one, which we criticized, on the proposition that natural languages are not regular. It is erroneous to conclude that a language is not context-free from the existence of non-context-free subsets.

Again a more convincing proof can be carried out along different lines (Brandt Corstius, personal communication). It has been proven by Bar-Hillel (see Hopcroft and Ulhman, 1969) that the intersection of a regular language and a context-free language is context-free. So, if L is a language, T is a regular language, and $T \cap L$ is non-context-free, then L is non-context-free. Assume for L the English language, and construct T as follows:

$$T = \{\underline{\text{The academics}}, \underline{\text{accountants}}, \underline{\text{actors}}, \underline{\text{admirals}}, \dots,$$
$$\underline{\text{in respectively}}\ \underline{\text{Belgium}}, \underline{\text{Bulgaria}}, \underline{\text{Burúndi}}, \underline{\text{Brasil}}, \dots,$$
$$\underline{\text{are respectively}}\ \underline{\text{calm}}, \underline{\text{candid}}, \underline{\text{canny}}, \underline{\text{careless}}, \dots,\}$$

or abbreviated

$$T = \{\underline{\text{The}}\ a^k, \underline{\text{in respectively}}\ b^m, \underline{\text{are respectively}}\ c^n \mid K, m, n \geq 0\}.$$

It is not difficult to write a regular grammar for T. Let

us now consider which sentences in T are grammatical English sentences. Intuitively these are the strings for which $K = m = n \geq 1$. However it is known (see Hopcroft and Ullman, 1969) that there is no possible context-free grammar for the language

$$\{a^n \; b^n \; c^n \quad n \quad 1\},$$

i.e. the intersection of T and English is not context-free. We therefore conclude that English is a non-context-free language. Again, this "proof" is as strong as the intuitions about the grammatical subset of T, which in this case are particularly weak. Much more convincing, at any rate, are other arguments against the context-free character of natural language. They are not based, however, on the above considerations about (weak) generative power, but on the less well defined notion of <u>strong generative power</u>.

For a context-free grammar $G = \; V_N, V_T, P, S$ we define its strong generative power as the set of terminal leftmost derivations it generates, i.e. the set of derivations of the form

$$S \Longrightarrow \gamma_0 \Longrightarrow \gamma_1 \quad \cdots\cdots \Longrightarrow \gamma_{n-1} \Longrightarrow \gamma_n$$

where $\gamma_n \in V_T^+$, and $\gamma_i = \varphi A \psi$ , $\gamma_{i+1} = \varphi \chi \psi$ ,

$A \longrightarrow \chi$ is in P, and $\varphi \in V_T^*$, for all $i = 0, 1, \ldots n-1$.

We may associate to each terminal leftmost derivation a labelled graph (also called "Phrase-marker);for example to $S \Longrightarrow a \; B \Longrightarrow abc$ we associate the following graph

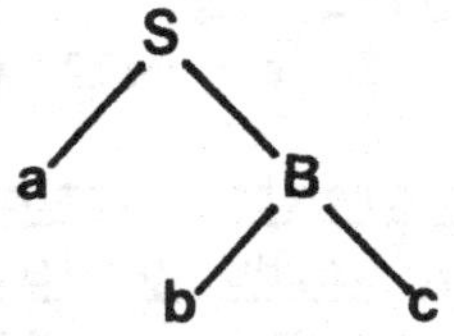


Each terminal leftmost derivation is a <u>structured description</u> of the terminal string or sentence it produces. The linguistic question, then, is whether a particular grammar can express in a satisfactory way what we feel the structu

re of a sentence is. Consideration about syntactic and semantic ambiguity in natural language often require that a sentence has two different structural descriptions. In some of these cases (e.g. for a sentence such as "Italian like opera as much as Germans") a context-free grammar cannot provide two different leftmost derivations which intuitively, correspond to the two readings of the sentence.

Moreover, also intuitive relations between different sentences (e.g. active and passive form of a statement) are often not directly expressible by means of type 2 and type 1 grammars. To express such relation linguists felt an increasing need for the possibility to simultaneously assign more than one phrase-marker to a sentence. These and many other similar problems led to abdication of the traditional context-free model, and for similar reasons of the context-sensitive model as well.

The next step in the Chomsky hierarchy is type-0 grammars. But these are equivalent to Turing machines, and there are good reasons not to give grammars such maximum power. This will be discussed in the next chapter.

## 1.3 Origins of the psycholinguistic approach.

Let us now, to conclude this general introduction, switch to psycholinguistics.

We have seen that the arguments in favour or against a certain variety of grammar were based on insights such as the grammaticality of strings, or the "fittingness" of a structural description. But when is a certain string of words "grammatical", and how "fitting" is a structural description? Clearly, these are linguistic intuitions, and Chomsky did not hesitate to state that linguistics is concerned with linguistic intuitions. These form the empirical domain in Chomskian linguistics. Not all linguists accept this view, but there are reasons to support it.

Two major problems, however, arise:

(1) Can we make explicit the relations between the formal linguistic theory on the one hand and linguistic judgements, i.e. expressions of linguistic intuitions on the ot

her hand? This will be the topic of the third chapter.

(2) What is the relation between a such defined grammar and models of the language user (speaker, listener)?

Initially, Chomsky, Miller and others conceived of this relation as follows. Intuitions, they said, express the (tacit) knowledge of speakers about their language; this knowledge, which they called linguistic *competence*, is at the basis of all actual language behavior or *performance*. So, if we have only determined the structure of linguistic competence, we can proceed to the study of performance, in which the competence plays a general and essential role. Of course in a theory of performance additional psychological factors come in, such as motivation, memory span, and so on. It is their interaction with linguistic competence which is to be studied by psycholinguists. In our view this distinction between competence and performance is far-fetched, if not fully untenable. The data for competence research are linguistic judgements, which are forms of language behavior. It is not clear why just this type of language behavior (linguistic judgement) should have the privilege of leading to a theory, which has then to be built into the models for various other types of language bahavior, such as speaking or listening. In fact, the latter forms are much more direct or "primary" forms of language use, whereas linguistic judgement is a very secondary or derived form of language behavior.

Though this approach could not stand the test of time, it did originally stimulate much research in psycholinguistics. In fact between 1963 and 1967 at Harvard and MIT a number of psychologists and linguists (among which the present author) tried to show that the competence or knowledge as described by the linguists in their grammars, is "psychologically real", i.e. could be shown to operate in sentence understanding, in memorisation and speech. Aspects of the formal grammar, such as different types of rewrite rules, transformations, and so on, were tested for their psychological relevance in experiment upon experiment.

Let us consider one or two examples of the subjects of these early developments.

The correspondence between the various types of grammars and automata led to considering various automata as models for the language user. In spite of the obvious finiteness of the human brain, the finite automaton was quickly dismissed as a model for the language user, as the regular grammar had been discarded as a linguistic model. More inspiring was the push-down automaton, which is in its non-deterministic form equivalent to a context-free grammar. The self-embedding property obviously attracted much attention; it was interesting to see if human finiteness would be reflected in a limited push-down capacity.

Severe limitations on the understanding of self-embedding were clearly demonstrated. One or two embeddings turned out to be disastrous for comprehension, as in the following examples:

(1) if if John comes Peter comes Charles comes.

(2) The dog the cat the mouse bit chased ate a lot.

Moreover, if limited push-down capacity (not lack of knowledge!) explained this, it should be equally hard to handle other types of embedding. But this turned out not to be the case, as it can be seen in the following examples:

(3) John, who saw everything, will tell it.

(4) John, who saw everybody you mentioned, will tell it.

So self-embedding seems to exhibit a special situation. It seems to be especially hard for the language user to interrupt a procedure by the same type of procedure.

In spite of this, the push-down automaton model is still of some use in psycholinguistics. Masters (1970), for instance, has studied in this way the language of schizophrenics. From the literature on schizophrenic language it was known that these patients use (1) less different words, (2) less adjectives, (3) shorter sentences, (4) more incomplete sentences, (5) more adjectives per verb, (6) more objects per subject, (7) less modifiers per verb, and so on. Masters wrote a context-free grammar of English and casted it in the format of a push-down automaton. By limiting the size of the push-down store to less there 6 elements it turned out that the language generated (or accepted) by it showed all the mentioned seven characteristics of schizophrenic language. However, the main interest of the model has gone to the study of transformations, i.e. how do people cope with passive sentences, negative sentences, question sentences and so on. A review of this work can be found in Levelt (1974).

These early developments of psycholinguistics eventually led to very little, and faded away. It was mainly due to extraneous developments, especially in Artificial Intelligence, that a new approach in psycholinguistic theory evolved. Computer scientists and linguists tried to develop programs for understanding and producing natural language. Thome's work in Edinburgh was a first big step. Others followed, in particular Sager, Woods and Vinograd.

At the basis of these programs is a structure called augmented transition network. In its simplest form it is a finite automaton expanded with a push-down memory. In a more sophisticated form all sorts of conditions on transitions can be specified, thus obtaining the power of a Turing machine. It is possible to write a transformational grammar in such terms. In this way the grammar is no more an abstract body of knowledge, which may or may not be "consulted" by the hearer or speaker, but it is, in a sense, the accepting (or generating) mechanism itself.

## 2. THE GENERATIVE POWER OF TRANSFORMATIONAL GRAMMARS.

In the first chapter we discussed how linguists felt the urge to move up in the hierarchy. Initially they tried to show that the more restrictive forms of grammar such as regular grammars and context free grammars could not be sufficient to generate all and only the sentences of a natural language. The main argument, however, to shift to more complicated grammars was the lack of descriptive adequacy of grammars up to the level of context-sensitive.

The next step, therefore, was to move to certain types of strictly type zero grammars. They were called transformational grammars for reasons that we will discuss presently.

Beforehand, we must make one or two remarks in order to show that this move is not without problems, and that certain precautions have to be taken. For this we have to consider again the fundamental aims of a linguistic theory. We mention two of them:

(1) A linguistic theory should be <u>descriptive</u> for the linguistic intuition of a native speaker. One intuition concerns grammaticality. Native speakers can recognize sentences from the language as being elements of the language. But at the same time, they can equally well recognize non-sentences as not belonging to the language. In terms of grammars this would mean that native speakers have the disposal of a decision procedure. For any string $x$ in $V_T^*$ they can in a finite time decide whether $x \in L$ or $x \notin L$. A linguistic grammar, therefore, should be <u>recursive</u>, not only recursively enumerable.

(2) A linguistic theory should be explanatory in the sense that it can explain how the grammar is caused. In formal terms: the grammar should be such that it is learnable-in-principle, i.e. there should be a conceivable inference procedure for the grammar. In the last chapter we will show that this requirement comes down to the condition that the grammar is <u>primitive recursive</u>.

Since the difference between recursive and primitive recursive is small, and has no linguistic interpretation we will conclude from these two aims that any grammar for a natural language should be decidable or recursive.

## 2.1 The structure of Chomsky's transformational grammar.

Various transformational grammars have been developed. Most influential has been (and is) Chomsky's formulation "Aspects of the Theory of Syntax" (1965), but there are interesting other examples such as Joshi's et al (1972) string adjunct grammar, and dependency grammars. The present discussion has to limit to Chomsky's model.

Chomsky wanted, on the one hand, to keep the various advantages of phrase structure grammars, such as Context Free Grammars and certain Context Sensitive Grammars (parsing, etc.) and at the same time expand the descriptive potentialities of the grammar. Necessary expansions, as we have seen in the first part, are required for generating more then one tree diagram or phrase marker per sentence in order to take account of certain ambiguities, deletions and relations between sentences. In all cases it is necessary to define relations between tree graphs or P-markers. These relations are called _transformations_. In principle a transformation maps a tree graph on a tree graph. It is a rule with tree graphs as input and output.

The rough structure of Chomsky's "Aspects"-grammar, then, is a context-sensitive grammar generating terminal tree graphs, which are called _base structures_. These base structures form the input for the transformational rules. For some of them these rules generate an output which is called a _surface structure_. Its terminal string is the sentence. Base structures transformationally leading to surface structures are called _deep structures_. All other base structures are said to have been _filtered out_.

The context sensitive base grammar generates an infinite set of strings. It is constructed in such a way that recursion can only take place through the recursive initial symbol S. Recursive rewriting of S leads to base P-markers of the form:

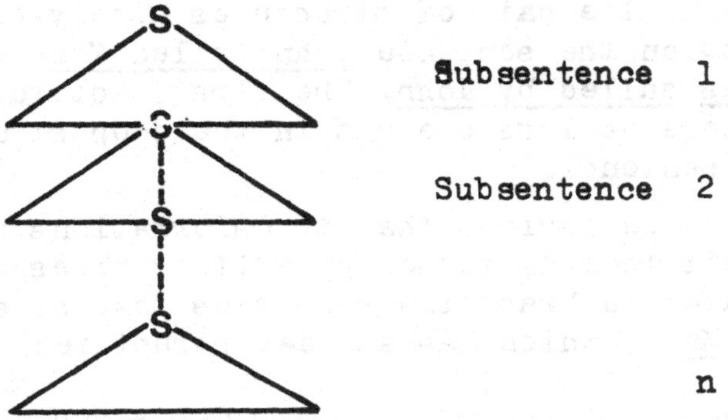


Were each triangle represents a subtree resulting from rewriting S up till recursion of S.

The transformation rules operate on such base structures in a special fashion. Transformations form an ordered list, they are tried out one by one, starting at the top of the list and ending at the bottom. This cycle is first applied to the most deeply embedded subsentence (_n_), then it turns to the next higher one (_n_ - 1), a.s.o. until the top sentence (1) has been reached. (Additionally it seems necessary to assume the existence of some pre- and post-cyclic rules). If there is an output, it is called a surface structure. Its terminal string is called a sentence.

The structural description of a sentence is the pair of tree graphs consisting of deep and surface structure. So, for instance for the sentence _Mary was called by John_ we have, in simplified form (node labels omitted) the pair:

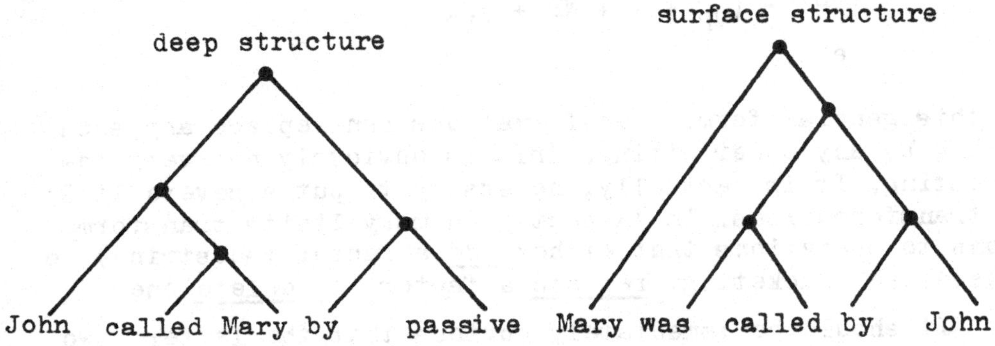

The mediating transformation here is called the passive transformation. The pair of structures nicely expresses the relation between the sentence John called Mary and the passive Mary was called by John. The first, active, sentence is already more or less present in the deep structure of the passive sentence.

It should be obvious that transformations are type-zero rules. This is easy to see by writing trees as strings, namely as labelled bracketings. Let us take as an example John called Mary, which has as deep structure:

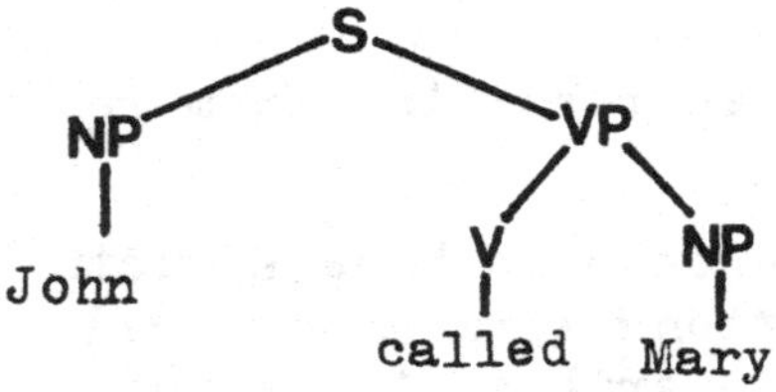


by rules

$$\begin{cases} S \rightarrow NP + VP \\ VP \rightarrow V + NP \\ NP \rightarrow \text{John, Mary} \\ V \rightarrow \text{called} \end{cases}$$

This can alternatively be written as:

$$({}_S\ ({}_{NP}\ \text{John}\ )_{NP}\ ({}_{VP}\ ({}_V\ \text{called}\ )_V\ ({}_{NP}\ \text{Mary}\ )_{NP}\ )_{VP}\ )_S$$

Transformations are rewritings of such strings. In fact, it is easy to replace the base grammar by a grammar which generates such labelled bracketings. Namely in the following way:

$$S \rightarrow ({}_S + NP + VP + )_S$$
$$VP \rightarrow ({}_{VP} + V + NP + )_{VP}$$
etc.

In this general form, transformations can replace any such string by any other string. This is obviously not very interesting. It is, actually, necessary to put a severe limit on transformations. In 'Aspects" Chomsky limits transformations to operations that either add a factor (substring) to a labelled bracketing, replace a factor, or delete one.

It should be immediately obvious that the latter two operations, which are essentially erasure operations can be strict type-zero rules, because they shorten a given string. It is at this point that our above mentioned caution is required. What sort of condition has to be put on transformations, in order to keep decidability? Or to state it differently: what sort of condition on transformations is required in order that a Turing Machine given a string can decide whether the string can or cannot be generated by the Transformational Grammar?

Chomsky was not very explicit about this problem. He formulated a condition, which he called the principle of recoverability of deletions. In essence, the condition states that given the string, and given the transformation from which it emerged, there should be only a finite set of strings that could have been the input to the transformation. This was secured by requiring that either (a) the deleted substring would after transformation still be present at some other place in the string, (b) the deleted string would be one of a finite set, i.e. the condition would specify the finite set for the transformations. An example of the former would be the derivation of John and Mary chased the dog from John chased the dog and Mary chased the dog by a coordination transformation. The first chased the dog is deleted, but this substring is still present at another place in the string. An example of the latter is the derivation of the imperative shut the door from you shut the door. The imperative transformation only allows for deletion of the element you (which is certainly a finite set).

It has been proven by Peters & Ritchie that this condition fails to preserve the recursiveness of the grammar. In fact they proved that transformational grammars of this sort are equivalent with type-zero grammars. They generate all and only the type-zero languages.

A rough outline of the proof is as follows: it has two parts. The first is to prove that every transformational grammar is type-zero. This we have more or less seen. The more interesting part is the converse, namely that every type-zero language can be generated by a transformational grammar of this type. It consists of 3 steps:

(1) Be L type-zero and G a grammar for L. We first construct a context-sensitive grammar G' which generates strings $xb^m$ for all x is L. It is derived from G by changing the shortening rules of G by adding a row of b's.

(2) Context-sensitive G' is equivalent to G" in Kuroda's normal form. Kuroda proved the theorem that context-sensitive grammars are equivalent to grammars with the limited rule format ($S \rightarrow SB$, $CD \rightarrow EF$, $G \rightarrow H$, $A \rightarrow a$). This is a format in which for generating $x = a_1 \ldots a_n$. One has first to apply $S \rightarrow SB$ n - 1 times giving $SB_1\ B_2 \ldots B_{n-1}$, which has the length of x, and then to replace or interchange the elements by applying further rules. In the Kuroda form, therefore, the string $xb^m$ has a structure such a

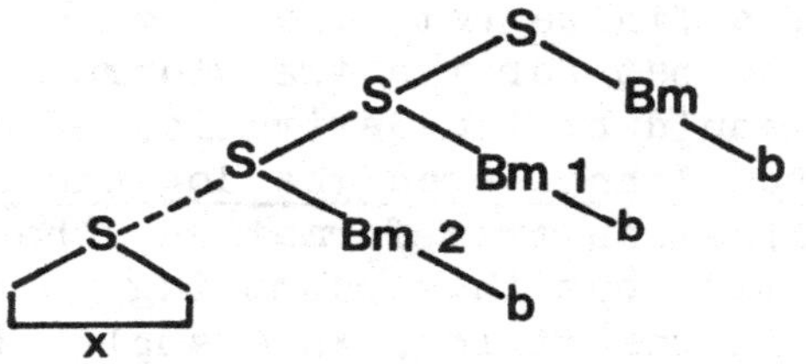


(3) We now create a transformational component by which the b's can be erased, in order to leave us with the set of strings {x} , which form the type-zero grammar L. This can easily be done. A single transformation suffices. It is constructed in such a way that it applies to a (sub-) sentence which is factorizable in two substrings, the last of which is a b. The transformation consists of erasing the b, i.e. the second factor of the sub-sentence. The nice thing about using Kuroda's normal form is that in this way indeed all b's get erased. It should be remembered that the transformations are first applied to the most deeply embedded subsentence. The b is erased and the next cycle starts. In this way all b's are erased because each b is a second and last factor of an S. By this procedure our TG can generate type-zero lan-

guage L. Does the transformation conform to the principle
of recoverability of deletions? Yes, bacause b is the only
element that can be deleted. Thus, given the output string
and the transformation, the input string can always be re-
contructed.

This equivalence of TG's and type zerogrammars shows
that they are not, in general, recursive as we had required. Such grammars, therefore, are unfit for linguistic de
scription or explanation.

It should be clear what makes the grammar undecidable
for a Turing Machine. Given a string and the transformation
it is possible to reconstruct the previous string, but the
problem is that the TM does not know the transformation and
worse, whether a transformation was applied at all.  There
is, given a string x of length $|x|$  no upper bound on the
size of the deep structure for x. It therefore requires an
infinite set of operations to test for all possible  deep
structures for x whether they are generated by the base
grammar.

One could be inclined to ascribe this state of affairs
to the combination of the apparently not adequate principle
of recoverability of deletions and the string (i.e. context
free) base grammar. This is only partly correct. In a furt
her paper Peters & Ritchie proved that even a regular gram
mar as base grammar was sufficient for the generation   of
all type-zero languages. In fact this could be  a  highly
trivial grammar, namely :

1. $\underline{S} \rightarrow \underline{S}\#$

2. $\underline{S} \rightarrow \underline{a}_1 \ldots \underline{a}_n \underline{b} \#$, where $\{\underline{a}_1, \ldots \underline{a}_n\}$ is  the
   terminal vocabulary of the language. It generates
   strings of the form $\underline{a}_1 \ldots \underline{a}_n \underline{b} \# \underline{n}$.

In order to proof this Peters and Ritchie had to make
use of the filter-function of transformations which we men
tioned above. So, one also has to repair the filter-mecha
nism.

A final objection one could make is that such trivial
grammars can never be descriptively adequate. But even  at

this point Peters and Ritchie were able to show that these grammars are able to account for grammaticality, ambiguity and paraphrase, i.e. for the most important structural intuitions.

In conclusion, the Chomskian transformational grammar severely fails both descriptively (it cannot account for ungrammaticality intuitions), and explanatory. It is not learnable and also it fails in handling the universal base problem. The idea of the latter is that what is universal to language is the base grammar. Languages would mainly differ with respect to their transformational structure. In Chomsk's formalism this is trivially true. The above trivial grammar can be used to generate any language. The universal base hypothesis is not any more an empirical issue.

At the present moment these problems of generative power have not yet been solved. There is only one other completely formalized transformational grammar, namely Joshi's mixed adjunct grammar. It goes back to the adjunction grammar of Harris. It is nicely recursive and it seems attractive to apply some of Joshi's notions to the Chomskian grammar. One is the so-called trace-condition. It says that each transformation leaves a <u>trace</u>, i.e. an element or string which cannot be erased by any further transformation. In this way for a given string <u>x</u>, there is an upper bound on the number of transformations which can have been applied in its derivation. A Turing Machine, therefore, has only to retrace a finite set of derivations, i.e. there exists a decision procedure. It has to be made convincing, however, that such a trace-condition can be linguistically interpreted, i.e. has a meaningful relation to linguistic data. This is still an open empirical issue.

Finally, it is amazing to see that younger linguists like McCawley and Lakoff are not at all bothered by the problem of generative power of their grammars. In fact, what they did was changing Chomsky's transformational grammar in such a way, as to even remove restrictions, i.e. to make the grammar more powerful. The resulting quibles between them and the Chomsky adherents are therefore clearly issues which are undecidable. Both have grammars as powerful as Turing Machines.

## 3. GRAMMARS AND LINGUISTIC INTUITIONS

### 3.1 The unreliability of linguistic intuitions

The empirical touchstone in the tradition of transformational linguistics is the linguistic intuition, either of the linguist himself or of an informant. This is also the case in other linguistic traditions, but not in all. Some linguists write grammars for a given corpus, at times on principle, and at times because they are forced to do so for lack of informants. Without taking position on the problem of whether or not intuitions constitute a sufficient basis for a complete language theory, we can in any case propose that their importance in linguistics is essentially limited by the degree to which they are unreliable. It is a dangerous practice in linguistics to conclude from the lack of psychological information on the process of linguistic judgment that intuitions are indeed reliable. Although incidental words of caution may be found in linguistic literature, their effect is negligible. Chomsky warns his readers that he does not mean "that the speaker's statements about his intuitive knowledge are necessarily accurate" (Chomsky 1965), and further states that

> in short, we must be careful not to overlook the fact that surface similarities may hide underlying distinctions of a fundamental nature, and that it may be necessary to guide and draw out the speaker's intuition in perhaps fairly subtle ways before we can determine what is the actual character of his language or of anything else.

Chomsky (1957) emphasizes that, as far as possible, grammars should be constructed on the basis of clear cases with regard to grammaticality. If the grammar is adequate for those cases, the status of less clear cases can be deduced from the grammar itself, and the intuitive judgment is no longer necessary.

After the first phase of the development of transformational generative linguistics, little seems to remain of these two directives in linguistic practice. Instead of an increasing number of cases in which the theory decides on the grammatical status of halfacceptable sentences, we find an enormous increase of examples in which sentences of doubtful grammaticality are applied as tests of syntactic rules.

Even if all problems of doubtful grammaticality just mentioned have been solved, we must still ask what the linguist can do with his reliable data. Data would offer the linguist the opportunity to test his theory, but this does not work only in one direction. The theory (grammar) determines which data are relevant, or, in other words, which linguistic intuitions must be investigated in order to justify certain conclusions. This theory may be said to indicate how the data (intuitions) are represented in the model (the grammar). In this respect the theory of interpretation fills the same function in linguistics as measurement theory in the social sciences (cf. Krantz, et al.1971).

For the direct investigation of the descriptive adequacy of a grammar, that is, for the investigation of the correctness of the structural descriptions, intuitive judgments of another nature are needed; we call them STRUCTURAL INTUITIONS.

Here we shall discuss a type of structural intuition which is sometimes used in linguistic practice and which can offer direct insight into the structure of the sentence: intuitions on syntactic cohesion. Cohesion intuitions are expressed in judgments on whether or not words or phrases belong together in a sentence. Chomsky (1965) uses cohesion intuitions for the study of relations between the main verb and prepositional phrases:

> It is well known that in Verb-Prepositional Phrase constructions one can distinguish various degrees of "cohesion" between the verb and the accompanying Prepositional Phrase.

He illustrates this with the sentence <u>He decided on the boat</u> which can be read in two ways. <u>On the boat</u> refers either to the place or to the object of the decision. This is clear when we compare it with the following nonambiguous sentence: He decided on the boat on the train. Chomsky writes that in the latter sentence "the first prepositional phrase ... is in close construction to the verb", and he modifies the base grammar to agree with this insight. Cohesion is a direct and potentially valuable structural intuition, but its use in linguistics demands a theory of interpretation which establishes the relation between syntactic structure and cohesion judgment.

### 3.2 The interpretation problem: some empirical studies

Let us start the discussion taking as example the simple sentence John breaks in. There is a gamut of methods for having subjects judge how strong the syntactic relations are among the three words of this sentence. For example the subject can be asked to rank the three word pairs - (John, braks), (breaks, in) and (John, in) - according to relatedness. The most probable result is (from strong to weak): (breaks, in), (John, breaks), (John, in). For longer sentences, where the number of pairs becomes quite large, the task can be facilitated in several ways. One of these is TRIADIC COMPARISONS, in which the subject must indicate for every triad of words from the sentence which pair has the strongest relation in the sentence, and which has the weakest. The triads may be presented, for example, as shown in Figure 2.1. The subject marks his judgment in every triangle by placing a plus sign (+) at the side of the triangle showing the strongest relation, and a minus sign (-) at the side showing the weakest relation. When every triad for the sentence has been judged, each word pair can be assigned a number which represents the relatedness judgment. This can also be done in various ways. One of these consists of counting the number of times a word pair is judged as stronger than other word pairs. Thus, in Figure 1., the pair (breaks, in) is judged as more strongly related than either (John, breaks) or (John, in); this gives a score of 2. The pair (John, breaks) has a score of 1, because it is more strongly related than only one other pair, (John, in), which in turn has a score of 0. If there are more than three words in the

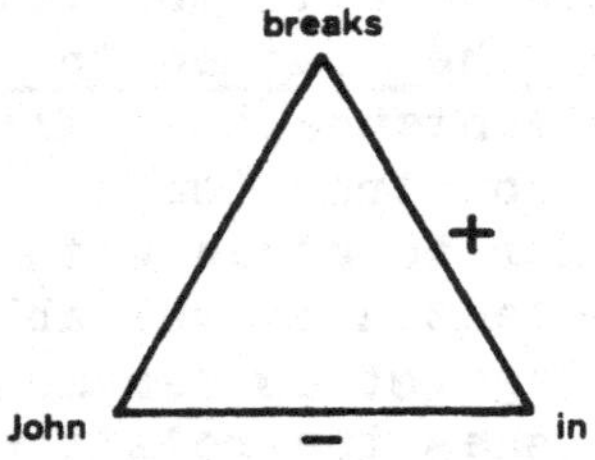


Fig. 1 An example of triadic comparison

sentence, the scores are added for all the triads in which the word pair occurs, yielding the final score for the pair. Other methods of determining the final score are also possible, but we need not describe them here.

An interpretation theory is necessary in order to connect relatedness judgments to a linguistic theory. The purpose is, of course, to test the linguistic theory on the basis of as plausible an interpretation theory as possible.

A general formulation as follows: the constituents of a sentence vary in cohesion, and the cohesion of a constituent is smaller than the cohesion of its parts. This is still nothing other than a faithful explicit representation of a more or less implicit linguistic notion. Without changing anything essential in the formulation, we can define the concept of cohesion mathematically as follows:

DEFINITION (Cohesion): A real-valued COHESION FUNCTION $\alpha$ is defines over the nodes of a phrase marker P, with the following property: if $A \rightsquigarrow B$, then $\alpha(A) < \alpha(B)$, for all nodes A, B in P, where $A \rightsquigarrow B$ means that there is a descending path in P from A to B. The COHESION of a constituent C, $\alpha$ (C), is defined as $\alpha$ (K), where K is the lowest node in P which dominates C and only C.

It follows from the definition that for every path from root to terminal element, the cohesion values of the nodes increase strictly. Consequantly the cohesion of a constituent is necesserily smaller than that of its parts.

The following step is the formulation of the theory of interpretation. This theory must indicate how the strength of the relation between two words, as judged by an informant, is connected with sentence structure. Let us imagine that we have performed such an experiment for a given sentence, and that the results of the experiment are summarized in a relatedness matrix R, in which the strength of the syntactic relation is indicated for every word pair in the sentence. Thus matrix element $r_{ij}$ in R is the score for the degree of relatedness between words i and j. The score is obtained in one of the ways described in the preceding paragraph. The interpretation theory must attempt plausibly to relate the observed r-values to the (theoretical ) cohesion values $\alpha$ . An obvious place to begin would be to find the smallest constituent for every word pair (i, j) to which both words belong, and to compare their degree of relatedness with the cohesion value of the constituent. Let us call that constituent the SMALLEST COMMON CONSTITUENT, SCC, of the word pair. Each word pair in the sentence evidently has one SCC and only one.

The most careful approach, therefore, is to establish no direct relationship between r-values and $\alpha$ 's, but only between the rank order of the r-values and the rank order of the $\alpha$ 's. The following interpretation axiom states that the rank order of the r-values must agree with the rank order of the $\alpha$ 's of the smallest common constituents concerned.

Interpretation axiom: For all words i, j, k, l in the sentence,

$$r_{ij} < r_{kl} \Longleftrightarrow \alpha(SCC_{ij}) < \alpha(SCC_{kl}).$$

In this axiom, $\Longleftrightarrow$ stands for "if and only if", and $SCC_{ij}(SCC_{kl})$ stand for the "smallest common constituent of words i and j (k and l)".

Given the interpretation axiom, we can study which phrase marker is most fitting for the observed relatedness values for a given sentence. If we have no particular theoretical expectation concerning the phrase marker, we can draw up a list of the predicted equalities and inequalities for every possible phrase marker in order to find the phrase marker which best agrees with the relatedness data. In doing so we should remember that different phrase markers for a single sentence do not always lead to the same number of equalities and inequalities. In general, however, we will certainly have particular theoretical expectations concerning syntactic structure, and it will be possible to limit the test to alternatives within that theoretical domain. The following is an experimental example of this.

For the sentence <u>the boy has lost a dollar</u>, only the phrase markers in Figure 2 are worth consideration. In an experiment described elsewhere (Levelt 1967a), twenty-four

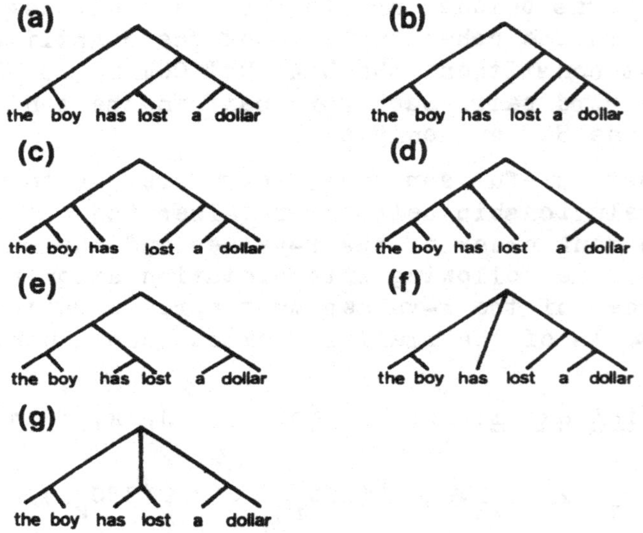


Fig. 2 Possible phrase markers for the sentence <u>the boy has lost a dollar</u> (node labels omitted).

native speakers of English judged this sentence by means of the method of triadic comparison.

Table 1. Shows the relatedness values obtained for the various word pairs. The value for a word pair was obtained by adding the scores for that pair in each triad and for each subject, it is expressed in a percentage.

Table 1. Relatedness Values for the Sentence <u>the boy has lost a dollar</u>.

| | the | boy | has | lost | a | dollar |
|---|---|---|---|---|---|---|
| the | - | 99 | 43 | 29 | 19 | 16 |
| boy | | - | 63 | 65 | 16 | 31 |
| has | | | - | 86 | 31 | 40 |
| lost | | | | - | 42 | 70 |
| a | | | | | - | 94 |
| dollar | | | | | | - |

Table 2. shows the number of inequalities predicted by means of the interpretation axiom for phrase markers (a) to (g), as well as the violations of these given Table 1. (also expressed in percentages in order to facilitate comparison of the models).

Table 2. Number of Predicted and Violated Inequalities for Phrase Markers (a) to (g) in Figure 3.

| Phrase marker | (a) | (b) | (c) | (d) | (e) | (f) | (g) |
|---|---|---|---|---|---|---|---|
| Predicted Inequalities | 64 | 67 | 58 | 67 | 64 | 46 | 36 |
| Violations | 9 | 11 | 7 | 12 | 8 | 5 | 0 |
| Percentage of Violations | 14 | 16 | 12 | 18 | 13 | 11 | 0 |

The predicted equalities are not taken into consideration here, but even without a statistical test it is quite clear that the results in this respect are in conflict with the expectations.

The problem is thus reduced to the following question:

given a formal grammar, which properties must matrix R of relatedness values have in order to be able to find an accurate structural description within that grammatical model?

We shall at this point find that critical property for the constituent model. Let a, b, and c be three random (but different) elements (words) of a sentence s.[1] Let us imagine the three smallest common constituents for a and b, b and c, and a and c, respectively.

It is quite clear that for the three smallest common constituents, one and only one of the four hierarchical relations in Figure 3 must apply.

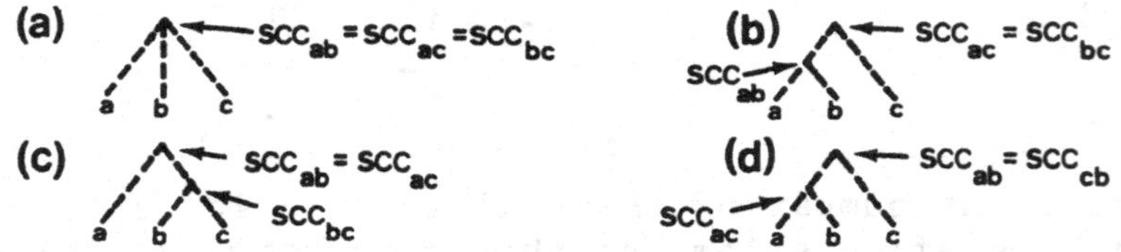


Fig. 3. The four possible hierarchies for the three elements in a phrase marker (dotted lines indicate paths which can contain other nodes)

If (a) is the case for the phrase marker of s, we have the following definition of cohesion:

(1) $\alpha(SCC_{ab}) = \alpha(SCC_{ac}) = \alpha(SCC_{bc})$

If it is (b) we have the following relation:

(2) $\alpha(SCC_{ab}) > \alpha(SCC_{ac}) = \alpha(SCC_{bc})$

If the hierarchical relation is as in (c), we have:

(3) $\alpha(SCC_{ao}) = \alpha(SCC_{ac}) < \alpha(SCC_{bc})$

If (d) is the case, we have:

(4) $\alpha(SCC_{ab}) = \alpha(SCC_{cb}) < \alpha(SCC_{ac})$

By the interpretation axiom, it follows from (1) to (4) that one and only one of the relations (5) to (8) must hold for the observed degrees of relatedness of a, b, and c.

(5) $r_{ab} = r_{ac} = r_{bc}$

(6) $r_{ab} > r_{ac} = r_{bc}$

(7) $r_{ab} = r_{ac} < r_{bc}$

(8) $r_{ab} = r_{cb} < r_{ac}$

These relations (5) to (8) simply mean that $r_{ab}$ must be equal to or greater than the smallest of the two other relations $r_{ac}$ and $r_{bc}$. This may be summarized as in (9):

(9) $r_{ab} \geqslant \min (r_{ac}, r_{bc})$

It follows from considerations of symmetry that the inequality also holds for every permutation of a, b and c. (9) is called the ULTRAMETRIC INEQUALITY. In whichever way a, b, and c are chosen, the relatedness values in R must satisfy the condition of ultrametric inequality, if representation by phrase marker is to be possible. In a different context, S.C.Johnson (1967) showed that this is not only a necessary condition, but also a sufficient one: if the matrix is ultrametric, there is a tree diagram which agrees with that matrix.

To summarize, then, it holds that the formal constituent model can be tested by establishing whether relatedness matrices satisfy the condition of ultrametric inequality (9) for all triads. If this is not the case within the measurement error, when the interpretation axiom is maintained, the constituent model must be rejected as such.

We shall limit the discussion to constructions of the type article+noun (<u>the child, a policeman, etc.</u>). Whether we test the parsing of the surface structure or that of the deep structure, article and noun in the cohesion determinant phrase marker will always be connected at a relatively low level in the hierarchy. Only at a higher level does the noun phrase as a whole come to be related to the other elements of the sentence. But this means that for every third element x in the sentence the smallest common constituent of article and x is the same as that of noun and x. It follows from the interpretation axiom that with the same degree of cohesion the same relatedness value should be expected for these pairs. For the sentence the child cried for help, for example, the theory predicts the following equalities:

r(the,cried) = r(child, cried)

r(the, for) = r(child, for)

r(the, help) = r(child, help)

This holds, no matter what the sentence structure is, provided that the smallest common constituent of the and child includes no other smallest common constituent. Any theory which allows the contrary is a priori in disagreement with current relatedness data, for the relation between the article and its corresponding noun is always stronger than any other relation in an experimental matrix. But the reader can clearly see that the predicted equalities conflict with intuition; one feels that the relations with the article are systematically weaker than those with the noun, and this is indeed what is regularly found in judgment experiments. For the dozens of sentences with article/noun pairs which we have investigated, we have always found, without exception, that the average strength of the relation between the noun and the other words of the sentence is considerably greater than that between the article and the other words. An example of this is the following. The Dutch sentence Meester geeft de doos aan Jetty of aan Thea ('Teacher gives the box to Jetty or to Thea') was presented to eight subjects, who judged the word pair relations on a seven-point scale. The relatedness values (total scores) for de 'the' and doos 'box' are given in Table 3.

Table 3. Experimental relatedness values for the relations between de 'the' and doos 'box' on the one hand, and on the other, the remaining words in the sentence Meester geeft de doos aan Jetty of aan Thea ('Teacher gives the box to Jetty or to Thea')

| | Meester 'Teacher' | geeft 'gives' | $aan_1$ 'to' | Jetty 'Jetty' | of 'or' | $aan_2$ 'to' | Thea 'Thea' |
|---|---|---|---|---|---|---|---|
| de 'the' | 10 | 11 | 9 | 9 | 9 | 10 | 9 |
| doos 'box' | 38 | 45 | 20 | 38 | 9 | 22 | 35 |

r (de, doos) = 55

The relations with doos 'box' are systematically stronger than those with de 'the'. Only the minimal relation with of 'or' shows the predicted equality. This result is also characteristic for the strength of the effect: the relations with the article are always close to the absolute minimum score (the minimum score is 8 for eight subjects), while those with the noun tend to cluster around the middle of the scale. It is possible to produce systematic deviations from ultrametricity by introducing article/noun constructions into the test sentence. In general, relations with the head of an endocentric construction are systematically stronger than those with the modifiers.

We may then conclude that the transformational extension of the constituent model must also be rejected when the interpretation axiom is maintained. The model is not capable of accounting for either the strong relation between the article and the corresponding noun, or the weak relation between the same article and the other words in the sentence. Yet this result is not surprising to the intuition. It shows that the relation between article and noun is asymmetric; the article is dependent on the noun, and the noun is the head of the noun phrase. A phrase struc ture grammar or constituent model is not suited for the representation of such dependencies. An obvious alternative is to use a dependency grammar as a linguistic theory, and to adapt the formulation of the interpretation axiom accordingly.

### 3.3 A Dependency Model for Relatedness Judgments (1)

In the preceding paragraph we found that relatedness judgments are more a reflection of the relations in the deep structure than of those in the surface structure. We suppose in the present paragraph that the dependency model must be a transformational model. Here, too, the theory has two aspects: a linguistic definition and an interpretation axiom. In a dependency grammar the equivalent of cohesion consists of the two notions of dependency and connectedness. We define a dependency function over the nodes of a dependency diagram:

DEFINITION (Dependency). A real-valued DEPENDENCY function $\alpha$ is defined over the nodes of a dependency diagram D, with the property that if $A \rightsquigarrow B$, then $\alpha(A) < \alpha(B)$ for all nodes A, B in D, where $A \rightsquigarrow B$ means that B is directly dependent on A.

The nodes of a dependency diagram thus have values expressed as real numbers; these values increase in all descending paths of the diagram. The head (the start symbol of the grammar) has the smallest degree of dependency.

If we suppose, by convention, that every element in a dependency diagram is dependent on itself, then for every pair of elements there is at least one element on which both are dependent. The FIRST COMMON HEAD FCH of two elements in a dependency diagram is the element with the high

(1) The suggestion of a dependency model as well as other considerations in this paragraph originated in the work of Mr. E.Schils.

est dependency value $\alpha$, on which both elements are dependent. This may be illustred by the following example.

Figure 4 gives a dependency diagram for the underlying structure of the sentence <u>the pianist plays beautifully</u>, and an <u>FCH</u> table for all pairs of elements in the diagram. N and A, for example, are both dependent on V, but also indirectly on T. The first common head of N and A is the element with the highest dependency value. It follows from the

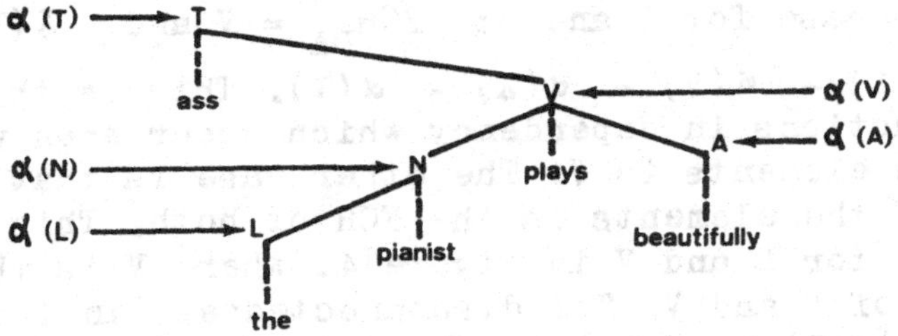


| FCH | T | D | N | V | A |
|---|---|---|---|---|---|
| T | T | T | T | T | T |
| D | T | L | N | V | V |
| N | T | N | N | V | V |
| V | T | V | V | V | V |
| A | T | V | V | V | A |

Fig. 4 Hypothetical dependency diagram for the sentence <u>the pianist plays beautifully</u>, with degrees of dependency and <u>FCH</u> table.

definition of the dependency function that V has a higher dependency value than T, and V is therefore the first common head of N and A. Or consider nodes D and N. They are both dependent on V, but also on N and T. Because $\alpha(N) > \alpha(V) > \alpha(T)$, $FCH_{DN} = N$, as may be seen in the FCH table.

We now define the notion of connectedness negatively as follows:

DEFINITION (Disconnectedness). The DEGREE OF DISCONNECTEDNESS of two elements A and B, $\delta(A, B)$ in a dependency diagram is defined as follows: $\delta(A,B) = [\alpha(A) - \alpha(FCH_{AB})] + [\alpha(B) - \alpha(FCH_{AB})] = \alpha(A) + \alpha(B) - 2\alpha(FCH_{AB})$.

Two situations can occur here. The first is that in which $FCH_{AB}$ is different from A and B themselves. In Figure 4, that is the case for D and A: $FCH_{DA} = V$ and $\delta(D,A) = \alpha(L) - \alpha(V) + \alpha(A) - \alpha(V)$. This is the sum of the two reductions in dependency which occur when we pass from the two elements to V. The other case is that in which one of the elements is the FCH of both. This holds, for example, for D and V in Figure 4, where V is the first common head of D and V. The disconnectedness in thus $\delta(D,V) = [\alpha(D) - \alpha(V)] + [\alpha(V) - \alpha(V)] = \alpha(D) - \alpha(V)$, which is the difference in the degree of dependency of D and V. In both cases $\delta$ is a nonnegative real number.

We must now give the interpretation theory which relates experimentally measured degrees of relatedness to this linguistic theory of dependency and connectedness.

<u>Interpretation Axiom</u>. $r_{ij} < r_{kl} \Leftrightarrow \delta_{ij} > \delta_{kl}$, for all words i, j, k, l, in a sentence.

It should be noted that the degree of connectedness of two words is considered to be equal to that of the syntactic category which dominates them directly.

The degree of relatedness of two words is therefore greater to the extent that their connectedness in the dependency diagram is stronger, and vice versa.

It is not difficult to see that, on the basis of the definitions of dependency and connectedness, the following should be the case: If two elements B and C lie in the path between two other elements A and D, then the connectedness between B and C is greater than that between A and D. By the interpretation axiom, it follows from this that $r(B,C) > r(A,D)$. This holds likewise when the two pairs have one element in common: with a path A-B-C we find $\delta(A,B) < \delta(A,C)$, and therefore $r(A,B) > r(A,C)$.

Within the context of the investigation of another problem, we examined the way in which degrees of relatedness behave under pronominalization (cf. Visser-Bijkerk, unpublished undergraduate thesis, 1969). Every reasonable linguistic theory recognized that <u>the boy gave the ice cream to a child</u> and <u>he gave the ice cream to a child</u> have the same structure, with the exception of the substitution of <u>he</u> for <u>the boy</u>. Likewise, the substitution of <u>it</u> for <u>the ice cream</u>, or <u>of him</u> for <u>a child</u>, will also leave the structure unchanged. Three noun phrases can thus be pronominalized in this sentence. Alternate pronominalization of one, two, or all three of those noun phrases will produce seven new sentences, beside the original complete sentence. The eight sentences (including the original) will all have the same structure, with the exception of the pronominalizations. We examined this in the context of the constituent model as well as within that of the dependency model. In the experiment this sentence (in Dutch) was used together with seven others, all with corresponding syntactic structure. The eight sentences were for following:

<u>de jongen gaf het ijsje aan een kind</u>
'the boy gave the ice cream to a child'

<u>de man betaalt het geld aan een agent</u>
'the man pays the money to a policeman'

<u>de miljonair schonk het schilderij aan een pastoor</u>
'the milionaire presented the painting to a priest'

<u>de directeur stuurde het honorarium aan een advocaat</u>
'the director sent the fee to a lawyer'

<u>de meester leende het boek aan een leerling</u>
'the teacher lent the book to a pupil'

<u>de slager overhandigde het vlees aan een klant</u>
'the butcher handed the meat to a customer'

<u>de eigenaar vermaakte het huis aan een invalide</u>
'the owner bequeathed the house to an invalid'

<u>de grossier leverde het hout aan een timmerman</u>
'the wholesaler delivered the wood to a carpenter'

With all the pronominalizations, this gave sixty-four experimental sentences. Each subject was presented with all the forms of pronominalization, and asked to judge them on seven-point scales. Each form was derived from a different sentence content, and the sixty-four sentences were distributed in such a way to eight subjects that each sentence was judged only once. We shall limit our discussion to the results of each form of pronominalization, that is, the totals for the various forms over subject and sentence content; therefore we shall indicate the various words with their category symbols. The sentences on which no pronominalization has been carried out have the form $D_1N_1VD_2N_2$ to $D_3N_3$; those in which the first noun phrase has been pronominalized have the form <u>he</u> $VD_2N_2$ to $D_3N_3$, and so forth. Note that the three articles are all different in Dutch (<u>de</u>, <u>het</u>, <u>een</u>), and thus no confusion was possible.

Analysis showed that the data obtained seriously conflicted with the constituent model. The principal deviation had to do with the predicted equalities for the relations with article and noun. With one exception, the relations with the noun are stronger than those with the corresponding article, quite in agreement with that which was discussed in the preceding paragraph.

There were also great deviations from the constituent model concerning inequalities. The ultrametricity of the matrices was limited, and alternative phrase markers were always found for the various forms of pronominalization.

The experiment, reported here by way of example, is no proof of the correctness of the dependency model. Further experimentation will certainly lead to modifications and additions. The purpose of this chapter was to show that to an explicitly formulated grammar an equally explicitly formulated interpretation theory could be added, making it possible to investigate the descriptive adequacy of the linguistic theory. We found that a transformational grammar with a phrase structure grammar as its base is not descriptively adequate in a number of regards, and that a dependency grammar as base avoids many of the difficulties. In both cases, the linguist can set these findings aside by rejecting the interpretation theory. To do so, however, will oblige him to find a better interpretation theory, and it is by no means excluded that this is possible. In that case, the linguist will finally have to attend to a matter which he usually neglects, namely, the theory of the relationship between formal linguistic model and concrete linguistic data.

I am deeply grateful to Dr. Paolo Legrenzi, who managed to compose this chapter from the written and printed parts and pieces that were handed in by me. W.L.

## 4. SYSTEMS, SKILLS AND LANGUAGE LEARNING

### 4.1 Language as skill

Language behavior, like any other complex human activity, can be approached from a variety of viewpoints. One could be mainly concerned with the actual or potential output of such behavior, i.e. with the structure of a corpus or language. Alternatively, attention could be directed to the communicative function of language, the transmission of intentions from speaker to hearer and the interpersonal variables that play a role in such communication.

Somewhere between the purely linguistic and the purely social-psychological points of view is the approach which considers language as a human skill. A skill analysis of language borrows from linguistic analysis in that the linguistic structure of the input or output message is systematically varied in order to measure its effects on speed, accuracy, timing and other aspects of linguistic information decoding and encoding. In its turn, knowledge of language as a skill is required for effective analysis of language as interpersonal communication. It is especially important to have an understanding of the mechanism of selective attention and motivation in the transmission of linguistic information in order to fully appreciate the facilitative or inhibitory effects of interpersonal variables in the functional use of language.

Apart from bridging the gap between a more structurally and a more functionally directed study of language, the skills approach to language behavior has the definite advantage of leading to a natural integration into an already existing body of psychological knowledge. The study of human skills, including symbolic skills, has been intensive and quite succesful since World War II. This is not the place to review the enormous developments in the post war study of "human factors", nor to outline the deep influence of cybernetic thinking on the analysis of skills. The reader may be referred to a recent volume on one symbolic skill, human problem solving (Newell and Simon, 1972)., to get an appreciation of this revolution in psychological thinking.

Herriot (1970), who was one of the first authors to stress the analogies between language behavior and other skills, especially mentioned the following features of skills which have been intensively studied, and which are equally central to language.

(a) Hierarchical organization. It is not necessary to convince linguists of the hierarchical nature of language, we will return to this in section 4.3. But many other skills are hierarchical in structure. The succesful completion of a task is, in almost all skills, dependent on the accurate performance of subtasks, plus the correct temporal or spatial integration thereof.

(b) Feedback. Nearly all human performance is controlled by comparing the behavioral effects with some internal standard or aim. The difference is then reduced by taking appropriate measures. This is especially salient in problem solving behavior, but it is also true for many aspects of language. A speaker's behavior, for instance, depends to a large degree on signs of understanding on the part of the listener.

(c) Automation. After a skill has been acquired it is to a large degree automatic, i.e. it does not require conscious control of each of its subtasks. Automobile driving is an example in case: during normal driving, one's attention is free for even rather complicated scussions. Skilled language use is similar in that there is no conscious attention to articulatory movements, or even to choice of sentence schemes. Attention is normally mainly with the semantic contents, and sometimes with the choice of appropriate lexical "core" terms.

(d) Anticipation. In skill research subjects often "react" <u>before</u> the appropriate stimulus is given. The accurate timing of the concert soloist is not by rapidly reacting to the conductor's sign, but by anticipating the critical moment. Any skill which involves planning also allows for anticipation. Speech perception is "being ahead of the speaker". This is possible because all speech is redundant. To the degree that the listener is familiar with the theme, he is able to anticipate by making hypotheses about what the speaker is going to say. As for any skill, this does not require much of a conscious effort. Anticipation is not necessarily a conscious phenomenon.

One could easily add other typical skill features that are equally essential in language behavior. Instead of expanding this issue any further in the present context we will finish this paragraph by mentioning two more reasons why the skill point of view can be especially fruitful for the study of language.

Of all psychological study of skill the major part concerns skill acquisition. Much is known about factors which facilitate or interfere with the learning of skills (see e.g. Bilodeau, 1966). It should be interesting to know how much of these findings can be generalized to language acquisition. Especially the study of second language learning should profit from this viewpoint, because almost all skills are learned on the basis of already existing skills, just as in second language learning. The degree of compatibility between the old and the new skill has been a very central issue in the study of skill acquisition.

Finally, the cybernetic revolution in skill research has led to a high degree of theoretical modelling in the analysis of skill, and especially to the introduction of very general formal systems for the description of skilled behavior. Skill research is increasingly profiting from what is known as systems analysis or system theory, of which some basic notions will be introduced in the next section. Such formal models are specifically developed for the theoretical representation of features such as feedback, hierarchy, anticipation, control, automation, learning. It is therefore, surprising that no systems analysis of (apects of) human language behavior has ever been envisaged. The remeinder of this chapter is intended to give some general thoughts on this issue. We will first introduce some central notions of system theory (section4.2). Next, we will devote a few words to a stratified description of the language user (section4.3). Instead of staying in this general mode, we will select one stratum, the syntactic level, for further analysis in terms of systems (section4.4). It will be shown that empiristic and rationalistic models of language acquisition can be theoretically analyzed in such terms and that both are wrong-in-principle (section4.5). Finally attention is given to some more global aspects of second language acquisition (section4.6). This chapter does not present any new empirical finding; its only aim is to present a way of thinking about matters of language acquisition which, though not new in itself, might lead to fruitful theoretical integration of grammar, skill research and applied linguistics.

## 4.2 System theory: some basic notions

There are many rather different definitions of the notion "system" (see e.g. Bertalanffy, 1969). Throughout this chapter we can neither be complete, nor go into much mathematical detail. In this section we will arbitrarily choose the following description of what we mean by a system. A system is any part of the real world which is considered apart from the rest of the world. This latter, the complement of the system, is called the system's environment. The environment may influence the system by means

Figure 1
System and environment

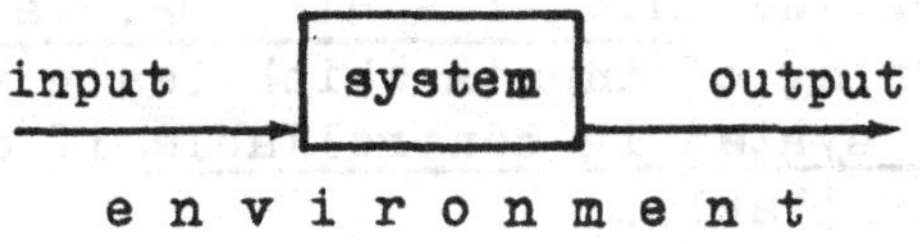


of what is called input into the system. In its turn the system may affect the environment by means of a certain output. The system may be in any of a finite or infinite number of states. The state is the present condition of the system. It is defined in such a way that for all possible cases it is true that given the state of the system as well as the input it receives in that state, it is fully determined what the next state and the next output will be.

Different classes of systems can be distinguished dependent on the types of input, output and state descriptions one chooses. If input, output and state transition is to be considered as occuring at discrete moments in time, the system is called a discrete-time system. Successive instants can then be numbered, and the behavior of the system can be completely described by the state transition function, which gives the state at the next instant as a function of the present state and the present input, and the output function, which gives the next output as a function of the present state and the present input. If moreover, the set of elementary inputs (i.e. inputs that can be applied at one given instant) and the set of elementary outputs are finite, the system is called an automaton. The automaton is finite if the set of states of the system is finite, it is infinite otherwise.

It is, in the present context, useful to think of systems in terms of automata, because most language behavior is characterized by discreteness in time and finiteness of input and output vocabulary. It should be kept in mind, however, that this limitation is not essential in system theory.

Essential in system theory is the notion of control. Assume that the state space of the system contains a designated initial state, $s_o$, as well as a desiguated arbitrary final state $s_f$. The initial state $s_o$, is controllable if there is a string of inputs which leads the system from $s_o$ to $s_f$. The system is controllable if every state of the system is controllable.

The idea of control is that we want to bring the system in a desired state (giving a desired output), and the question is whether we can do it, and if so, what string of inputs should be applied in order to obtain this goal. This can be depicted as follows:

Figure 2 - Diagram of system control

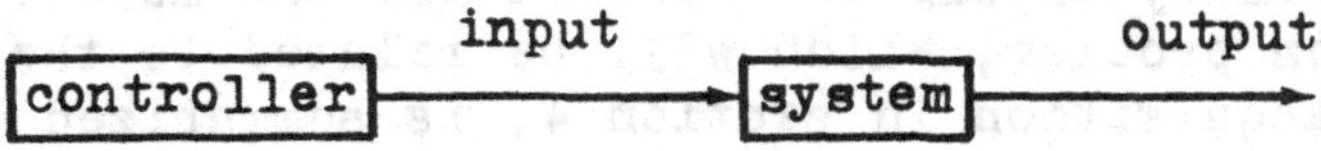


This notion of control will be used in section 4, where we will consider the listener as the system, the state of the listener in which he accepts the message as the desired state, and the speaker as the controller who has the task of leading the listener into this desired state, by choosing an appropriate input string of words.

The notion of feedback comes in if the controller is able to compare the factual output of the system with the desired or reference output. This is depicted in Figure 3: For the purpose of

Figure 3 - Diagram of control through feedback

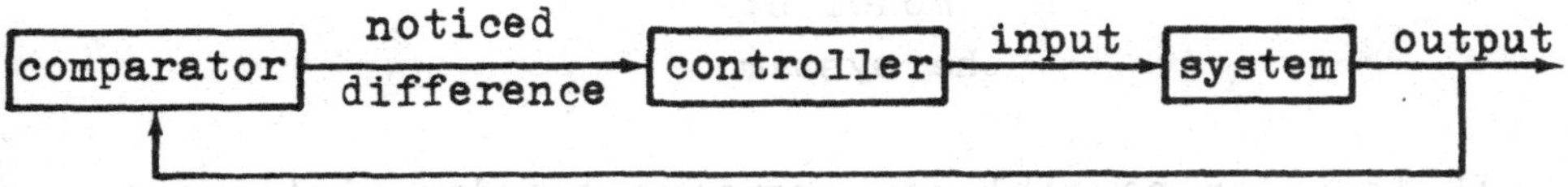


clarity the comparison of factual and comparison of factual and desired output has been set apart in a separate box. The controller acts on the basis of the noticed difference and chooses an input which may lead to a decrease of the difference.

An interesting chapter of system theory is concerned with the so-called identification problem. If our knowledge of a certain system is limited, how can we learn to control the system without opening it? In that case we have to estimate as accurate as possible the structure, or parameters, of the system by sistematically sampling input/output pairs. Another way of formulating the identification problem is: can we devise a procedure which gives us an accurate model of the system, by observing a finite set of input/output strings. If an accurate model, i.e. a model which simulates the system perfectly, can be derived, we can approach the control problem by trying to solve it for the model. The identification problem, which will be related to the problem of language acquisition in section 4, is summarized in the diagram of Figure 4.

Figure 4 - Diagram of system identification

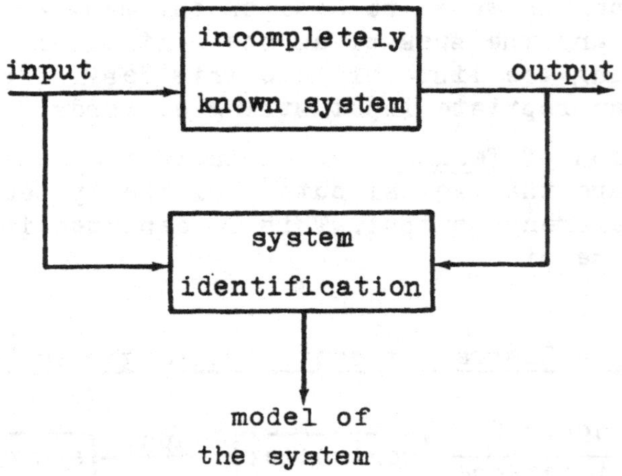


It is often possible to organize the description of a system in terms of sub-systems and their interrelations. There are several different notions of hierarchy in system theory, we will limit ourselves to one: the notion of a stratified hierarchical system. One can consider the same system on different levels of detail. Figure 5 is not taken from a linguistic or psycholinguistic text, but from a text on hierarchical systems (Mesarović et al., 1970).

One may consider one and the same system, for instance a speaker delivering a lecture, from a very detailed point of view (e.g. as a producer of a sequence of elementary sounds), or from a global point of view (as a producer of a certain textual composition), or from several intermediate levels of detail. Each level of description has its own sets of inputs, outputs and states. On the level of sentences, for instance, the elements are words (or morphemes),

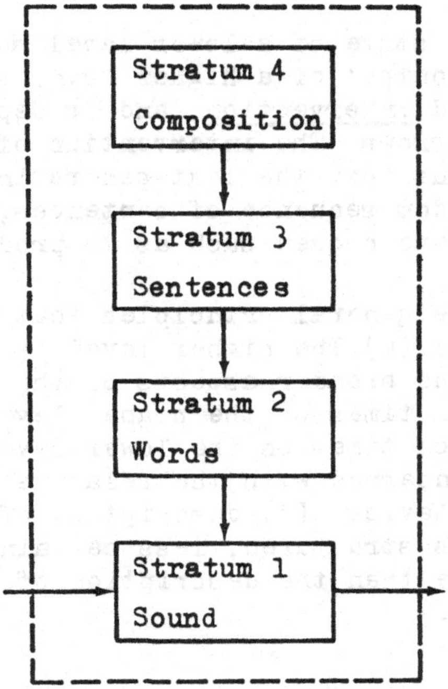


Figure 5 - A four-strata diagram of a text generating system.

but it is irrelevant whether these words are written or spoken, or spoken by a male or a female voice, etc. The latter features, however, are essential for a stratum 1 - description.

In general, the description of one stratum cannot be derived from the description on another stratum. Each level has its own concepts and principles. It is, especially, impossible or unfeasible to describe a high level stratum in terms of a low level stratum. One cannot derive processes of human problem solving from principles of neural interaction, or the principles of text composition from syntax. But one should keep in mind that in a stratified description it is the same system which is described on different levels. A state of this system is the composition of the different states of the subsystems at a certain in stant in time. The state of a lower level subsystem is co-determined by the output of a higher level stratum. This influence is called <u>intervention</u>, and is depicted in Figure 5 by downward arrows. The intervention of stratum 4 upon stratum 3 means that the text generating system does not generate a random sequence of sentences, but that successive sentences are chosen such as to produce a coherent text.

There are some general principles that hold for all stratified systems: (a) The higher level is concerned with larger positions and broader aspects of the system's behavior, (b) decision times on the higher level are usually longer than decision times on the lower level, (c) the higher level is concerned with the relatively slow aspects of the system's behavior (d) description of a higher level is usually less structured, less certain, and more difficult to formalize than the description of low level behavior of the system.

### 4.3 <u>The language user as a system</u>

The structure of a human language user is so complicated that we have little a priori knowledge about its possible states, state transition function or output function. A complete and detailed description of such a huge and complew system is excluded from the beginning. On the one hand one wants to create a model of the language user's global behavior, i.e. his communication with other language users about certain aspects of the real world. On the other hand, one has to fill in all the details of such behavior on all levels of functioning. In such cases the system theorist resorts to a stratified description. He defines different levels of detail and tries to create more explicit models for each of the sybsystems. The subsystems should be chosen in such a way that their functioning is as much as possible independent from other subsystems. This description can then be extended by a specification of the intervention and other relations between levels and subsystems. It is, therefore, completely legitimate to choose a certain stratum for further analysis. One should only keep in mind that it is a part of a larger system, and that its description should, in the long run, be integrated in a more general characterization of the system.

There is nothing new here for linguists. Linguistics is a highly stratified science with various levels of description such as phonology, morphology, syntax, semantics, more or less comparable to the strata of the system in Figure 5.

Also in psycholinguistics the use of hierarchical models for speaker or listener are increasingly common. This is especially so in studies directed toward computer simulation of natural language understanding. The reader is referred to Winograd's (1972) system as a recent example. It consists of a hierarchy of subsystems, each having its own principles of functioning, but nevertheless cooperating in a global and sometimes surprisingly "human" manner.

In this section we will not propose any stratified model for a language user. Instead, we will arbitrarily select one level of description, the syntactic level, for the purpose of discussing the contributions system theory can make to the problem of (second) language acquisition. The syntactic level is selected because results are most clearcut in that area, not because this stratum is the most important for understanding language acquisition. In fact it will be shown in the next paragraph that a syntactic account of language learning is unfeasible. But the syntactic level is certainly the highest level for which such results could be obtained through formalized analysis.

## 4.4 Some system aspects of the syntactic stratum

Consider the listener as a system. Though for the system as a whole the usual input is a text, and the desired final state is one of understanding of that text, on the syntactic level this input/output relation reduces to a sentence as input and a syntactic structural description as output. The syntactic subsystem reaches a final state if a correct structural description of the sentence has been ereated. One calls this state the accepting state. Generally, the listener does not overtly output the structural description, so that the speaker does not know whether the accepting state has been reached. However, control is nevertheless often possible since the speaker shares the language with the listener and can therefore plan the input in such a way as to be sure that an accepting state is indeed obtained. The speaker/listener situation so far can be represented by the elementary control-diagram of Figure 2; where the system is the listener, and the controller the speaker. If we call the state of the listener before the utterance is presented the initial state, according to system theory this initial state is controllable if there is an input string which brings the listener into the accepting state. It is interesting to notice that in the ideal case, i.e. where the listener has unlimited memory, etc., the set of all input strings by which the system can be controlled in the initial state is the language itself. The linguistic notion of grammaticality, therefore, is a special case of the notion of controllability in system theory.

The notion of feedback comes in if the speaker is not completely with the listener's linguistic outfit. Important cases are the child, talking to his mother, and the beginning second language learner who tries to make himself understood by a native speaker of thet language, or more typically by his language teacher. In such cases it is very important for the controller to get feedback, as in Figure 3, about the state of the listener. If a certain utterance is not understood or accepted by the listener, the speaker could try a different wording if only the listener gives some clue with respect to his state of understanding. From the purely syntactic point of view this amounts to feedback with respect to whether a certain input string has led the listener into the accepting state or not.

This brings us to our main theme, the systems approach to language acquisition. In terms of system theory, language learning is a case of the identification problem. The language learner is confronted with an incompletely known system, the fluent language user, i.e. speacker/listener. In order to "control" this system, i.e. to communicate in the new language, the learner has to make hypotheses about the system's structure and parameters and test such hypotheses by checking sample of input/output pairs. This is exactly the situation depicted in Figure 4. The system identification box represents the language learner, who infers a model of the system by observing a set of input/output pairs. Again limiting our attention to the syntactic stratum, such a pair consists of, on the one hand, a string of morphemes or words and, on the other hand, some indication of whether the string is acceptable or non-acceptable to the system. If the system is a syntactically ideal system, this indication simply means, as we have noticed before, that the corresponding string is either grammatical or ungrammatical. Here it is immaterial whether the unknown system is a listener or a speaker of the language. Syntactically this amounts to an inversion of input and output, whichdoes not affect the essential character of the pairs: they always consist of a string and a plus or minus-sign. If the sign is positive, the particular pair is called a *positive example*, i.e. the learner knows that the particular string is a sentence in the language. Because a syntactically ideal speaker always producs grammatical text, a positive example is best imagined as drawn from a speaker-system. If the learner is exclusively presented with positive examples, i.e. a sequence of grammatical sentences, one calls such a sequence a *text presentation*. If, however, the sign is negative, i.e. if the string is not a sentence of the language, the pair is called a *negative example*. If we consider the unknown system as an informant to whom we present strings with the question whether they belong to the language or not, we will sample a mixture of positive and negative examples: some strings turn out to be grammatical and others are faulty. Such a mixture of positive and negative examples is therefore called an *informant presentation*.

As we have seen in section 2, the essential problem of system identification is whether we can devise a procedure which can generate an accurate model of the system by observing a finite set of examples. On the syntactic level, such a model is called a grammar of the language, and the question is then if a correct grammar of the language can be derived from a finite text or informant presentation. If the answer is affirmative, such a procedure could be an ideal model of the language learner, and actual language acquisition could be studied on the basis of such an ideal model (1). If the answer is negative, however, it makes no sense whatsoever to even try to understand the acquisition of syntax as a relatively autonomous process. Before we study processes of language acquisition, we should first solve what Chomsky (1965) called the adequacy in principle of a theory of language learning. If there is no conceivable procedure to output a grammar on the basis of a finite presentation of the language, be it text of informant presentation, then any theory in such terms must be wrong, since children and adults do acquire languages.

Before we introduce, in the next paragraph, some substantial results with respect to this adequacy-in-principle, we must add two more notions which are essential for a discussion of theories of language acquisition.

System identification is impossible without some a priori knowledge of the structure of the system. One should, for instance, have some knowledge of the sort of input accepted by the system, or linguistically speaking, the learner must have some idea about the class of languages that should be considered.

The set of models, or syntactically speaking: grammars, which agree with this a priori knowledge is called the hypothesis space in system identification. It is obvious that language acquisition is greatly facilitated if the hypothesis space is made very narrow. This means that the learner already has very detailed a priori knowledge of the language to be learned.

(1) The construction and testing of ideal models is common practice in many areas of psychology. Compare for instance the ideal perceiver models in signal detection theory.

Another way to speed up learning is to make the learner very "clever". He could be endowed with very powerful heuristics which allow him to scan the hypothesis space in a very systematic way, and to process huge amounts of observations in very short time.

## 4.5 Adequacy of empiristic and rationalistic acquisition models

The system identification procedure presented so far can be seen as a schema for organizing the discussion about language acquisition in terms of the syntactic stratum. It corresponds to what Chomsky and Miller became to call a language acquisition device, LAD (Miller and Chomsky,1957; Chomsky, 1962). But there are two important points to keep in mind before we proceed this discussion.

First, LAD is a schema which is limited to the syntactic stratum. As we have seen in section 2, concepts and principles can be quite different for different strata of the system and there is no reason whatever to expect that substantial results for the syntactic stratum will be valid for other strata as well. We should not expect to solve the language acquisition by solving it at the syntactic level. This is in sharp disagreement with Chomsky's position. Chomsky (1962) tries to minimize the additional role of the semantic stratum in language acquisition. He writes "For esample, it might be maintained, not without plausibility, that semantic information of some sort is essential even if the formalized grammar that is the output of the device does not contain statements of direct semantic nature. Here care is necessary. It may well be that a child given only the input of Figure 2 (i.e. of LAD) as nonsense elements would not come to learn the principles of sentence formation. This is not necessarily a relevant observation, however, even if true. It may only indicate that meaningfulness and semantic function provide the motivation for language learning, while playing no necessary part in its mechanism, which is what concerns us here. And Chomsky repeats this argument in *Aspects* (1965, p. 33). In a moment we will discuss how much of this position can be maintained.

Second, LAD is *nothing else* than a schema for the discussion of language acquisition procedures. LAD is only meant to be a hypothetical system identification procedure endowed with a hypothesis space and a set of heuristics, with a text or informant presentation as input and a grammar, i.e. a model of the system, as output. At this point the literature is badly confused and quite misleading. The confusion mainly relates to the distinction between *empiricistic* and *retionalistic* acquisition models, which we will now introduce. In *Aspects*, Chomsky formulates this distinction in terms of LAD as follows.

The *empiricistic model* of language acquisition says that there is hardly any limitation with respect to the hypothesis space of LAD, it has little a priori knowledge of the system's grammar. Language learning occurs through strong heuristic principles by which the grammar is derived from observations.

The *relationalistic model*, on the other hand, assumes that LAD's hypothesis space is very narrow or specific; there is a large a priori knowledge of the system's grammar. A relatively small set of observations will suffice for LAD to derive the system's grammar.

Both models, therefore, are special conceptions of LAD's structure. The main confusion in the literature resulted from contaminating the LAD discussion schema with the rationalistic assumptions about LAD. The most outstanding example in this respect is McNeill (1970), but many others made the same short circuit, often to their own disadvantage. Braine (1971), for instance, weakened his argument against syntactic acquisition models by making the same contamination, as we will see.

A second source of confusion is the identification of *rationalistic* with *innate*, and *empiricistic* with *learned*. Though it is not implausible that the a priori knowledge of the grammar is innate in some sense, it is exactly equally plausible to suppose that the strong heuristics in an empiricistic model are innately given. Innateness has no intrinsic relation with the dichotomy under concern. Here we will not go into the innateness issue. We refer the rea der to Levelt (1973), where it is treated in much detail.

Let us put the discussion straight. The first question concerns the adequacy-in-principle. Can one conceive of whatever procedure which derives the grammar from a finite text or informant presentation? Only in the affirmative ca se it makes sense to pose the second question: how does the child, or second language learner, compare with such an ideal procedure? Chomsky (1965) makes a very one-sided statement with respect to these questions. He writes: "In fact, the second question has rarely been raised in any se rious way in connection with empiristic views... since stu dy of the first question has been sufficient to rule out whatever explicit proposals of an essentially empiricist character have emerged in modern discussions of language acquisition". The facts are, however, that the question of constructability of a language acquisition procedure had not been solved at all in 1965. Substantial results in this respect have only been obtained by Gold in 1967 and by Hor ning in 1969. These latter solutions have been completely ignored by both linguists and psycholinguists, so that it makes sense to give a very short summary of the main re- sults. Technical detail, however, must be left out in the present context. The interested reader is referred to the original publications, or to Levelt (1973), chapter 8.

Gold (1967) could prove the following. With text pre sentation an error-free acquisition procedure can only be constructed if the hypothesis space is limited to finite languages. That is, with text presentation, a language can be learned in principle if and only if the learner knows in advance that the language is finite.

Since natural languages are quite clearly not finite, they cannot be learned by text presentation in Gold's sen- se. Gold's mathematical results were extended by Horning. Instead of discussing the error-free case, Horning discus sed a stochastic version of the identification procedure. He proved that the difference between the grammar derived by LAD, and the "real" grammar of the system can be made arbitrarily small in the case of (stochastic) text presentation, if LAD knows in advance that the system's grammar is of the non-ambiguous context free type. Natural languages are clearly of a more complicated type, be it alone for the fact that natural languages are ambiguous,and the question is what the results would be for more complicated stochastic languages. This has not yet been solved. But for our purpose it is not too important to wait for such solutions. With respect to the second question, the factual properties of the acquisition procedure, Horning could prove that even for the context free case, where acquisition is possible in principle, the procedure is so time-consuming as to be completely unrealistic as a model for human language acquisition: "grammars as large as the ALGOL-60 grammar will not be attainable simply by improving the deductive processing"."But adequate grammars for natural languages are certainly more complex than the ALGOL-60 grammar". So, even with the strongest heuristics, a text presentation model for natural language acquisition is excluded as a realistic model.

How is the situation for informant presentation?This is very much better. Gold could prove that even if LAD only knows that the language is primitive recursive,which is probably true for all natural languages, it can derive a correct grammar for the language. Though this might seem to be a hopeful alternative to the text presentation model, in this case we hit upon too much empirical counterevidence. This has most clearly been formulated by Braine (1971). He argues that the language learning child is at best presented with positive examples. If presented with ungrammatical utterances, these are hardly ever marked as such. In our terms, Braine argues that the child is, at best, in a text presentation situation. We mention some of several arguments: (1) The speech of many children is never corrected, i.e. marked as grammatical or ungrammatical. Nevertheless all children finally acquire their language. (2) If such marking occurs, it seems to be highly ineffective as a means for language improvement. This is clear from experiments by Braine (1971) and Brown (1970). Therefore, the "this-is-ungrammatical" -output of the adult can hardly be considered as input for the language identification procedure. It should be noted that the same is true for second language acquisition. Experiments by Crothers and Suppes (1967) show that presentation of negative syntactic information does not improve the acquisition of certain syntactic forms in Russian. (3) Informant presentation in Gold's sense requires, roughly speaking, that every ungrammatical string will, in the long run, occur in LAD's observations. This, however, is highly unrealistic, since it is known (see Ervin-Tripp, 1971) that the speech directed to young children is highly grammatical and hardly ever contains negative instances. It seems to me that this is also very much true for the second language learning situation in so-called natural teaching methods. Students are almost exclusively presented with positive examples. (4) One could think that non-reaction of adults to ungrammatical strings might constitute implicit negative information for the language learning child. This can certainly not be the case. Initially, almost all utterances of the child are ungrammatical in the adult's sense. Nevertheless, the adult reacts if he can derive the child's intention. This means that many ungrammatical strings are "marked" as positive. This should confuse any language acquisition procedure. This situation is fully comparable to the learning of a language in a foreign country, or by means of most "natural" methods. Conversation is not interrupted for reasons of ungrammaticality, but mostly for inunderstandability only.

If these arguments are sufficiently convincing,it follows that the language learning child, as well as the second language learner in a foreign country (still the quickest way to learn a second language!), are essentially in a text presentation condition.

But since the work of Gold and Horning we know that there is no conceivable real-time acquisition procedure for natural languages within the syntactic stratum. The conclusion therefore must be that the adequacy-in-principle question must be answered in the negative for all modeld of the LAD-family, i.e. not only for the empiristic models, but also for the rationalistic models.

It is now interesting to look back at the literature. From the citation above, it is clear that Chomsky (1965) rejects the empiristic model, without answering the adequacy-in-principle question. Even according to his own writing, however, the latter issue should have been solved first. It is only due to this lack of substantial results that Chomsky, and with him McNeill and many others, could keep believing in the adequacy of a rationalistic model. On the other hand Braine (1971) quite correctly rejected the rationalistic model by arguing that it is unfeasible with text presentation. He then made a case for an empiricistic model. But it should by now be clear that the test argument relates to the adequacy-in-principle of the LAD-schema as such, and that Braine's argument therefore leads to rejection of both versions of LAD, i.e. including his own empiristic version.

The only safe conclusion is that all exclusively syntactic accounts of language acquisition must fail for principled formal reasons, be they empiricistic or rationalistic. Chomsk's assumption which was cited at the beginning of this section, saying that an essentially syntactic account of language learning might suffice, cannot be maintained. This is, moreover, little surprising from the system theoretical point of view, and even less so from what we know about language teaching.

One note could be added. This discussion did not solve the rationalist/empiricist controversy. It can be reformulated on another, especially a higher stratum of the system description. Even about the level of intention and meaning one could ask whether a child or second language learner acquires such structures by analyzing his observations by means of strong heuristic principles, or alternatively, whether he has strong advance knowledge of such structures and can easily select the correct structure by only making a relative small amount of observations.

## 4.6 Some global aspects of second language learning

In this final section we return from the syntactic stratum to some more global aspects of the language learner. More specifically, we will make some remarks on three points. The first is the question of facilitation and interference due to the first language. The second issue relates to the acquisition of hierarchical skills and possible conclusions for language learning. The third issue is some possible causes of failures in second language learning.

(a) Facilitation and interference.

One of the most intensively studies phenomena in skill research is the role of compatibility in skill acquisition (see for instance Bilodeau, 1966, Fitts and Posner, 1967, Welford, 1968). The question is how much the learning of a new skill is facilitated by similarity with an already existing skill. If one has learned to perform some task (e.g. writing) with the right hand, how easy is it to learn to do the same task with the left hand? If a child wants to learn to drive a bicycle, is it advantageous if he already has some skill on the scooter? A very general summary of numerous experimental findings is the following: compatibility between old and new task is facilitatory in the sense that the initial skill at the new task is higher. However, compatibility hardly affects the speed of learning. Therefore, compatibility is not reflected in speed of learning, but only in the maintainance of the initial advantage.

If this general result can be extended to second language learning, one should expect that the learning of Japanese is not slower than the learning of French, but that, throughout learning, the proficiency in Japanese will be less than the fluency in French. The large effect of compatibility on second language learning has been demonstrated by Carroll and Sapon (1959), see also Carroll (1966).

Little is known about the causes of the compatibility effect. In terms of system theory one would suppose that the facilitatory effect of language similarity is due to the restriction of the hypothesis space that the language learner can allow himself. An interesting aspect of such restriction is that there is no a priori lower limit. The apparent similarity between first and second language can easily induce the learner to over-restrict his hypothesis space. This results in what is known as <u>interference</u> in skill and second language research: the learner keeps making intrusions from his native language. I would not be surprised if it were shown that there exists an optimal similarity between languages: if the second language comes too close to the first, interference may become more important than facilitation. In that case the task for the language teacher would be to expand the hypothesis space by contrastive teaching. Newmark and Reibel (1968) reject this approach, but much more research is required to give a definite answer.

(b) Acquisition of a hierarchical skill

Fitts and Posner (1967) distinguish three stages in the acquisition of hierarchical skills. The first stage is <u>learning of individual components</u>. Each component initially requires full attention, therefore they can only be trained in succession. The second stage is called <u>integration</u>. Dependent on the depth of the hierarchy different or all components are organized in larger wholes. The learner tries to get familiar with the spatial and temporal relations between the subtasks. Finally the stage of <u>automation</u> is reached. In section 2 we noticed that in a stratified system slow decisions are feasible at the higher levels where the broader aspects of planning take place. All skilled behavior is characterized by full automation at lower levels, so that the subject's attention is available for controlling the performance as a whole.

All this applies to language learning as well. Initially the language learner has to give attention to all sorts of minor components of the skill: the pronunciation of individual sounds, the meaning of individual words, etc. Only then integration becomes possible. In its turn this leads to a higher level integrated component, e.g. a correctly pronounced and understood word, which requires further syntactic integration, etcetera.

Horning (1969), after his negative conclusions with respect to language learning from text presentation, remarks that, in the case of the child, language learning probably proceeds quite differently. The child is not presented with the full blown language, but with a very limited subset of the language. Probably the child initially does have an extremely limited hypothesis space and the parents are nicely matching it by presenting the child with a very simple language. One could say that the child is learning a mini-grammar. Recent research (Ervin-Tripp,1971) has indeed shown that the language which adults direct to their very young children is extremely simple in structure: it does not contain conjunctions, passives, subordinate clauses, etc. Moreover, sentences are very short. Therefore Horning may be correct: the child is learning a mini-language, which is gradually expanded in later stages. In terms of skill integration: the initial language becomes a higher level component of the language in a later stage. In this way a growing set of already automated sentence schemes becomes available to the child, who in his turn keeps expanding his hypothesis space for whatever reason.

It is noteworthy that his idea has been around since a long time in second language learning practice. This is especially the case for the Berlitz-method (1967). Right from the first lesson a mini-language is learned which suffices to discuss some little subject. In later lessons this is gradually expanded by new words and forms, but at each stage one aims at maximal automation or fluency before proceeding to the next stage. This is fully comparable to the teaching of other symbolic skills such as arithmetic. One preferably starts with one operation (addition) in a limited domain (1-9), and gradually expands if sufficient automation has been acquired.

But again, much more research is required with respect to the optimal organization of the training of hierarchical skills. No general principles are as yet available.

(c) Some causes of failures in second language learning. From the systems point of view failures in language learning can be due to a variety of factors. We already mentioned interference through a too restricted choice of the hypothesis space. Contrastive teaching might be helpful. Also, certain parts of the system's behavior might not have been observed by the learner, and his model of the fluent language user would therefore remain incomplete. An example which has often occurred to me, but which does not seem to get much attention in language teaching is lip position. It is well known that in many cases exactly the same sound can be produced with different lip positions. In a language course one does learn to make the correct sound, but one is not taught that the natuve speaker makes a characteristic lip position with the sound. People tend to keep their "native" lip positions even if they pronounce faultlessly. Since looking at the speaking face is an important addendum to language understanding (see e.g. Campbell, 1970), such people may always be hampered in their verbal communication, as well ad recognized as foreigners.

As long as a task is not too difficult, performance may appear to be fully automated, whereas in fact the learner is still giving attention to several low level components. This is immediately revealed if the subject's attention is distracted, either by a secondary task or by stress (speeding up performance or otherwise). The less a skill is automated, the earlier it will break down. If tasks during second language teaching are kept too easy, the subject may seemingly acquire a high level of skill, but nevertheless fail at a stressful examination. During language courses, the teacher should from time to time "test the limits" in order to detect which components are most likely to break down, and are thus least automated.

Finally, some errors persist because the learner intends to "control" the native speakers in a very special way. He does not only want to make his intentions understood, but also the fact that he is a foreigner. This can often be quite advantageous for all sorts of social reasons. (See Diller, 1971, for discussion of this point).

REFERENCES


Bar-Hillel, J., Perles and Shamir, On formal properties of simple phrase structure grammars, Z. Phonetik Sprachwiss Kommunikationsforschung, 14, 143, 1961.

Berlitz Publication Staff, English: First Book, Berlitz Publications, New York, 1967.

Bertalanffy, L. von, General System Theory, Braziller, New York, 1968.

Bilodeau, E.A., Acquisition of skill, Academic Press, New York, 1966.

Braine, M.D.S., On two models of internazionalization of grammars, in The Ontogenesis of Grammar. A Theoretical Symposium, Slobin, D.I., Academic Press, New York, 1971.

Brown, R., Psycholinguistics. Selected Papers, Free Press, New York, 1970.

Campbell, H.W., Hierarchical ordering of phonetic features as a function of input modality, in Advances in Psycholinguistics, Flores d'Arcais, G.B. and Levelt, W.J.M., Eds., North-Holland, Amsterdam, 1970.

Carroll, J.B., Research in Language teaching: the last five years, Reports of the Working Committees, North east Conference on the Teaching of Foreign Languages, M.L.A. Materials Center, New York, 1966.

Carroll, J.B. and Sapon, S.M., Moderne Language Aptitude Test, Manual, The Psychological Corporation, New York, 1959.

Chomsky, N.A., Three models for the description of language, IRE Transaction on Information Theory, IT-2, 113, 1956.

Chomsky, N.A., Syntactic Structures, Mouton, The Hague, 1957.

Chomsky, N.A., Explanatory models in linguistics, in Logic, Methodology and Philosophy of Science, Proceedings of the 1960 International Congress, Nagel, E., Suppes, P. and Tarsky, A., Stanford University Press, Stanford, 1962.

Chomsky, N.A., Aspects of the Theory of Syntax, MIT Press, Cambridge, Mass., 1965.

Chomsky, N.A. and Miller, G., Introduction to the formal analysis of natural language, in Handbook of Mathematical Psychology, Luce, R.D., Bush, R.R., and Galanter, E., Eds., vol. 2, chap. II, 1963.

Crothers, E., and Suppes, P., Experiments in Second Language Learning, Academic Press, New York, 1967.

Diller, K.C., Generative Grammar. Structural Linguistics and Language Teaching. Newbury, Rowley, Mass., 1971.

Ervin-Tripp, S., An overview of theories of grammatical development, in The Ontogenesis of Grammar. A theoretical Symposium, Slobin, D.I., Academic Press, 1971.

Gold, E.M., Language identification, Information and Control, 10, 447, 1967.

Herriot, P., An Introduction to the Psychology of Language, Methuen, London, 1970.

Hopcraft and Ullman, S., Formal languages and their relation to automata, Reading, Addison-Wesley, USA, 1969.

Horning, J.J., A study of grammatical inference, Technical Report CS 139 Stanford Artificial Intelligence Project, Computer Science Developments, Stanford, 1969.

Johnson, S.C., Hierarchical Clustering Schemes, Psychometrica, 32, 241, 1967.

Joshi, A.K., Kosaraju, S., and Yamada, H.M., String adjunct grammars: I local and distributed adjunction, II Equational representation, null symbols and linguistic relevance, Information and Control, 21, 93-235, 1972.

Krantz, D., Luce, R.D., Suppes, P., and Tversky, A., Foundation of Measurement I, Academic Press, New York, 1971.

Levelt, W.J.M., Psychological Representations of Syntactic Structures, in The Structure and Psychology of Language (in preparation). Available as Heymans Bulletin HB-69-36 Ex, Department of Psychology, Groningen University, 1967.

Levelt, W.J.M., Formele Grammaticals in Linguistick en Taalpsychologie, 3 vol., Kluwer, 1973, in English traslation, Formal grammars in linguistics and psycholinguistics, 3 vol., Mouton, The Hague, 1974.

Masters, J.M., Pushdown Automata and Schizophrenic Language, unpublished report, University of Sydney, 1970.

McNeill, D., The acquisition of language. The study of developmental psycholinguistics, Harper and Row, New York, 1970.

Mesarovic, M.D., Macko D., and Takahara, Y., Theory of Hierarchical, Multilivel, Systems, Academic Press, 1970.

Miller, G.A., and Chomsky, N.A., Pattern Conception, Paper for Conference on Pattern Detection, University of Michigan, 1957.

Miller, G.A., and Chomsky, N.A., Finitary Models of Langua ge Users, in Handbook of Mathematical Psychology, Luce, R.D., Bush, R.R., and Galanter, E., Eds., vol. 2, chap. 13, 1963.

Newell, A., and Simon, H.A., Human Problem Solving, Englewood and Cliffs, Prentice-Hall, 1972.

Newmark, L., and Reibel, D.A., Necessity and sufficiency in language learning, International Review of Applied Linguistics in Language Teaching, 6, 145, 1968.

Peters, P.S., and Ritchie, R.W., A note on the universal base hypothesis, Journal of linguistics, 5, 150, 1969.

Peters, P.S., and Ritchie, R.W., On restricting the base component transformational grammars, Information and Control, 18, 483.

Peters, P.S., and Ritchie, R.W., On the generative power of transformational grammars, Information Sciences, 6, 49, 1973.

Postal, P.M., Limitations of phrase structure grammars, in The structure of language: Readings in the philosophy of language, Fodor, J.A., and Katz, J.J., Eds., Prentice-Hall, Englewood Cliffs, USA, 1964.

Sager, N., Syntactic Analysis of Natural Language, in Advances in Computers, Alt, F., and Rubinoff, M., Academic Press, New York, 1967.

Thorne, A computer model for the perception of syntactic structure, Proc. Royal Society, B. 171, 377, 1968.

Winograd, T., Understanding natural language, Cognitive Psychology, 3, 1, 1972.

Woods, Transition network grammars for natural language analysis, Comm. ACM, 13,591, 1970.

## LIST OF CONTRIBUTORS

J.L. KULIKOWSKI : Institute of Applied Cybernetics of the Polish Academy of Sciences, Warszawa, Poland.

W.J.M. LEVELT : Psychology Laboratorium Katholieke Universiteit Nijmegen, Nijmegen, The Netherlands.

D. MANDRIOLI : Artificial Intelligence Project, Politecnico di Milano, Milano, Italy.

A. MARZOLLO : Istituto di Elettrotecnica ed Elettronica, Università di Trieste, Trieste and CISM, Udine, Italy.

B. MELTZER : School of Artificial Intelligence, Department of Computational Logic, University of Edinburgh, Edinburgh, Great Britain.

A. SANGIOVANNI VINCENTELLI : Artificial Intellingence Project, Politecnico di Milano, Milano, Italy.

M. SOMALVICO : Artificial Intelligence Project, Politecnico di Milano, Milano, Italy.

W. UKOVICH : Istituto di Elettrotecnica ed Elettronica, Università di Trieste, Trieste, Italy.

Printed in the United States
By Bookmasters